Collins

GCSE Maths
2 tier-foundation
for Edexcel A
TEACHER PACK

GREG BYRD

LYNN BYRD

PHIL DUXBURY

WILL FERGUSON

GILLIAN READ

William Collins' dream of knowledge for all began with the publication of his first book in 1819. A self-educated mill worker, he not only enriched millions of lives, but also founded a flourishing publishing house. Today, staying true to this spirit, Collins books are packed with inspiration, innovation and a practical expertise. They place you at the centre of a world of possibility and give you exactly what you need to explore it.

Collins. Freedom to teach.

Published by Collins
An imprint of HarperCollins*Publishers*
77–85 Fulham Palace Road
Hammersmith
London
W6 8JB

Browse the complete Collins catalogue at
www.collinseducation.com

© HarperCollins*Publishers* Limited 2006

10 9 8 7 6 5

ISBN-13 978-0-00-721561-4
ISBN-10 0-00-721561-4

Commissioned by Marie Taylor and Vicky Butt

Publishing Manager Michael Cotter

Project managed by Nicola Tidman

Edited by Joan Miller and Peta Abbott

Proofread by Amanda Whyte

Internal design by Gray Publishing

Cover design by JPD

Cover illustration by Andy Parker

Page make-up by TECHSET Composition Ltd

Illustrations by TECHSET Composition Ltd

Production by Natasha Buckland

Printed and bound by Martins the Printers, Berwick upon Tweed

Acknowledgements
Whilst every effort has been made to trace the copyright holders, in cases where this has been unsuccessful or if any have inadvertently been overlooked, the Publishers will be pleased to make the necessary arrangements at the first opportunity.

Contents

Introduction

Welcome to Collins GCSE Maths!

Collins GCSE Maths uses a stimulating approach to Maths that really appeals to pupils, and features straightforward guidance on grade performance for clear progression. Written by experienced teachers and examiners, the series provides perfect coverage of the new 2 tier Edexcel GCSE Linear A Maths Specification.

This Teacher Pack has been developed to make teaching GCSE Maths much easier. It not only supports the Collins GCSE Maths textbook, but also provides a wealth of resources such as homework activities, worked examples and extra prior knowledge "Check-in" tests.

Developed by the team behind the highly popular and successful Maths Frameworking series, Collins GCSE Maths is the easiest way to achieve success in 2 tier Mathematics.

Teacher Pack

Chapter Overviews
Each chapter commences with a Chapter Overview. These provide a summary of the work pupils will encounter, and offer context for the key mathematical ideas – this will help explain "why is this topic useful to us?"

Links to the specification are given, followed by a Route mapping grid through the Exercises to indicate the level of work pupils will meet. The grid will show, for example, that questions 1–6 in Exercise A are set at around Grade F difficulty level.

In addition, answers to the diagnostic Check-in test are provided.

Check-in tests
Each chapter has a short diagnostic test which can be copied and distributed to the class, before main teaching of the topic begins. This will help quickly establish if pupils have the appropriate level of understanding to tackle the topic.

Lesson plans
Each section in the textbook is supported by a Lesson plan. The Lesson plan provides:

- Key words, Learning objectives and Links to other Pack resources for each section.
- Engaging oral and mental starter activities to involve the whole class. These are designed to work with minimal specialised equipment, although of course the use of whiteboards, digital projection, OHPs, target boards, counting sticks, etc. can make the activities easier to present and more accessible to pupils.
- Main teaching points to help lead pupils into exercise questions.
- Notes on common mistakes that pupils may make.
- Notes on differentiation – advising how to direct pupils of varying ability to the work that best suits them.
- Plenary guidance to complete the structured lesson.

Homework answers
The Teacher Pack provides Homework activities for every section. The answers to these activities are provided towards the back of the Pack.

Textbook Examination questions answers
Answers to the exam practice questions in the textbook are provided towards the back of the Pack.

Teacher Pack CD-ROM

All of the printed materials in the Teacher Pack are also supplied on the CD-ROM, to allow customisation and easy access. The structure of the CD-ROM matches the structure of the textbook, and by navigating to the required section, you will find the Chapter Overviews, Check-in tests and Lesson plans in Adobe Acrobat PDF form.

In addition, the CD-ROM also features:

Homework activities

Each section in the textbook is accompanied by a homework activity. These can be printed out and distributed to the class. Note that answers to these activities are listed at the back of the Pack.

Worked examples

Most of the sections in the textbook are accompanied by at least one Worked example on the CD-ROM. Use these to provide extra support if needed to help pupils grasp key ideas.

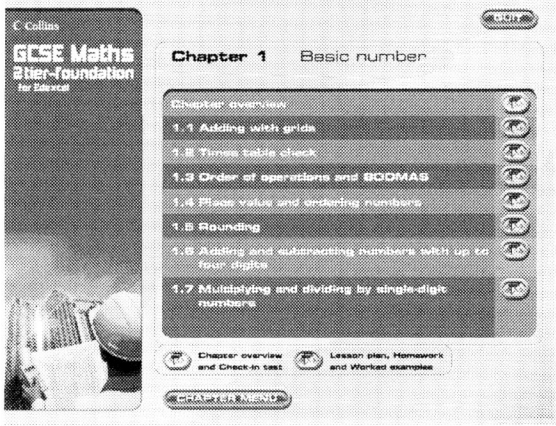

Bonus content online

In order to further assist you in your teaching, Collins will provide ongoing updates on a dedicated section of its website. For access to this FREE bonus content, such as editable MS Word™ versions of the Lesson plans, go to:

www.collinseducation.com/gcsemaths/mathsbonuscontent

This area of the website can also be accessed by clicking through the hyperlink on the CD-ROM.

We do hope you enjoy using Collins GCSE Maths, and wish you good luck in your teaching!

Greg Byrd, Lynn Byrd, Phil Duxbury, Will Ferguson and Gillian Read

Basic number

This chapter covers work on numbers with up to four digits, and multiplying and dividing by a single-digit number. It also includes place value, ordering and rounding to given numbers of integers. The chapter includes work at grade G, with Sections 1.1, 1.3, 1.6 and 1.7 moving onto work at grade F.

Context

It is vital for pupils to have a good understanding of the work in this chapter, as it is essential in all the arithmetic that occurs in everyday life. Basic number work forms the building blocks upon which the global society operates. Imagine a world without numbers. All GCSE examinations have a non-calculator paper. Quick, accurate recall of basic number facts and a good grasp of non-calculator methods is essential if marks are not to be lost in examinations.

Edexcel A references

Ma2 Number and algebra: Calculations

1.1, 1.2	2.3a "add, subtract, multiply and divide integers ..."
1.3	2.3b "use brackets and the hierarchy of operations"
1.6	2.3j "use standard column procedures for addition and subtraction of integers ..."
1.7	2.3k "use standard column procedures for multiplication and division of integers ..."

Ma2 Number and algebra: Numbers and the number system

1.4, 1.5	2.2a "use their previous understanding of integers and place value to ... round them to a given power of 10; ... order integers; ..."

Route mapping

Exercise	G	F
A	1	2
B	all	
C	1–6	7
D	all	
E	all	
F	1–5	6
G	1–3	4–5

1

×	2	4	7	8
3	6	12	21	24
5	10	20	35	40
9	18	36	63	72
6	12	24	42	48

2 a 15   **b** 8   **c** 15   **d** 9   **e** 7

3 a 4   **b** 6   **c** 9   **d** 49   **e** 45

4

	× 10	× 100
4	40	400
23	230	2300
60	600	6000
28	280	2800

1 Complete the multiplication grid.

×	2	4	7	8
3				
5				
9				
6				

2 Write down the answers to these calculations.

a $7 + 8 =$ ☐   **b** $19 - 11 =$ ☐   **c** $3 + 5 + 7 =$ ☐

d $15 - 6 =$ ☐   **e** $12 -$ ☐ $= 5$

3 Work out the answers to these calculations.

a $24 \div 6 =$ ☐   **b** $18 \div 3 =$ ☐   **c** $54 \div$ ☐ $= 6$

d $7 \times 7 =$ ☐   **e** $9 \times 5 =$ ☐

4 Complete the following grid.

	×10	×100
4		
23		
60		
28		

Incorporating exercise:	1A		Key words	
Homework:	1.1		add	grid
Example:	1.1		column	row

Learning objective(s)

- add and subtract single-digit numbers in a grid
- use row and column totals to find missing numbers in a grid

Prior knowledge

Pupils need to know the number bonds to 20.

Starter

Put a list of five numbers across the bottom of the board, for example 1   3   4   2   5.

Add each adjacent pair and write the result on the line above.

       4   7   6   7

    1   3   4   2   5

Ask pupils to continue this to form a pyramid.

Repeat with a different arrangement of the five numbers, for example 1   2   3   4   5.

Ask pupils to pick their own arrangement. Who can get the biggest total at the top of the pyramid?

Main teaching points

Make sure pupils understand how to complete the tables in the activity on page 2 of the Pupil Book, which can be used as a practical introduction to the topic.

Pupils must know how important it is to be able to use mental maths to add quickly and accurately. Ask them where they use basic addition and subtraction in everyday life.

Differentiation

This comes through the questions. Brighter pupils may only need to answer parts g to i of question 1 before moving onto question 2. They can then make grids for other pupils.

Plenary

Read out three different numbers from one to nine, for example 1, 6, 7. Ask the pupils to add them mentally and write down their answer. Repeat with different sets of three numbers. Include some that have complements of 10, for example 7, 3, 2 or 8, 5, 2. Discuss whether pupils used complements of 10 to aid their mental calculations.

Incorporating exercise:	1B
Homework:	1.2

Learning objective(s)

● recall and use your knowledge of times tables

Prior knowledge

Pupils should be familiar with the multiplication tables up to 10×10.

Starter

Show the pupils a completed times-table wheel. Choose, or let them choose, a times table and ask them to make their own times-table wheels.

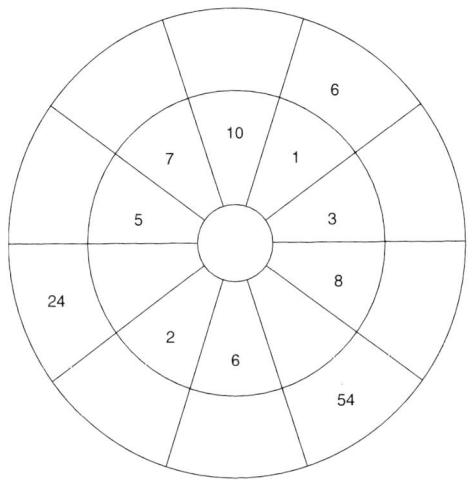
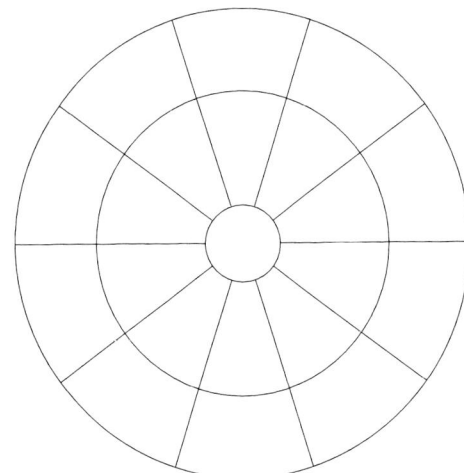

Main teaching points

Pupils should understand that multiplication is repeated addition and that division is repeated subtraction. Quite commonly, pupils do not realise that they can divide by finding the inverse of a multiplication. Help them to make the link by suggesting that, for example, if a question asks them to divide 27 by 9, another way of putting it is, 'How many 9s are there in 27?'

Show pupils shortcuts for multiplying, for example:

● to multiply by 4, simply double and double
● to multiply by 5, multiply by 10 and then halve the answer.

Ask pupils to find easy ways of multiplying by 8 or by 6.

Differentiation

The 6, 7 and 8 times tables are the most difficult. The activity that precedes Exercise 1B in the Pupil Book demonstrates a good method of learning the most troublesome pairs of products.

Plenary

Ask pupils for multiplication questions that give the answers 24, 36, 18.
Practise multiplying by 4 by doubling and doubling.

Incorporating exercise:	1C	Key words	
Homework:	1.3	brackets	sequence
		operation	

Learning objective(s)

- work out the answers to a problem with a number of different mathematical operations

Prior knowledge

Pupils should know the number bonds to 20 and the times tables up to 10×10.

Starter

Ask pupils to work out:

$$4 \div 4 + 4 - 4 \ (= 1)$$
$$(4 + 4) \div (4 + 4) \ (= 1)$$
$$(4 \div 4) \times (4 \div 4) \ (= 1)$$

Make sure pupils are happy with the meaning of the brackets.

Now ask pupils to make any other numbers from 1 to 10 using only four 4s. Collect answers for numbers 2 to 10. Discuss any that use brackets incorrectly or have brackets missing.

Main teaching points

Explain to the class that there is a convention for the order in which calculations are worked out and they must follow it. As an example, ask pupils to find the answer to $7 + 3 \times 4$. Many will give an answer of 40. Explain that the correct answer is 19 and ask if anyone can see how this was achieved.

Talk about the order of working through the calculation and ask how the problem needs to be set out, to make the answer 40. Pupils may suggest putting an equals sign after the 3. Accept that this would work but then move on to introduce the brackets.

Introduce BODMAS, giving examples to show how to use it. The exercise provides practice.

Common mistakes

Pupils can usually cope with questions that have only two signs, but a calculation such as $4 \times 6 + 2 \times 7$ causes problems as pupils often add the 2 to 24 before multiplying by 7.

Differentiation

Brighter pupils could omit question 1. Question 7 is grade F, questions 1 to 6 are grade G.

Plenary

Play 'Countdown'. For example, use 25 6 3 10 4 1 and allow pupils 30 seconds to make 254 $(25 \times 10 + 4)$, or 60 seconds to make 287 $(25 \times 10 + (6 + 3) \times 4 + 1)$.

Pick other target numbers of varying difficulty depending on the ability of the class.

Incorporating exercise:	1D	Key words
Homework:	1.4	digit place value

Learning objective(s)

- identify the value of any digit in a number

Prior knowledge

Pupils should know the size order of the words *unit, ten, hundreds, thousands, 10 thousands, 100 thousands* and *million,* and understand the relative values of the terms.

Starter

Have ready two sets of digit cards, each from 0 to 9, large enough for pupils to see the numerals when you hold them up. Shuffle them and place them face down. Ask the pupils to draw four boxes next to each other, i.e. ☐☐☐☐. Tell them you are going to pick four numbers at random, one at a time, and they have to write them down, deciding where to place each digit in the boxes in order to make the biggest four-digit number possible. Play this several times, giving a point to pupils who make the biggest number each time.

Main teaching points

Remind pupils that numbers go on for ever – however large a number they think of, they can always add one more.

It is the number and order of digits in a number, not the value of the individual digits, that determines the size of a number.

Zeros are very important and pupils should not miss them out.

When writing numbers with more than four digits, the convention is to leave narrow spaces between groups of three digits, starting from the right. These replace the commas that were used previously. This helps to identify the number. For example, 2 678 000 is two million, six hundred and seventy-eight thousand.

Common mistakes

Pupils may find it difficult to identify and say very large numbers, particularly those with zeros in such as 70 403.

Plenary

Read out some numbers, for example 109, 7043 or 4508 and ask the pupils to write them down in figures. If there is time, ask pupils to make up a number with a zero in one of the place values and read it out for the rest of the class to write down.

Incorporating exercise:	1E	Key words	
Homework:	1.5	approximation	rounded up
		rounded down	

Learning objective(s)

● round a number

Prior knowledge

Pupils should know that numbers are not always given exactly but are sometimes approximated.

Starter

Give pupils two numbers and ask for the number that is halfway between them. Begin with simple examples and then give more complicated numbers, according to the ability of the class.

Main teaching points

Explain that it is not always sensible to use exact numbers, so approximations are used. Give examples, such as numbers of people attending a pop concert or a sports event, times taken to travel large distances, population, measurements, cooking times. Ask pupils if they can think of any more examples.

Talk about average amounts, such as the weight of the contents in a packet of cornflakes, the life of a light bulb, the number of small sweets in a tube or packet.

Common mistakes

Pupils need to be reminded what to do when the number to be rounded is halfway between two possible values.

Differentiation

Brighter pupils could omit question 1 and low achieving pupils need not do question 5.

Plenary

Use examples from real life (taken from the teaching points above) to ask questions.

For example, if the number of sweets in a tube is 30, to the nearest 10, how many could there be in the tube?

Adding and subtracting numbers with up to four digits

Incorporating exercise:	1F	**Key words**	
Homework:	1.6	addition	digit
Example:	1.6	column	subtract

Learning objective(s)

● add and subtract numbers with more than one digit

Prior knowledge

Pupils should know the number bonds to 10.

Starter

Let pupils use mini-whiteboards. Give them a two-digit number and ask them to write on their boards the number that must be added to this number to make 100.

Main teaching points

Pupils need to realise that when they add two positive whole numbers the answer will be bigger than the larger number they are adding.

Explain that when they are adding in columns, they must always add the units column first, and remind them that it is a good idea to show any carried figures so they do not forget to add them in.

Explain that when using column addition to add a three-digit number to a two-digit number, it is important to write both numbers with the units in the same column, one below the other.

Pupils need to realise that when they subtract one positive whole number from another positive whole number the answer will be smaller than the first number.

They must subtract the units first and 'decompose' a number from the next column to the left, if necessary.

Common mistakes

When subtracting, pupils sometimes take the smaller digit from the larger in a column rather than 'bottom from top'. This seems to be a throw-back from early instructions where pupils learn to subtract by taking smaller from larger.

Pupils often have difficulty subtracting when the larger figure has several zeros. Pupils are now taught several methods, including counting on in stages. This is useful to overcome the problems with carrying, especially with zeros.

Differentiation

Brighter pupils should do the last half of each of the first four questions and less able pupils should do the first half of each question. All pupils should try questions 5 and 6 of the exercise.

Plenary

Check pupils' understanding of the rules, concentrating on subtraction. Start with subtracting one-digit numbers from two-digit numbers, for example 25−9, asking pupils to do this mentally. Now move on to two-digit numbers from two-digit numbers, two-digit numbers from three-digit numbers and so on.

Incorporating exercise:	1G
Homework:	1.7
Examples:	1.7

Key words
division
multiplication

Learning objective(s)

● multiply and divide by a single-digit number

Prior knowledge

Pupils should know the times tables up to 10×10.

Starter

Do some mental multiplying and dividing and practise doubling and halving. Ask questions such as: 'If 7×10 is 70, what is 70×10?'

Main teaching points

When they are multiplying two numbers, encourage pupils to write the bigger number first. They should start by multiplying the units, and must expect a bigger answer than either of the numbers they started with.

For division, the answer will be smaller than the number they are dividing into. They must always start division at the left-hand side. It is sometimes easier for pupils to understand what is required if they are asked, 'How many fives in 60?' rather than, 'What is 60 divided by 5?'

Common mistakes

One common mistake is to ignore zeros. Another is to forget to add in any carried digits.

Differentiation

Questions 1, 2 and 3 are grade G, questions 4 and 5 are grade F.

Plenary

Do some mental problems, for example 4×32. Pupils could write their answers on mini-whiteboards. Discuss how to break the problem down into $4 \times 30 + 4 \times 2$. Repeat with other two-digit by one-digit problems.

Fractions

Overview

This chapter covers all aspects of work with fractions. It begins by looking at fractions of shapes and showing what is meant by equivalence, and how to simplify fractions. It then moves onto finding a fraction of a quantity and expressing a quantity as a fraction. Next there is a section about adding, subtracting and multiplying fractions and solving problems. Finally, the chapter covers reciprocals and recurring decimals.

Context

Why are fractions useful in the real world? A fraction is a quantity that is not a whole number. It is useful for splitting quantities into equal parts. It is often easier to use a fraction, rather than a decimal or percentage, when finding a part of an amount. We either find a fraction of one whole unit, for example cutting a pizza into half or quarters, or we share amounts in given fractions, for example a pack of 30 sweets divided into thirds. Generally, measurements cannot be expressed simply as integers, so the parts that are left over, as remainders, must be expressed as fractions.

Edexcel A references

Ma2 Number and algebra: Numbers and the number system

2.1, 2.3, 2.4, 2.5   2.2c: "understand equivalent fractions, simplifying a fraction by cancelling all common factors; order fractions by rewriting them with a common denominator"

Ma2 Number and algebra: Calculations

2.2, 2.6, 2.7, 2.8, 2.10   2.3c: "calculate a given fraction of a given quantity, expressing the answer as a fraction; express a given number as a fraction of another; add and subtract fractions by writing them with a common denominator;…"

2.9   2.3d: "understand and use unit fractions as multiplicative inverses; multiply… a fraction by an integer, by a unit fraction…"

2.11   2.3a: "…understand 'reciprocal' as a multiplicative inverse, knowing that any non-zero number multiplied by its reciprocal is 1 (and that zero has no reciprocal, because division by zero is not defined);…"

All   2.3l: "use efficient methods to calculate with fractions, including cancelling common factors before carrying out the calculation, recognising that, in many cases, only a fraction can express the exact answer"

Route mapping

Exercise	G	F	E	D	C
A	all				
B	all				
C	all				
D	all				
E	1–30	31–60			
F	1–2	3	4		
G		all			
H	1–2	3–12			
I			all		
J				all	
K					all

Answers to diagnostic Check-in test

1	42	**2**	27	**3**	30	**4**	4	**5**	9
6	16	**7**	9	**8**	5	**9**	4	**10**	8

1 $7 \times 6 =$

2 $3 \times 9 =$

3 $5 \times 6 =$

4 $28 \div 7 =$

5 $72 \div 8 =$

6 What is half of 32?

7 What is half of 18?

8 What is a quarter of 20?

9 What is a fifth of 20?

10 What is a third of 24?

Incorporating exercise:	2A
Homework:	2.1
Example:	2.1

Learning objective(s)

- recognise what fraction of a shape has been shaded
- shade a given simple fraction of a shape

Prior knowledge

Pupils should understand what the term 'fraction' means.

Starter

Give each pupil a sheet of A4 plain paper. Using coloured paper makes the activity more interesting. Ask pupils to fold their paper in half. Discuss the different ways this can be done. Repeat with quarters, eighths, and then thirds.

Main teaching points

Make sure that pupils are clear about the main features of a fraction.

- The denominator determines the number of parts into which a shape is divided.
- The numerator determines how many parts of the shape are shaded.
- Each part or division of the shape must be the same size.

Common mistakes

Pupils do not always realise that when a whole is divided into fractions, each fractional part must be the same size. A common question is, 'Do you want the bigger half?'

Pupils cannot always write fractions correctly.

Plenary

Draw a diagram on the board.
Ask pupils to find ways of dividing the shape into half. Ask, 'What do all the ways have in common?'

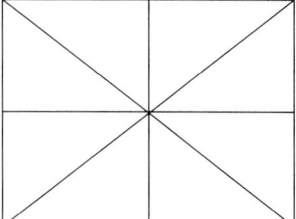

2.2   Adding and subtracting simple fractions

Incorporating exercise:	2B
Homework:	2.2
Example:	2.2

Key words
denominator
numerator

Learning objective(s)

● add and subtract two fractions with the same denominator

Prior knowledge

Pupils should be able to recognise shaded fractions of shapes.

Starter

Give each pupil a sheet of A4 plain paper. Using coloured paper makes the activity more interesting. Ask pupils to fold their paper in half, in half again and then again, so there are eight equal parts. Ask pupils to shade two of these parts. Discuss the different ways pupils do this. Explain that two-eighths of the paper have been shaded. Ask if pupils can tell you another way of saying 'two-eighths'.

Main teaching points

Using the appropriate mathematical words, explain how to add and subtract fractions with the same denominator. Emphasise that they must not add the denominators.

Common mistakes

Some pupils will add the denominators as well as the numerators.

Plenary

Write the following on the board:

$$\frac{1}{3} + \frac{1}{6}$$

Ask if any pupils know the answer. They will probably reply two-ninths. Emphasise the rule that fractions can only be added if they have the same denominator. Ask pupils if they can see any way of solving the problem. Guide them to turn one-third into sixths. Get the answer of three-sixths and cancel down. Another way of showing this is to use a shape split into six parts.

Repeat with other examples if there is time.

Incorporating exercise:	2C	**Key words**
Homework:	2.3	equivalent
Example:	2.3	

Learning objective(s)

- recognise equivalent fractions

Prior knowledge

Pupils should know what a fraction is and understand the word 'equivalent'. They also need to know the times tables to 10×10.

Starter

Give pupils a copy of the '100 club' multiplication square. Give them 10 minutes to fill in as many answers as they can. Any pupil with 100 correct answers becomes a member of the 100 club and receives a certificate.

The '100 club' multiplication square

×	7	9	4	3	8	5	2	6	10	11
3										
5										
2										
7										
9										
10										
8										
11										
4										
6										

Main teaching points

The aim for this section is for pupils to learn what equivalent fractions are. They need to understand that two or more fractions that look different can represent the same part of a whole. One good method of showing equivalence is given in the activity 'Making eighths', in the Pupil Book. This could be demonstrated to the class or pupils could do it themselves. Pupils must understand that they have to multiply both the numerator and the denominator of the initial fraction by the same number, to produce a fraction that is equivalent.

Plenary

Go around the class asking pupils to suggest fractions that are the same size as two-fifths.

Ask pupils to tell you the simplest way of showing $\frac{50}{100}$. Explain that this is the sort of work they will be doing in the next section.

			Key words
Incorporating exercise:	2D		denominator
Homework:	2.4		lowest terms
Examples:	2.4		numerator

Learning objective(s)

- create equivalent fractions
- cancel fractions, where possible

Prior knowledge

Pupils must be able to recognise equivalent fractions.

Starter

Go around the class asking pupils to give fractions that are the same size as one half. Repeat, asking for fractions that are the same size as one quarter.

Main teaching points

Pupils must understand that fractions can only be simplified by dividing the numerator and denominator by the *same* number. A simplified fraction has the same value as the original fraction. Simplification should be continued until it is impossible to divide by the same number any more, for example, $\frac{36}{72}$ can be simplified to $\frac{18}{36}$ by dividing both numerator and denominator by 2. To reach its most simple form, the denominator and numerator must be divided by 18 to get $\frac{1}{2}$.

Common mistakes

Pupils do not always give their answers in the lowest terms. They may not identify all of the common factors of the numerator and denominator.

Plenary

Check pupils' understanding of 'most simple form' by asking them to simplify fractions such as $\frac{56}{100}$ and $\frac{36}{72}$.

Encourage pupils to look for other common factors once fractions have been cancelled. For example, 56 and 100 divide by 2 to give $\frac{28}{50}$. These also divide by 2 to give $\frac{14}{25}$, which will not cancel any further.

Incorporating exercise:	2E
Homework:	2.5
Examples:	2.5

Key words
mixed number
proper fraction
top-heavy

Learning objective(s)

- change top-heavy fractions into mixed numbers
- change a mixed number into a top-heavy fraction

Prior knowledge

Pupils should know that it is possible to have fractions greater than 1 and that, for example, $1\frac{1}{4}$ means one whole one plus one quarter of a whole.

Starter

Give pupils some practice in factorising by asking questions such as, 'What is the largest number that will divide exactly into 12 and 18?' Repeat with other pairs such as 12 and 15 or 18 and 24.

Ask, 'What is the rule for finding the highest number? How is this useful with simplifying fractions?'

Use a simple fraction such as $\frac{20}{75}$. Ask, 'How can you simplify this?' Repeat for $\frac{75}{15}$.

Main teaching points

Make sure that pupils understand that not all fractions are proper fractions. A fraction in which the numerator is greater than the denominator is called an 'improper' or 'top-heavy' fraction.

Stress that any top-heavy fraction can be converted into a mixed number that is made up of a whole number and a fraction. The fraction should be simplified to its lowest terms.

Make sure pupils understand that a whole number can be represented by a fraction with a denominator of one.

Common mistakes

Pupils find it much more difficult to change mixed numbers into top-heavy fractions than the other way round. They often use the whole number as the denominator of their improper fraction.

Differentiation

Questions 1–30 of exercise 2E are grade G and questions 31–60 are grade F. Lower attaining pupils may need to draw diagrams to help them understand the conversions.

Plenary

Ask questions such as, 'Maria has three and three-quarter pizzas. How many quarters does she have?'

Incorporating exercise:	2F	Key words	
Homework:	2.6	lowest terms	top-heavy
Example:	2.6	mixed number	fraction
		proper fraction	

Learning objective(s)

● add and subtract two fractions with the same denominator, then simplify the result

Prior knowledge

Pupils should understand equivalent fractions and be able to simplify by cancelling.

Starter

Draw a 6 × 4 grid. Ask someone to shade one-sixth, then ask someone else to shade one-eighth and then one-quarter. Ask, 'What fraction is shaded altogether?' Tell pupils that this is the same as $\frac{1}{6} + \frac{1}{8} + \frac{1}{4}$. Let pupils draw a different grid and use it to add together simple fractions.

Main teaching points

You can only add and subtract fractions that have the same denominator. It is therefore necessary to use equivalent fractions to make the denominators the same before adding and subtracting them. Then it is important to add only the numerators. See also the notes on page 36 of the Pupil Book.

Common mistakes

Pupils do not always give the answer in its lowest terms.

Some pupils will add or subtract both the numerators and the denominators.

Differentiation

Questions 1 and 2 of Exercise 2F are grade G, question 3 is grade F and question 4 is grade E. Lower achieving pupils will find equivalence difficult and they may need a fraction number line to help them. They should complete all of question 1. Higher achieving pupils could just do questions 3 and 4.

Plenary

Check pupils' understanding, particularly of subtracting a fraction from a whole number. Use questions such as $3 - \frac{5}{8}$.

Incorporating exercise:	2G
Homework:	2.7
Example:	2.7

Learning objective(s)

● solve problems that have been put into words

Prior knowledge

Pupils will need to know how to add and subtract simple fractions.

Starter

Use mini-whiteboards or simply ask questions such as:

What fraction of a week is 1 day?
What fraction of a year is 1 week?
What fraction of a year is 1 month?
What fraction of a circle is a right angle?
What fraction of a pound is 50p, 25p or 30p?
What fraction of an hour is 1 minute?
What fraction of a metre is 33 centimetres?

Main teaching points

Pupils need to realise that their examination questions and most real-life problems involving fractions will be set out in words. They have to read the question and decide what they need to do to answer it correctly. They should then write down the calculation they are going to perform and work it out. They will gain marks for doing this in the examination.

Common mistakes

Examiners complain that the most common mistake pupils make is just to write down answers with no write-up of the method they have used. Pupils must be discouraged from doing this.

Plenary

Do some mental calculations of the complements to 1, for example one minus three-fifths. After a while ask pupils if they can see a simple rule for doing this. Mention that this type of problem occurs in a topic called probability, which they will meet later in the course.

Incorporating exercise:	2H
Homework:	2.8
Example:	2.8

Learning objective(s)

○ find a fraction of a given quantity

Prior knowledge

Pupils need to know how to use the fraction button on a calculator. They should also know how to use a calculator to multiply and divide.

They must know the times tables to 10×10.

Starter

On the board, draw a line that is 60 centimetres long. Say to pupils, 'I want to mark a point that is halfway along the line. Where should I put it?' Discuss their answers and then mark the point in the correct position. Repeat with other fractions such as one-third, one-tenth, one-fifth.

Main teaching points

Remind pupils how to use their calculators for these questions. Stress that they should always divide by the denominator and multiply by the numerator.

Differentiation

Questions 1 and 2 of Exercise 2H are grade G, questions 3 to 12 are grade F. There is a lot of reading involved in this exercise; lower achieving pupils may need help accessing the mathematics.

Plenary

Check pupils' understanding by asking quick-fire questions such as 'What is three-quarters of eight centimetres? What is two-thirds of 90°? What is three-fifths of 60 minutes?'

Discuss the mental process. For example, for two-thirds of 90°, first find one-third of 90 and then multiply it by two.

> Incorporating exercise: 21
> Homework: 2.9
> Example: 2.9

Learning objective(s)

● multiply a fraction by a fraction

Prior knowledge

Pupils should know the times tables up to 10×10.

Starter

Ask pupils, 'What is a half of a half?' Many will answer one.

Ask pupils to draw a 2×2 grid and then shade half of it. Then ask them to shade half of the half they shaded before. Ask, 'What fraction of the original shape has been shaded twice?'

Repeat with a 3×2 grid, first shading half then a third of the same half. Ask, 'How much is shaded now?' Then ask, 'Do you notice anything about the fractions you have shaded? Who can use the three fractions to make up a number sentence or a problem?'

Main teaching points

It is essential for pupils to understand that when they are multiplying by a proper fraction, the answer will be smaller than the original number. Multiplying fractions is quite simple, as they just multiply the numerators together and multiply the denominators together. Remind them that they can cancel and simplify the answer if necessary.

It is often easier to cancel before doing the multiplication. Show pupils an example of this, such as $\frac{3}{5} \times \frac{25}{33}$, using both methods. Advantages of cancelling before the multiplication are that the tables facts required are easier and the answer does not need to be cancelled.

Plenary

Put the following multiplication on the board: $\frac{2}{15} \times \frac{5}{9} \times \frac{5}{6} \times \frac{3}{4} \times \frac{12}{25}$

Discuss why it may not be a good idea to multiply all the numerators and denominators (easy to make a mistake, difficult calculations).

Ask pupils if they can see any numbers, top and bottom, that will cancel. Cancel as much as possible. You should end up with all the top cancelled and 5 and 3 on the bottom. Make sure pupils understand that there are ones left on top and not zero. The final answer is $\frac{1}{15}$.

Incorporating exercise:	2J
Homework:	2.10
Example:	2.10

Learning objective(s)

- express one quantity as a fraction of another

Prior knowledge

Pupils should be able to simplify fractions.

Starter

Use a metre rule or draw one on the board. Show a length of 20 centimetres on the rule and ask what fraction this is of the whole rule. Ask, 'Can this be simplified?' Repeat with other numbers of centimetres and then ask questions such as, 'What fraction is 20 centimetres of two metres?' Bring in other measures, such as money or time.

Main teaching points

Encourage pupils to see that the first number in the problem becomes the numerator of the fraction and the second the denominator. They should simplify their answers where possible.

Make sure pupils know that the two numbers must be in the same units.

Plenary

Ask pupils for numbers that go into 360. Ask them to form a pair of numbers, such as $1 \times 360 = 360$, $2 \times 180 = 360$. Write them on the board and then ask for fractions of 360, for example, 'What fraction of 360 is 36?'

Discuss the connection between the multiplications and the fractions.

Incorporating exercise:	2K
Homework:	2.11
Examples:	2.11a, 2.11b, 2.11c

Key words

rational number   terminating
reciprocal   decimal
recurring
    decimal

Learning objective(s)

- recognise rational numbers, reciprocals, terminating decimals and recurring decimals
- convert terminal decimals to fractions
- convert fractions to recurring decimals
- find reciprocals of numbers or fractions

Prior knowledge

Pupils will need to know how to round decimals and how to convert fractions into decimals using a calculator.

Starter

Ask pupils what one-half is as a decimal, then one-quarter and then one-eighth. Look at what is happening to the decimal as the denominator is doubling. Explain that this is a way of working out other decimals when you know that 0.5 is a half. Ask. 'What is three-eighths? Five-eighths? ... How about one-fortieth? One-eightieth? One-sixteenth?' Discuss the answers.

Write fractions on the board and discuss them with the pupils. Ask them what one-third is as a decimal. Make sure they understand the difference between $\frac{1}{3}$ and $\frac{3}{10}$.

Main teaching points

Pupils need to understand that fractions can be expressed as either terminating or recurring decimals. Terminating decimals are finite and have denominators that have only prime factors of 2 and 5. All other fractions convert to recurring decimals. Recurring decimals contain a digit or a block of digits that repeats. This is indicated by a dot on top of the single recurring digit, or over the first and last digits in a block.

Examiners expect pupils to know $\frac{1}{3}$ and $\frac{2}{3}$ as recurring decimals, and that these are usually rounded to 0.33 and 0.67. When using a calculator with recurring decimals pupils need to remember that answers will be rounded and so will not be true answers.

The reciprocal of a number is the result of dividing the number into one. Reciprocals of fractions are easy as they are simply the number turned upside down. Reciprocals of decimals can be found by converting into fractions.

Plenary

Pupils will have found out that $\frac{1}{9} = 0.11111\ldots$ and $\frac{2}{9} = 0.2222\ldots$. Establish that $\frac{3}{9} = 0.3333\ldots$ and ask pupils

what common fraction this recurring decimal represents. Show that $\frac{3}{9}$ cancels to $\frac{1}{3}$.

Carry on with $\frac{4}{9}, \frac{5}{9}, \frac{6}{9}$ (again, establish the link to $\frac{2}{3}$), $\frac{7}{9}, \frac{8}{9}$ and $\frac{9}{9}$.

Pupils will have no problem seeing that $\frac{9}{9} = 0.9999\ldots$. Ask them what fraction is represented by $\frac{9}{9}$.

Leave them with the apparent fallacy that $1 = 0.99999\ldots$.

Negative numbers

Overview

3.1 Introduction to negative numbers
3.2 Everyday use of negative numbers
3.3 The number line
3.4 Arithmetic with negative numbers

This chapter is in two parts. It begins with an introduction to negative numbers and how they are used in everyday life. The second part of the chapter shows how negative numbers fit on the number line and then covers arithmetic involving negative numbers.

Context

Pupils need to understand that, when they are counting down, numbers do not end at zero. It is possible to have numbers with values that are less than zero. Negative numbers are used in everyday life, for example for temperatures below freezing and depths below sea level, when diving, exploring caves or going down a mine. They can also denote a negative bank balance, showing when a customer owes money to the bank.

Edexcel A references

Ma2 Number and algebra: Numbers and the number system

3.1, 3.2, 3.3   2.2a "... order integers; ..."

Ma2 Number and algebra: Calculations

3.4   2.3a "add, subtract, ... integers ..."

Route mapping

Exercise	G	F	E	D	C
A	all				
B	all				
C		all			
D		1–15	16–17		
E		all			

Answers to diagnostic Check-in test

1 2, 24, 27, 57, 75, 100

2 0, 16, 28, 36, 51, 60, 106

3 1, $5\frac{1}{2}$, 6, 12, 15, 16, 48

4 13, 42, 103, 111, 130, 209, 286

Put the numbers in each list in order, smallest first.

1 75, 24, 27, 57, 2, 100

2 60, 16, 106, 36, 28, 0, 51

3 15, $5\frac{1}{2}$, 12, 48, 16, 1, 6

4 103, 13, 130, 42, 111, 286, 209

Incorporating exercise: –	**Key words**
Homework: 3.1	negative number
Example: 3.1	

Learning objective(s)

- negative numbers can represent depths

Prior knowledge

Pupils must know the order of positive numbers.

They may also understand what a negative number is.

Starter

Hold a class discussion about what negative numbers are and where they fit on the number line.

Main teaching points

Numbers carry on below zero. Negative numbers can be used to represent actual amounts or measurements. Depending on the location of your school, pupils may not have a clear idea of caves, mountains or mines, but they may be familiar with shops that have basement floors, or car parks.

Common mistakes

Pupils sometimes confuse negative numbers with decimal numbers thinking that, for example, -6 is bigger than -2.

Plenary

Check pupils' understanding by going through the activities.

Make sure that pupils understand the table they have completed as they will need to work on it for their homework.

Incorporating exercise:	3A
Homework:	3.2
Examples:	3.2

Key words

after	loss
before	negative number
below	profit

Learning objective(s)

- using positive and negative numbers in everyday life

Prior knowledge

Pupils should understand what a negative number is and be able to order numbers.

Starter

Use the data below to set questions for the class about positive and negative temperatures.

Melting points		Boiling points	
oxygen	$-218\ °C$	sulphuric acid	$340\ °C$
nitrogen	$-210\ °C$	acetic acid	$118\ °C$
hydrogen	$-259\ °C$	nitric acid	$83\ °C$
helium	$-272\ °C$		

Information for teachers
Absolute zero is the lowest temperature that is theoretically possible. Its value is equivalent to $-273.15\ °C$ or zero on the Kelvin scale.

Main teaching points

Pupils need to know where they are likely to need to use negative numbers in real life. The most common examples include temperature, sea level and below, and credit and debt. They will also have met negative scales on graphs, but will only have used them to plot coordinates. It is important that pupils realise that negative numbers are smaller than positive numbers and they should ignore the value of the digit, for example, -10 is smaller than $+2$.

Plenary

Talk about the temperatures used in the starter. Check that pupils understand which is the lowest and which the highest. Ask if anyone could find a way of showing them in order.

Explain that the topic for the next lesson will be number lines that do not end (or start) at zero.

Incorporating exercise:	3B		Key words	
Homework:	3.3		greater than	negative
Example:	3.3		inequality	number line
			less than	positive
			more than	

Learning objective(s)

- use a number line to represent negative numbers
- use inequalities with negative numbers

Prior knowledge

Pupils will need to have a basic understanding of the value of negative numbers.

Starters

Go around the class starting at 40 and counting down in threes. Encourage pupils to keep going when they reach negative numbers.

Ask quick-fire questions such as, 'What is three less than seven? What is five less than one? What is four more than minus two?'

Main teaching points

Emphasise that numbers to the right of zero on a number line are positive and those to the left of zero are negative. Some pupils prefer a number line that goes up and down rather than across. Remind pupils of the inequality signs ($<$ and $>$) and make sure that they understand them. For example, -7 is smaller than 4. Stress that it is the sign that is important with negatives not the value of the digit.

Common mistakes

Pupils may miss out zero altogether.

When comparing numbers, pupils often look at the value of the digit and not its sign.

Plenary

Draw a number line the other way from how you have been working. Check that pupils can fill in missing numbers on this line.

Incorporating exercises:	3C, 3D, 3E
Homework:	3.4
Examples:	3.4
Resource:	3.4

Key words
add
subtract

Learning objective(s)

● add and subtract positive and negative numbers to both positive and negative numbers

Prior knowledge

Pupils need to be able to add and subtract positive numbers and to be familiar with a number line.

Starter

Ask pupils to complete the addition pyramids on Resource 3.4.

Answers:

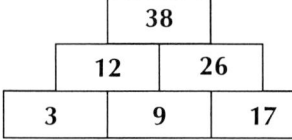 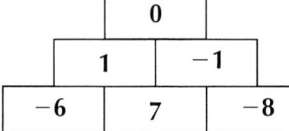 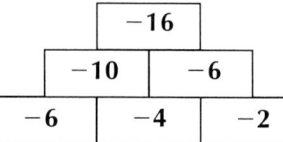 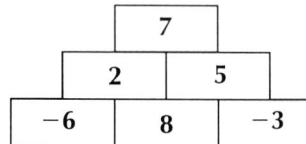

Main teaching points

Use a thermometer scale and/or a number line to compare negative numbers and positive numbers. Stress that when you add on positive numbers these move the answer up the scale, and subtracting positive numbers moves the answer down. When dealing with negative numbers this is not the case. Help pupils to see that subtracting a negative number is equivalent to adding ($- - = +$), and that adding a negative number is equivalent to subtracting ($+ - = -$).

Show pupils how to use a calculator to add and subtract negative numbers.

Common mistakes

This is a confusing concept for low achieving pupils, who commonly cannot learn the rules. When using a calculator they may press the minus button instead of the $+/-$ button.

Differentiation

The whole of Exercise 3C is grade F, Exercise 3D is mainly grade F except for questions 16 and 17, which are grade E. The whole of Exercise 3E is grade F.

Plenary

Make up some more pyramids for pupils to complete together, to test their understanding.

More about number

4

This chapter begins by looking at multiples and factors of whole numbers. It then looks at special numbers, such as primes, squares and square roots. It moves on to the different powers and then the effects of multiplying and dividing by powers of 10. Next it covers how to work out prime factors and finally the rules for multiplying and dividing powers.

Context

This chapter contains material that is interesting and valuable for its own sake. Factors and multiples relate to the multiplication tables and instant recall of these is a useful tool in life. Knowledge of factors also helps when cancelling or multiplying and dividing fractions. Squares and roots are used in patterns, for example when tiling a floor or wall.

Edexcel A references

Ma2 Number and algebra: Numbers and the number system

4.1, 4.2, 4.3   2.2a "... use the concepts and vocabulary of factor (divisor), multiple, common factor ..."
4.4, 4.5, 4.6   2.2b "use the terms square, positive ... square root, cube ...; use index notation for squares, cubes and powers of 10; ..."
4.8   2.2a "... use the concepts and vocabulary of ... highest common factor, least common multiple, prime number and prime factor decomposition"
4.9   2.2b "... use index notation ...; use index laws for multiplication and division of integer powers; ..."

Ma2 Number and algebra: Calculations

4.1, 4.2, 4.3   2.3g "... recall all multiplication facts to 10×10, and use them to derive quickly the corresponding
4.4, 4.5, 4.6   division facts; ... recall the cubes of 2, 3, 4, 5 and 10, ..."
   2.3o "use calculators effectively and efficiently; know how to ... use function keys for ... squares and powers"
4.7   2.3a "... multiply or divide any number by powers of 10 ..."
4.8   2.3a "... find the prime factor decomposition of positive integers ..."

Route mapping

Exercise	G	F	E	D	C
A	all				
B	all				
C		1–2	3–6		
D	1	2–3	4–7	8–13	14
E		all			
F		1–2	3–4	5–9	10
G				all	
H					all
I					all
J					all

Answers to diagnostic Check-in test

1 6	**2** 45	**3** 9	**4** 7	**5** 18
6 25	**7** 9	**8** 8	**9** 30	**10** 72
11 1200	**12** 36	**13** 12	**14** 121	**15** 4
16 150	**17** 7	**18** 16	**19** 24	**20** 4

Write down the answers to the following questions.

1 36 ÷ 6 = ☐

2 5 × 9 = ☐

3 ☐ × 9 = 81

4 63 ÷ 9 = ☐

5 2 × 9 = ☐

6 5 × 5 = ☐

7 ☐ × 3 = 27

8 64 ÷ 8 = ☐

9 6 × 5 = ☐

10 9 × 8 = ☐

11 300 × 4 = ☐

12 6 × 6 = ☐

13 60 ÷ 5 = ☐

14 11 × 11 = ☐

15 ☐ × 9 = 36

16 10 × 15 = ☐

17 49 ÷ 7 = ☐

18 4 × 4 = ☐

19 3 × 8 = ☐

20 12 × ☐ = 48

			Key words
Incorporating exercise:	4A		multiple
Homework:	4.1		times table
Examples:	4.1		

Learning objective(s)

- find multiples of whole numbers
- recognise multiples of numbers

Prior knowledge

Pupils will need to know the times tables to 10 × 10.

Starter

Ask pupils, around the class, to take turns to increase an amount by a given number, for example the first person may say, "Six," the next, "Twelve," the next, "Eighteen," and so on. Continue until someone makes a mistake.

Draw 'multipillars' of different tables. These also make good displays of the tables.

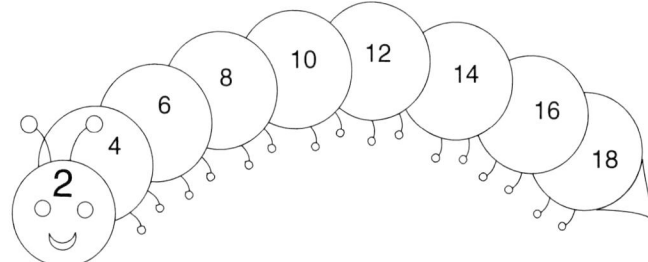

Main teaching points

Encourage pupils to look at the numbers in various times tables and try to identify patterns or rules. For the 10 times table, the answer always ends in 0, numbers in the five times table always end in either 0 or 5, numbers in the two times table are always even. The digits in multiples of three always add up to a multiple of three, the digits in multiples of nine always add up to a multiple of nine. Multiples of six are always even numbers and the digits add up to a multiple of three.

Make sure that pupils know how to use a calculator to find multiples.

Plenary

Put the number 392 on the board. Ask the pupils which of the numbers from one to ten this number is a multiple of. Clearly two is one answer. Half of 392 is 146 so four is also a multiple, but what about other numbers? Three and nine are not answers as 3 + 9 + 2 is not a multiple of three. Also five and ten are not answers as the number does not end in 0 or 5.

Using calculators test whether seven is a multiple (it is).

Repeat with further examples, such as 630 or 720.

Incorporating exercise:	4B	Key words
Homework:	4.2	factor
Examples:	4.2	

Learning objective(s)

● identify the factors of a number

Prior knowledge

Pupils will need to know the times tables to 10×10.

Starter

Ask pupils to draw rectangles, each with an area of 12 cm^2. Look at the different possibilities and list the lengths of the sides. Repeat with other areas.

Show pupils how to draw factor bugs and let them complete their own bugs for different numbers.

Main teaching points

Make sure that pupils realise that factors always come in pairs, so when they have found one factor they can find the other. The exception to this is when they are finding factors of square numbers, where one pair is the same number repeated.

Draw out the fact that every number has one and itself as a factor pair.

In order not to miss any factors, it is sensible to start with one and work upwards, matching the pairs. Using this method, when they have tried all the numbers up to half the number itself, pupils will have found all the factors.

Common mistakes

Pupils often miss out one and the number itself.

Plenary

Give pupils a number, for example 48. Ask them to write it as a multiplication, for example 6×8. Carry on breaking down the separate values as multiplications (do not allow $1\times$), for example $2 \times 3 \times 8$, then $2 \times 3 \times 2 \times 4$, then $2 \times 3 \times 2 \times 2 \times 2$.

Repeat with 20 ($2 \times 2 \times 5$), 60 ($2 \times 3 \times 2 \times 5$), 100 ($2 \times 2 \times 5 \times 5$), etc.

Incorporating exercise:	–	Key words
Homework:	4.3	prime number
Example:	4.3	

Learning objective(s)

- identify prime numbers

Prior knowledge

Pupils will need to know the times tables to 10×10 and the prime numbers up to 50.

Starter

Ask pupils to give numbers that have only two factors.

Main teaching points

A prime number has only two factors, itself and one.

One is not a prime number because it only has one factor.

Make sure that pupils know or can find the prime numbers up to 50.

Common mistakes

Sometimes pupils confuse prime numbers with odd numbers.

They frequently also include 1 and forget 2.

Plenary

Check pupils' understanding by playing 'True and false'. Say a number and ask pupils to put their thumbs up if it is prime and down if it is not prime.

Incorporating exercises: 4C, 4D	**Key words**
Homework: 4.4	square
Examples: 4.4	square number

Learning objective(s)

- identify square numbers
- use a calculator to find the square of a number

Prior knowledge

Pupils will need to know the times tables to 10×10.

Starter

Put the sequence 1, 4, 9, 16, 25 on the board. Ask the pupils if they can give the next two terms.

Ask them how the pattern is building up. They may say that it goes up by 3, 5, 7, 9, ... but make sure they eventually spot that it is 1×1, 2×2, 3×3, etc. Carry on the sequence as far as possible without a calculator.

Pupils are expected to know up to 15×15 for the GCSE exam.

Main teaching points

Square numbers can form square patterns when they are drawn as arrays of dots.

When any integer is multiplied by itself, the result is called a square number.

The short way of writing 'squared' is to put a small 2 after and above a number. For example, 12 squared is written as 12^2.

There is a button on a calculator that can be used to square the input number or the number on screen. It is usually shown as $\boxed{x^2}$.

Common mistakes

Pupils may multiply the number by two instead of squaring it.

Plenary

Put the following on the board:

$1 = 1$
$1 + 3 = 4$
$1 + 3 + 5 = 9$

Ask pupils if they can continue the pattern, for example:

$1 + 3 + 5 + 7 = 16$

Ask pupils to describe each side of the equals sign (sum of consecutive odd numbers, square numbers.

Ask if they can fill in the missing square number for:

$1 + 3 + \cdots + 17 + 19 = ?$ $(= 100$, as the value is $((19 + 1) \div 2)^2)$

Incorporating exercise:	4E	Key words
Homework:	4.5	square root
Example:	4.5	

Learning objective(s)

- find a square root of a square number
- use a calculator to find the square root of any number

Prior knowledge

Pupils will need to know the times tables to 10×10.

Starter

Draw a function machine on the board, but leave the operation blank. Give the pupils three inputs and outputs, for example (1, 3), (5, 7), (10, 12), and then ask them to give the output for a given input and the input for a given output. Once they have spotted the rule, ask them to describe it and give you the inverse rule.

Repeat with other rules such as 'double', 'divide by 3' and 'double and add 3'.

Finish with the operation square. Pupils should have an intuitive idea of a square root, but may not know how to describe it.

Main teaching points

Finding a square root is the inverse of finding a square. Because it is difficult to put a simple explanation into words, the best way to teach pupils about roots is to use examples. It is particularly helpful to use the concept of an inverse operation.

There is a 'square root' button on every calculator and it looks like this $\boxed{\sqrt{}}$. Pupils need to know how to use this button.

Common mistakes

Pupils may divide by two instead of finding the square root.

Plenary

Allow pupils to use calculators, or tell them to start with the number three.

Ask them to think of an odd number, say nine. Square the number, *add* one to the answer and divide by two: $(81 + 1) \div 2 = 41$

Now square the odd number, *subtract* one from it and divide by two: $(81 - 1) \div 2 = 40$

Ask pupils to square the first result, subtract the second result from it and then square root the answer: $41^2 - 40^2 = 81, \sqrt{81} = 9$

If they have done it correctly they will get the number they started with.

		Key words	
Incorporating exercise:	4F	cube	power
Homework:	4.6	indices	square
Example:	4.6		

Learning objective(s)

- use powers

Prior knowledge

Pupils will need to know the times tables to 10×10.

Starter

Show the pupils this puzzle and ask them to find the number in the middle.

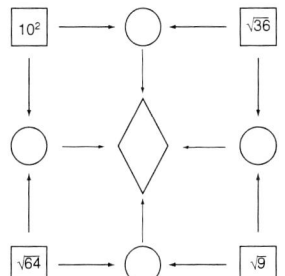

They must multiply the number in each square by the number in the next square, and put the answer in the circle between the two squares.

They should then add the numbers in the circles and write the answer in the diamond in the middle.

Ask them to estimate the square root of the number in the middle.

(The answer is 1442, with a square root of approximately 38.)

Main teaching points

This work is an extension of Section 4.4, which covers square numbers.

A power defines how many times to multiply a number by itself, but the language needs care. For example, 4^5 means $4 \times 4 \times 4 \times 4 \times 4$ and is pronounced as, "Four to the power of five." However, it is not "four multiplied by itself five times", which would be 4^6.

When working with powers of 10, the power is the same as the number of zeros in the calculated answer, for example $10^3 = 1000$.

For the GCSE examination, pupils are expected to know by heart the cubes of 1, 2, 3, 4, 5 and 10.

Common mistakes

Pupils often calculate, for example, 4^5 as 4×5.

Plenary

Show the pupils this puzzle. Ask them to find the middle number and estimate its square root.

(The answer is 2072, with a square root of approximately 46.)

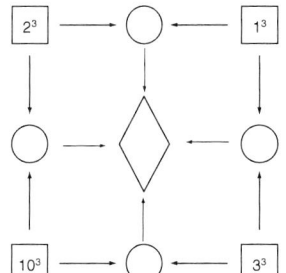

Incorporating exercise:	4G
Homework:	4.7
Examples:	4.7

Learning objective(s)

● multiply and divide by powers of 10

Prior knowledge

Pupils will need to know the times tables to 10×10.

Starter

Ask quick-fire questions around the class, involving multiplying integers and then decimals by 10, 100, 1000. Include questions using powers of ten.

Discuss topics from the beginning of Section 4.7, for example, "How many zeros must you write for a million?"

Main teaching points

Remind pupils about index notation.

Multiplying and dividing by powers of 10 is not just a matter of adding or subtracting zeros. When multiplying a decimal by 10 the rule is *move all the digits in the number* one place to the left. Multiplying by 100 moves them two places to the left, and so on. Make sure the pupils realise that it is the number that moves and not the decimal point. Similarly for division, numbers are moved the required number of places to the right, decreasing in value by a factor of 10 with each move. When multiplying multiples of tens, hundreds and so on, simply multiply the non-zero digits and then append the same number of zeros as there are in the question. For example, $200 \times 300 = 60\ 000$. Cover examples such as $200 \times 50 = 10\ 000$, explaining that the extra zero is required because $2 \times 5 = 10$.

Common mistakes

Pupils sometimes just add zeros, even when they are working with decimals.

They don't allow for the extra zero, as in the example $200 \times 50 = 10\ 000$.

Plenary

Do some mental multiplications, for example 20×30, using the rules learnt in the lesson. If possible, do some simple divisions, for example $800 \div 20$, $600 \div 30$, etc.

Incorporating exercises:	4H, 4I
Homework:	4.8
Examples:	4.8

Key words

highest common factor   prime factor

lowest common multiple   prime factor tree

Learning objective(s)

- identify prime factors
- identify the lowest common multiple (LCM) of two numbers
- identify the highest common factor (HCF) of two numbers

Prior knowledge

Pupils will need to know the times tables to 10×10, and be able to identify prime numbers.

Starter

Give pupils a number, for example 36. Ask them to write it as a multiplication, for example 4×9. Carry on breaking down the separate values as multiplications (do not allow $1\times$), for example $2 \times 2 \times 9$, then $2 \times 2 \times 3 \times 3$.

Repeat with 40 ($2 \times 2 \times 2 \times 5$), 42 ($2 \times 3 \times 7$), 150 ($2 \times 3 \times 5 \times 5$), etc.

Main teaching points

This section assumes a knowledge of factors and prime numbers. It shows how to express a number as a product of its primes. Pupils may have met this at KS3 and already have a method with which they are comfortable. If their method is successful then let them use it. The two methods shown in the Pupil Book are similar; one will suit kinaesthetic learners more.

The lowest common multiple (LCM) of two numbers is the smallest number that appears as an answer in both times tables. The Pupil Book shows two ways of finding the LCM, a third way is to use Venn diagrams.

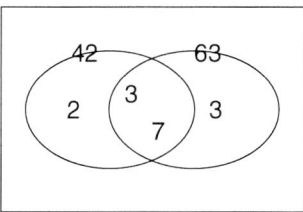

Multiply all the numbers that appear in the various regions of the diagram:

$2 \times 3 \times 3 \times 7 = 126$

This method may appeal to the visual learners in the class.

The highest common factor (HCF) of two numbers is the biggest factor shared by both numbers. An alternative way to find this is again to use the Venn diagram. From the diagram above, the HCF is the product of the numbers that appear in the intersection of the sets.

Common mistakes

A common mistake, when pupils are using the division method, is to miss out the last factor when rewriting the answer in index notation.

Plenary

Write on the board $3^2 \times 2 \times 5$. Ask pupils what the value of the expression is. Repeat with other examples, such as $2^2 \times 5^2$, $2 \times 3 \times 5^2$, $2^3 \times 5$, etc.

Incorporating exercise:	4J
Homework:	4.9
Example:	4.9

Learning objective(s)

○ use rules for multiplying and dividing powers

Prior knowledge

Pupils will need to know the times tables to 10×10 and the meaning of a number expressed to a power.

Starter

Write out the powers of 2 as a table:

| 2^1 | 2^2 | 2^3 | 2^4 | 2^5 |
| 2 | 4 | 8 | 16 | 32 |

Ask pupils to work out the following and write the full calculation on the board:

$2 \times 4 = 8$ $4 \times 8 = 32$ $2 \times 8 = 16$ $2 \times 16 = 32$

Ask pupils if they can see any connection between the calculations and the powers.
If not, write the powers underneath the original calculations:

$2 \times 4 = 8$ $4 \times 8 = 32$ $2 \times 8 = 16$ $2 \times 16 = 32$
$2^1 \times 2^2 = 2^3$ $2^2 \times 2^3 = 2^5$ $2 \times 2^3 = 2^4$ $2 \times 2^4 = 2^5$

They may spot the connection in this form.

Main teaching points

This section covers two simple rules of indices, how to multiply them and how to divide them. The technique can be demonstrated by writing out the index form in full, for example $2^3 \times 2^2$ is $2 \times 2 \times 2 \times 2 \times 2 = 2^5$. Pupils can then see that a quicker way of working is to add the indices. Similarly, when dividing, the rule is to subtract. Pupils need to appreciate that these rules only work when the numbers they are multiplying or dividing are expressed as powers of the same algebraic unknown.

Plenary

Talk about division expressed as: $\dfrac{2^3 \times 2^2}{2^4}$

Talk about division expressed as: $3^2 \div 3^3$.

Overview

5.1 Perimeter
5.2 Area of an irregular shape
5.3 Area of a rectangle
5.4 Area of a compound shape
5.5 Area of a triangle
5.6 Area of a parallelogram
5.7 Area of a trapezium
5.8 Dimensional analysis

This chapter consists of the methods required to find the perimeters and areas of simple 2-D shapes (excluding the circle).

Context

Areas and perimeters of simple shapes occur widely in everyday life. For example, a garden might be modelled as an irregular shape whose area needs to be known. If a room in a house were to be decorated, one would need to know the area of the floor (before buying a carpet) and the areas of the walls (before buying paint).

Edexcel A references

Ma3 Shape, space and measures: Measures and construction

5.1–5.7 3.4f "find areas of rectangles, recalling the formula, understanding the connection to counting squares and how it extends this approach; recall and use the formulae for the area of a parallelogram and a triangle; find the surface area of simple shapes using the area formulae for triangles and rectangles; calculate perimeters and areas of shapes made from triangles and rectangles"

Route mapping

Exercise	G	F	E	D	C
A	1–6	7–12			
B	all				
C		1–6	7–13	14–15	
D				all	
E			1	2–4	
F			1–2	3–5	
G				all	
H				all	
I				1–8	9
J				1–5	6–9
K				1–3	4–6
L					all

Answers to diagnostic Check-in test

1 a 100 cm   **b** 1000 m   **c** 10 mm

2 a 12 cm   **b** 9

3 a 18 cm   **b** 20

4 Square of sides 6 cm

5 Any rectangle whose dimensions add to 8, for example a rectangle 5 cm by 3 cm

1 Write down the answers to the following.

   a 1 m = _____ cm

   b 1 km = _____ m

   c 1 cm = _____ mm

2 This square is 3 cm by 3 cm.

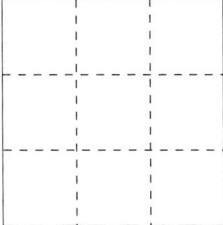

   a What is the total length of all the sides? . . . .

   b How many small squares make up the larger square? . . . .

3 This rectangle is 5 cm by 4 cm.

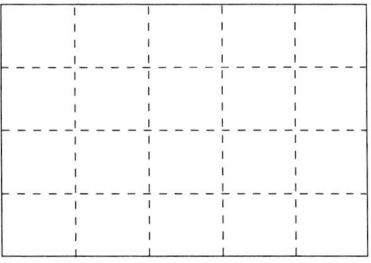

   a What is the total length of all the sides? . . . .

   b How many small squares make up the rectangle? . . . .

4 Draw a square whose sides have a total length of 24 cm.

5 Draw a rectangle (but not a square!) whose sides have a total length of 16 cm.

Incorporating exercise:	5A	Key words
Homework:	5.1	compound shape rectangle
Examples:	5.1	perimeter

Learning objective(s)

- find the perimeter of a rectangle and compound shapes

Prior knowledge

Pupils need to be aware of the idea of the perimeter as being the distance round a shape.

Starter

Draw a rectangle on the board. Ask pupils what they can say about the shape, for example there are four sides, opposite sides are parallel, opposite sides are the same length.
Draw a 3 × 2 rectangle. Ask pupils for the perimeter. Double the lengths of the sides of the rectangle. How does the perimeter change?

Main teaching points

Emphasise the dimensions of perimeter. For example, perimeter is a *length* (that is, the 'distance' round a shape) and so its units will be centimetres (or metres).

Encourage pupils to write their full working out. For example, in Exercise 5A question 1, perimeter = 4 + 1 + 4 +1 = 10 cm. For the first few questions, it would also be advantageous for them to copy out the diagrams and label the lengths of each side clearly.

Common mistakes

Many pupils should have come across area and/or perimeter before and often confuse the two. Pupils will often find the product of the two sides when asked to find the perimeter or just add one length to one width.

Plenary

Draw a compound shape with all dimensions on, for example:

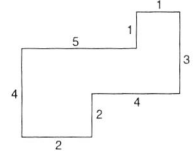

Ask pupils how many dimensions can be removed before it becomes impossible to work out the others. The answer is one 'horizontal' dimension and one 'vertical' dimension: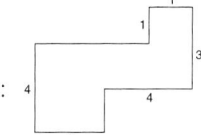

Now split the shape into rectangles and ask for the dimensions of each:

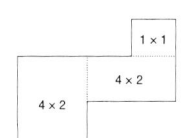

Emphasise the need to be able to break shapes down and find the dimensions of the separate parts.

			Key words
Incorporating exercise:	5B		area
Homework:	5.2		estimate
Example:	5.2		

Learning objective(s)

● estimate the area of an irregular 2-D shape by counting squares

Prior knowledge

Pupils need to be aware of the idea of area as the amount of space a 2-D shape holds.

Starter

On an OHP or using two cut out shapes stuck on a board, show pupils a circle and a rectangle (or an irregular shape) with approximately the same area. Discuss how to find out which has the largest area. Pupils will be familiar with the idea of splitting a shape into centimetre squares and counting them, or cutting shapes up. If possible, have the shapes with squares drawn on the back (i.e. 5 cm by 5 cm squares), so the shapes can be 'turned over' and the areas compared.

Main teaching points

It would be useful to emphasise that the area of an irregular shape can only be estimated, and there might be more than one correct answer, depending on pupils' estimations.

Emphasise the difference between an estimate and a guess. A guess is just that, while an estimate usually requires a certain procedure to be followed. In this case, it is to count the number of whole squares within the shape first.

Common mistakes

Many pupils often count a square as being within the shape, even if it is only, say, 90% within.

Plenary

Extend the idea of counting squares to find an area, where partial squares are simple fractions of a whole square. For example, draw a 4 × 4 right-angled triangle as follows:

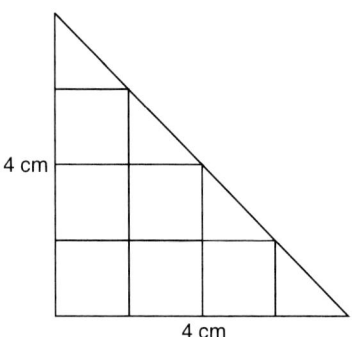

Ask the pupils for the area of this triangle. (Calculate by counting squares.)
Some pupils may remember the formula, area = half base × height, and can see that this will provide the same answer.

Incorporating exercise:	5C	**Key words**	
Homework:	5.3	area	width
Examples:	5.3	length	

Learning objective(s)

- find the area of a rectangle
- use the formula for the area of a rectangle

Prior knowledge

Pupils need to be aware of the idea of area as the amount of space covered by a 2-D shape.

Starter

Draw a 5 × 3 rectangle on the board. Ask pupils, "How do I find the area of this rectangle?" Repeat for two more rectangles.

Main teaching points

When calculating the area of each rectangle, ensure pupils write down the formula before substituting in their values for length and width.

Conversion between area units is often a difficult idea for foundation pupils to grasp and should be taught to the class as a whole before such questions are attempted. Even after being guided through with an example, the idea of changing square metres to square centimetres is often simply taken as multiplying by 100 rather than 100^2.

Question 15 in Exercise 5C, for example, could be emphasised.

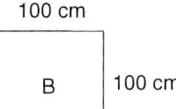

Area of A = 1 × 1 = 1 m^2
Area of B = 100 × 100 = 10 000 cm^2

Therefore, to change metres to centimetres, you multiply by 100. But to change square metres to square centimetres, you multiply by 10 000. For example, an area of 5 m^2 is the same as 50 000 cm^2 and an area of 8.2 m^2 is the same as 82 000 cm^2.

Plenary

Summarise the work done so far in finding the area of a rectangle, that is: $A = LW$, $W = A \div L$, $L = A \div W$

Summarise the calculations needed for unit change of length and area, that is:

- to change metres to centimetres, multiply by 100
- to change centimetres to millimetres, multiply by 10

- to change square metres to square centimetres, multiply by 10 000
- to change square centimetres to square millimetres, multiply by 100.

Compare the areas of these two rectangles:

A = 40 × 60 = 2400 cm^2
A = 0.4 × 0.6 = 0.24 m^2

Incorporating exercise:	5D	**Key words**
Homework:	5.4	area
Examples:	5.4	compound shape

Learning objective(s)

● find the area of a compound shape by splitting it into rectangles

Prior knowledge

Pupils need to be able to find the area of a rectangle, as covered in Section 5.3.

Starter

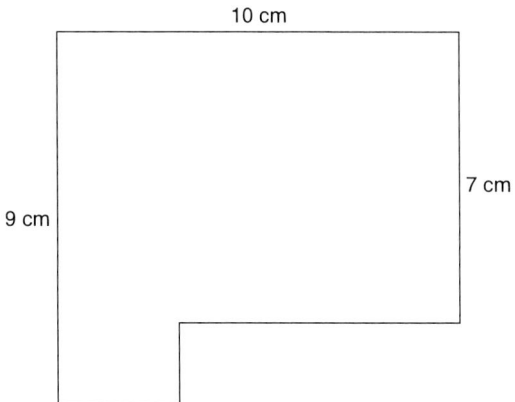

Ask pupils, "How might I find the area of this shape?" Split the shape into two rectangles and find the area of each before adding them. Ask, "Is there another way to find the area of this shape?" Show that by splitting the shape into another two rectangles, the same answer is obtained.

Main teaching points

Ensure pupils copy down the diagrams for each question and show precisely how they are splitting up the compound shape. Label each rectangle clearly, with A, B, etc., and calculate the area of each before finding their sum (or difference). It is important that pupils set out their working clearly, as in example 5, as they will still pick up method marks if they get a dimension wrong.

Common mistakes

Pupils will often fare badly when asked to calculate the area of a compound shape. Ensure they have drawn a good diagram to avoid obtaining incorrect dimensions. For example, in question 5 of the homework sheet, it will be common to see their dimensions of the swimming pool and path as 16 × 9 rather than 17 × 10.

Plenary

Draw this shape on the board:

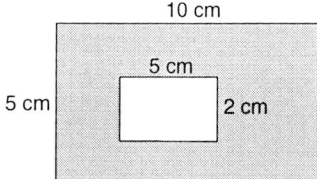

Ask pupils if they can see a way to calculate the shaded area. They will probably come up with the idea of subtracting the two values.

Now draw this shape:

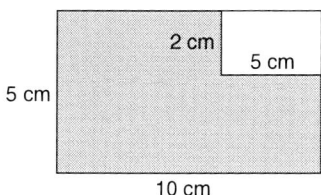

Ask them if they can see a similar method of calculating the shaded area. Point out that sometimes the area of a compound shape may be worked out by subtracting areas rather than adding.

Show how to set out the working:

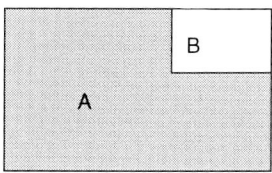

Area of rectangle A = $5 \times 10 = 50$ cm^2
Area of rectangle B = $2 \times 5 = 10$ cm^2
Area shaded = Area of A $-$ Area of B = $50 - 10 = 40$ cm^2

Incorporating exercises:	5E, 5F	Key words	
Homework:	5.5	area	perpendicular
Examples:	5.5	base	height
		height	triangle

Learning objective(s)

- find the area of a triangle
- use the formula for the area of a triangle

Prior knowledge

Pupils should know how to find the area of a rectangle, as covered in Section 5.3.

Starter

Ask pupils, "What is meant by a 'right-angled triangle'? How many types of triangle are there and what are they called?"
Ask them, "What do we mean by 'perpendicular'? What do we mean by 'height'?" It might be useful to emphasise that other 'heights' exist, for example slant heights in cones.

Main teaching points

The area of a triangle is given by $A = \frac{1}{2}$ base × height, although it must always be emphasised in this context that height means perpendicular height.

Given that the formula for the area of a triangle can easily be seen from halving that of a parallelogram, one option may be to cover Section 5.6 first.

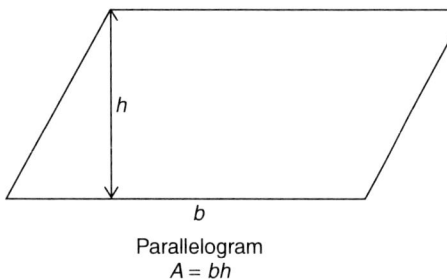

Parallelogram
$A = bh$

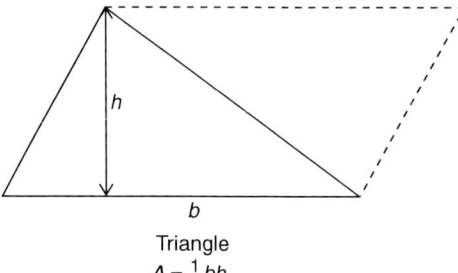

Triangle
$A = \frac{1}{2}bh$

Common mistakes

The most common error is to use a height other than the perpendicular height. However, there is unlikely to be any ambiguity at this level as the pupils will have no way of working out the perpendicular height if it were not given to them.

Plenary

Ask pupils to draw as many triangles as they can that have an area of 24 cm^2, but with different-sized bases.

Incorporating exercise:	5G	Key words	
Homework:	5.6	area	parallelogram
Examples:	5.6	base	vertices
		height	

Learning objective(s)

- find the area of a parallelogram
- use the formula for the area of a parallelogram

Prior knowledge

Pupils should know how to find the area of a rectangle, as covered in Section 5.3.

Starter

Ask pupils, "What is meant by a 'parallelogram'?" (It is a quadrilateral with two pairs of parallel sides.)
Ask them, "Does this mean that a rectangle is a parallelogram? Is a square a parallelogram?"

Main teaching points

The area of a parallelogram is given by A = base $\times$ height. As in the previous section for the area of a triangle, it must always be emphasised in this context that height means perpendicular height.

The formula for the area of a parallelogram can be shown in two ways:

Area of parallelogram = area of a rectangle = base $\times$ height

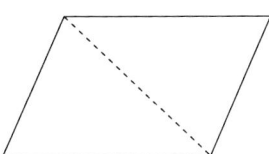

Area of parallelogram = area of two congruent triangles

$$= 2 \times \frac{1}{2} \times \text{base} \times \text{height} = \text{base} \times \text{height}$$

Ensure final answers are given to a suitable degree of accuracy, normally 3 significant figures.

Pick's Theorem (1899)

The 'activity' in this section is an investigation based on Pick's Theorem (1899). George Pick (1859–1942) was an Austrian mathematician and a close friend of Einstein.

Suppose that P is a lattice polygon, and that there are $I(P)$ lattice points in the interior of P, and $B(P)$ lattice points on its boundary.

Then Pick's Theorem states: $A(P) = I(P) + \dfrac{B(P)}{2} - 1$, where $A(P)$ is the area of P.

Common mistakes

The most common error in calculating the area of a parallelogram is to use the length of another side of the parallelogram rather than a perpendicular height. Questions might be given where all sides of the parallelogram are given, along with the height. Extra care must be taken in these cases (see Worked example 5.6).

Plenary

Ask pupils to draw several parallelograms, each with an area of 12 cm^2 and the same base. Then ask them to draw parallelograms with an area of 12 cm^2, but with different sized bases.

Incorporating exercise:	5H
Homework:	5.7
Examples:	5.7

Key words

area   trapezium
height

Learning objective(s)

- find the area of a trapezium
- use the formula for the area of a trapezium

Prior knowledge

Pupils should know how to find the areas of triangles, rectangles and parallelograms, as covered in previous sections in this chapter.

Starter

Ask pupils, "What is meant by a 'trapezium'?" (It is a quadrilateral with one pair of parallel sides.)
Ask them, "Does a rectangle count as a trapezium? What about a square?"

Main teaching points

The area of a trapezium is given by:

A = half the sum of the parallel sides × height

$A = \dfrac{1}{2}(a + b)h$

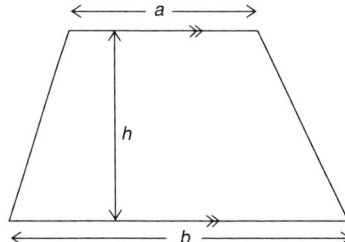

This can be seen to be the case by splitting the trapezium into two triangles:

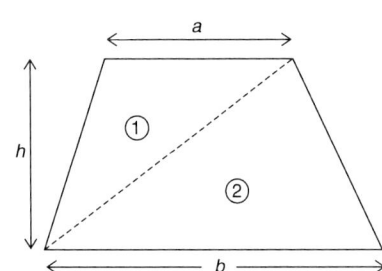

Area of triangle 1 = $\dfrac{1}{2}$ × base × height = $\dfrac{1}{2}ah$

Area of triangle 2 = $\dfrac{1}{2}$ × base × height = $\dfrac{1}{2}bh$

Total area = $\dfrac{1}{2}ah + \dfrac{1}{2}bh = \dfrac{1}{2}h(a + b) = \dfrac{1}{2}(a + b)h$

As in the previous section for the area of a parallelogram, it must always be emphasised in this context that height means perpendicular height and that we add the two *parallel* sides.

Common mistakes

The most common error is to calculate $(\frac{1}{2}a + b)$, which is generally down to lack of understanding in the use of the calculator. This can be avoided by encouraging pupils to label their trapezium with letters, a, b and h, before commencing the question and to set out their working appropriately as shown in the worked examples.

Plenary

Draw the following on the board:

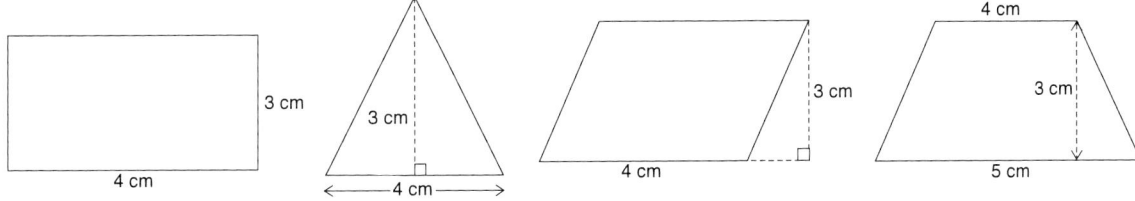

Which has the largest area?

Key words
area	volume
dimension	
length	

Learning objective(s)

- recognise whether a formula represents a length, an area or a volume

Prior knowledge

Pupils should know the formulae for perimeters of various shapes, and the metric units commonly used to express length: mm, cm, m and km. They should know the formulae for areas of standard shapes and how to find the volumes of simple and compound solids, including prisms.

Starter

Ask pupils for perimeter formulae for various shapes. For example, suggest to them a circle of radius r, or a rectangle of dimensions l by w. Ask them to give expressions for the perimeters.

Ask pupils for area formulae for various shapes. Ask them to calculate expressions for areas.

Ask pupils to recall the volume formulae for standard shapes.

Main teaching points

The main teaching point is the difference between volumes (having three dimensions), areas (having two dimensions), lengths (having one dimension) and numbers (which are dimensionless).

Illustrate the dimensions of length using the fact that length + length = length, while number × length = length. The dimensions of area might be illustrated using the fact that area = length × length, while number × area = area.

The dimensional aspects of volume should be illustrated by focusing on these examples:
- volume = area × length can be seen from the general formula for the volume of a prism
- volume = length × length × length can be illustrated by looking at the volume of a cube or cuboid
- number × volume = volume can be seen by taking a cuboid of lengths l, w and h, calculating its volume, then changing the length of w to $2w$, for example.

Explain to the class that scientists use dimensional analysis to check if complicated formulae are consistent, but they should only be concerned with length, area and volume. Tell them that it is possible to recognise if a formula is for length, area or volume by looking at the number of variables in each term.

Plenary

Summarise the dimension notes for pupils as used throughout this section:
- number × length = length
- length + length = length
- length × length = area
- area + area = area
- length × length × length = volume
- area × length = volume
- volume + volume = volume
- volume + area is inconsistent
- area + length is inconsistent

Overview

6.1 Frequency diagrams
6.2 Statistical diagrams
6.3 Bar charts
6.4 Line graphs
6.5 Stem-and-leaf diagrams

This chapter addresses two areas of Data Handling: organising and representing data. The first exercise covers organising data into frequency tables and grouped frequency tables. The other exercises cover diagrams and representations of data.

Context

The usefulness of this topic should be evident from the nature of the exercises and questions. It may be worthwhile to provide examples from the national and local press of representations of data as a discussion point. One national newspaper does a weekly statistical graphic on a current news topic. The misuse of statistical techniques is worth exploring, so that the importance of a good understanding of this topic is reinforced. Pupils could be asked to bring in examples of their own choosing, allowing them the opportunity to relate the topic to their own interests. Any discussion that encourages understanding and interpretation of tables and diagrams is very useful, as this is a common area of weakness.

Edexcel A references

Ma4 Handling data: Collecting data

6.1   4.3a "design and use data-collection sheets for grouped, discrete and continuous data; collect data using various methods, including observation, controlled experiment, data logging, questionnaires and surveys"
4.3b "gather data from secondary sources, including printed tables and lists from ICT-based sources"
4.3c "design and use two-way tables for discrete and grouped data"

Ma4 Handling data: Processing and representing data

6.2, 6.3, 6.4, 6.5   4.4a "draw and produce, using paper and ICT, ... diagrams for continuous data, including line graphs for time series, ... frequency diagrams and stem-and-leaf diagrams"

Route mapping

Exercise	G	F	E	D	C
A	1	2	3–5	6	
B	1–2	3–5			
C		all			
D			1–2	3–4	
E			1–2	3–4	

Answers to diagnostic Check-in test

1 a Fiction   **b** 94   **c** £925.60   **d** 51
2 13, 17, 10, 8, 5
3 a 22   **b** Bekki   **c** 90   **d** 9

1 Use the information in the table to answer the following questions.

Type of book	Number sold this week	Total money taken (£)
Fiction	43	327.65
Health	27	286.70
Travel	16	205.40
Biography	8	105.85

a Which type of book was the top selling? ....

b How many books were sold altogether in that week? ....

c How much money was taken altogether in that week? ....

d How many of the books sold that week were non-fiction? ....

2 Complete the frequency column of this table.

Number of visitors	Tally	Frequency
0	ⵏ⵰ ⵏ⵰ |||	
1	ⵏ⵰ ⵏ⵰ ⵏ⵰ ||	
2	ⵏ⵰ ⵏ⵰	
3	ⵏ⵰ |||	
4	ⵏ⵰	

3 Josie recorded how many text messages she received from five of her friends one week and made this bar chart.

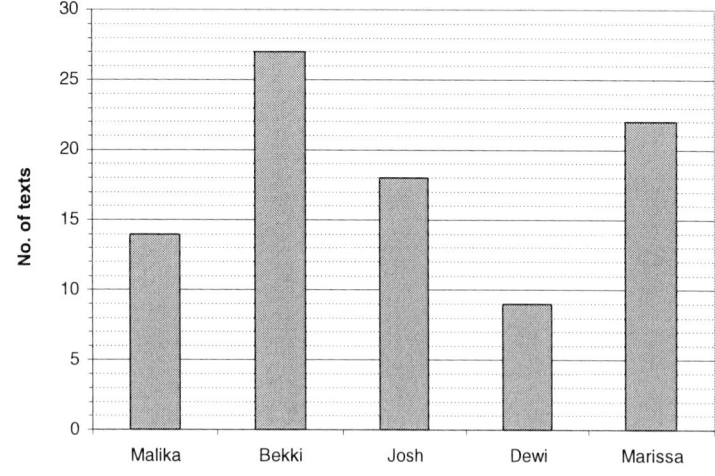

a How many texts did she receive from Marissa?

....

b Who sent her the most texts?

....

c How many texts did these five send her altogether?

....

d How many more did Josh send than Dewi?

....

Incorporating exercise:	6A
Homework:	6.1
Examples:	6.1

Key words

class	frequency table
class interval	grouped data
data collection	grouped
sheet	frequency table
experiment	observation
frequency	sample
	tally chart

Learning objective(s)

● collect and represent discrete and grouped data using tally charts and frequency tables

Prior knowledge

Pupils must know how to use a tallying process accurately (with both discrete and grouped data) and must be able to understand information that has been presented in tabular form.

Starter

Tell the class that you are going to collect information about how many siblings they have (they can include half brothers and sisters, etc.). Go round the class asking each pupil individually for their answer. Write the results on the board as a list. Once all of the data has been collected, discuss how it could be analysed. Mention that this is raw data at the moment. Ask if there are better ways to show the data. Putting it in order may be suggested. This would give ordered data. A table may be mentioned. Organise the data into a table, using tallies to record each value. Compare the advantages of raw data, ordered data and a table.

Main teaching points

Pupils should understand the need for a methodical approach to collecting and organising data. It is important to cover clearly the three methods for collecting data: sampling, observation and experiment. The benefits and potential pitfalls of sampling should be discussed.

It is also important that they use a correct tallying procedure. Ideally, the starter activity should provide some support for this, as it should be clear that tallying data items one at a time, rather than scanning for all the records for a class, is much more likely to give accurate results.

The final important skill covered concerns ensuring that pupils can retrieve relevant information from a table.

Common mistakes

Pupils often find it difficult to distinguish between the types of situation which suit the different methods of data collection. Plenty of examples and clear explanations are helpful here.

It is also very common for pupils to try to find shortcuts in the tallying process, as the correct method is often seen as very time consuming. It is worth comparing results of tallying, as you are likely to find differences in what should be a straightforward activity. If pupils can see that differences occur so easily, it gives them more reason to follow the correct procedure and to be more careful than they might think is necessary.

Differentiation

Question 6 offers a lot of scope for differentiation. Suitable topics for surveys can be selected, depending on the ability of the pupil or the amount of time available, and could perhaps be set as a homework, in which case the dice activity could be used instead of question 6 during the lesson.

Plenary

Ask for examples of occasions when sampling, observation and experiment should be used.
Discuss the results of the Double dice activity.

Incorporating exercise:	6B
Homework:	6.2
Examples:	6.2

Key words

key	symbol
pictograms	

Learning objective(s)

● show collected data as pictograms

Prior knowledge

Pupils must be able to understand data presented in tabular form. It is also helpful to have a good command of the times tables for this exercise.

Starter

Draw a number line on the board, divided into 10. Write 0 at one end and any multiple of 10, for example 30, at the other.

Point at different marks on the line and ask pupils to give the value.

Point at some positions between marks and ask for the value (all values are integers). Repeat with other multiples of 10, but end with 40.

Now draw the following on the board:

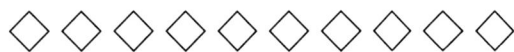

Tell the class that each diamond is worth four and we are counting from left to right. Point at a diamond and ask what the value is. The link between this and the previous activity should be clear.

Ask how we could show 10 with this notation. A half diamond may be suggested, but make the point that using symbols is not always as useful as a continuous line.

Main teaching points

Pupils should understand that, when designing a pictogram, they need to think carefully when choosing how many of the data items a particular symbol is going to represent. They should look through all the frequencies that are to be represented and, if possible, choose a number which is a factor of all of them. It may be necessary, on occasion, to use half symbols but, with careful planning, other fractions can be avoided.

Pupils should also be reminded that the choice of symbol should be something that is relevant to the data being represented, and that only one symbol should be used throughout the pictogram.

Common mistakes

Weaker students often simply use a symbol to represent 1 unit of data. This should be avoided wherever possible. A common mistake is to use different symbols in the different classes of the pictogram.

Differentiation

Since the questions in this exercise are all grade G or F, higher achieving pupils should find it straightforward. It may be more appropriate to use only one lesson on a selection of questions from Exercises 6B and 6C for these pupils, as 6C is aimed at grade F as well.

Plenary

Recap with small groups of numbers and a symbol unit, and ask for the quantity of symbols to represent each number. For example, 'How many symbols are required for the numbers 18, 21, 36 and 42, with each symbol representing 6?' Repeat with variations.

Incorporating exercise:	6C	Key words	
Homework:	6.3	axis	class interval
Examples:	6.3	bar chart	dual bar chart

Learning objective(s)

● draw bar charts to represent statistical data

Prior knowledge

Pupils must be able to understand data presented in tabular form. One question in this exercise requires pupils to be able to express one number as a fraction of another.

Starter

Select some newspaper clippings with bar charts. Distribute these among the class (this works best in pairs or small groups). Ask for a summary of what each bar chart is depicting. Discuss why the journalists have decided to use bar charts.

Main teaching points

These are, perhaps, the most commonly used diagrams for statistical representation and it is likely that pupils will be familiar with them. The teaching should be to ensure that pupils know how to use bar charts correctly and that they are familiar with the different varieties that they may encounter.

Pupils should be aware that bars should be of the same width and it is usual (although not strictly necessary) to arrange them so that the bars are vertical. Pupils should be shown bar-line graphs as an alternative method of presentation.

Pupils should understand when to use dual bar charts and how to read them, ensuring that they are aware of the necessity to have a key to identify the different sets of data.

Common mistakes

Less able pupils sometimes confuse the two axes and consequently draw the bars the wrong way round, possibly without a correctly spaced frequency axis. This is most likely to happen if the data is numerical.

Differentiation

As mentioned in Section 6.2, all questions in this exercise are grade F and could be combined with Exercise 6B for the higher achieving pupils, as the work is likely to be familiar to them. They could move quickly to question 7 if newspapers are available, as this type of work is good practice for Data handling coursework.

Plenary

Ask pupils to summarise the main points of the lesson. Focus on the fact that the bars are drawn from the data axis and extend to the length of the frequency value.

Review and discuss the findings from question 7.

Incorporating exercise:	6D	**Key words**
Homework:	6.4	line graphs
Examples:	6.4	trends

Learning objective(s)

● draw a line graph to show trends in data

Prior knowledge

Pupils must be able to understand data presented in tabular form. Pupils need to be able to plan and read scales on axes in a variety of situations.

Starter

Present the class with a number of line segments, with different numbers of sections along them (2, 4 and 5 sections are the most usual). Put a number at each end of the line and ask for the numbers that go at other positions along the line segment.

Repeat the above with units of time along the line segments (for example, minutes, years, dates).

Main teaching points

Pupils should understand that the use of line graphs to represent statistical information is usually restricted to time series. The reason for this is that line graphs allow estimates to be made at intermediate points. Some discussion is useful concerning the use of suitable scales on axes. If times are measured from a 'zero' or 'starting time', then the horizontal axis may start at zero, whereas if times are years, days of the week or times of day, then it is impracticable to start at zero. Times are always plotted on the horizontal axis.

Pupils should understand that line graphs are useful because they give a picture of how something is changing over a period of time. This is what allows intermediate values to be estimated and it may allow future predictions to be made, although these should always be treated very cautiously.

Common mistakes

The most common mistakes are the poor choice, or incorrect use, of scales to represent times.

It is also common for pupils to make intermediate or future estimates without giving the data realistic thought.

Differentiation

As these are grade E and grade D questions, low achieving pupils may well find some of this work quite difficult. They are likely to find the interpretation of the information being presented the most challenging and these parts may require some discussion so that what is actually being asked is made clear.

Plenary

If the activity has been used, ask groups to give feedback on their findings to the class.
Ask for a summary of line graphs, for example when they can be used and why they can be useful.

Incorporating exercise:	6E	Key words	
Homework:	6.5	discrete data	raw data
Examples:	6.5	ordered data	unordered data

Learning objective(s)

⬤ draw and read information from an ordered stem and leaf diagram

Prior knowledge

Pupils must be able to order a set of numbers. They must have a clear understanding of place value in order to classify the digits of a set of numbers into the same category.

Starter

Show the class this set of numbers: 23, 54, 20, 48, 26, 58, 41. Ask them to suggest ways of forming a group of numbers that have something in common from this collection. Examples might be: (54 and 48), where both numbers are multiples of 6, and (23 and 41), where both numbers are odd numbers. Hopefully, someone will suggest (20, 23 and 26), (41 and 48) and (54 and 58), where each group has the same tens digit.

Main teaching points

Pupils should understand that the benefit of this method of representation is that it shows how the range of data is distributed, in a similar way to a grouped frequency table, but maintains all the detail of the original data.

Perhaps the most difficult skill here is in reading the data from a stem-and-leaf diagram and it would be beneficial for pupils to have as much practice in this as possible, ideally as a whole-class activity so that it generates discussion and brings out the most common mistakes. Pupils should understand that a stem-and-leaf diagram is much easier to read if the 'leaf' digits are well spaced and kept in distinct columns.

Common mistakes

The most common mistake is to forget to recombine the stem and leaf and just give the leaf as the value. Pupils often forget to provide a key.

Differentiation

As this is a grade E and grade D exercise, some of the less able pupils will find it quite difficult and may need more examples to reinforce the concepts. Question 2 of this exercise may need extra explanation as it uses a back-to-back stem-and-leaf diagram and pupils may find this a little confusing without some initial discussion.

Plenary

As this is the end of the chapter, it is worth asking for summaries of the techniques covered, for example, "What different statistical diagrams have been covered?", "When are line graphs used?", "Which way round should a bar chart be drawn?", and "Why would someone use a dual bar chart?".

Overview

7.1 The language of algebra	**7.4** Factorisation
7.2 Simplifying expressions	**7.5** Quadratic expansion
7.3 Expanding brackets	**7.6** Substitution

The work in this chapter covers the language of algebra, including writing algebraic expressions from words, writing formulae by using letters, and solving problems. It then looks at simplifying expressions, collecting like terms, combining like terms into groups and expanding brackets. The next section deals with factorising both numbers and letters, followed by expansions of the product of two sets of brackets. Finally the chapter covers substitution.

Context

One of the advantages of using algebra is that it allows you to generalise, rather than limiting you to specific occurrences. Rules can be formulated that apply every time to a given situation. Everyday examples include finding areas and volumes, converting between different units and calculating household bills, such as those for telephone, water, gas and electricity, where the standard charge is constant and the numbers of units consumed are variable. Once the rule is known, numbers can be substituted so that calculations may be made.

Edexcel A references

Ma2 Number and algebra: Equations, formulae and identities

7.1	2.5a "distinguish the different roles played by letter symbols in algebra, ... knowing that letter symbols represent definite unknown numbers in equations, defined quantities or variables in formulae ..."
7.2, 7.3, 7.4, 7.5, 7.6	2.5b "understand that the transformation of algebraic expressions obeys and generalises the rules of generalised arithmetic, expand the product of two linear expressions; manipulate algebraic expressions by collecting like terms, by multiplying a single term over a bracket, and by taking out common factors ..."

Route mapping

Exercise	G	F	E	D	C
A		1–6	7–17		
B			1–20	21–40	
C			all		
D			1–24	25–42	
E			1	2–4	5–6
F				1–16	17–39
G				all	
H			1–6	7–12	
I			1–5	6–8	

Answers to diagnostic Check-in test

1 39	**2** 39	**3** 16	**4** 22	**5** –210
6 18	**7** 25	**8** Annie is correct because you multiply before you add.		

1 $5 \times 7 + 4 =$

2 $4 + 7 \times 5 =$

3 $\dfrac{18}{2} + 7 =$

4 $24 - \dfrac{12}{6} =$

5 $90 - 50 \times 6 =$

6 $2(3 + 6) =$

7 $5 \times (7 - 2) =$

8 Bill says the answer to $3 + 7 \times 2$ is 20. Annie says it is 17.
Who is right? Explain why.

Incorporating exercise:	7A	**Key words**	
Homework:	7.1	expression	symbol
Example:	7.1	formula	

Learning objective(s)

● use letters, numbers and mathematical symbols to write algebraic expressions and formulae

Prior knowledge

Pupils need to know the order of operations for arithmetic. This is known as the BODMAS rule and should be used whenever different arithmetic operations occur together.

Starter

Throw three dice. Tell pupils the numbers, say 6, 3, 5, and ask them to make up five calculations using mathematical signs, including brackets. For example:

$$6 + 3 + 5 = 14, (6 - 3) \times 5 = 15, 6 \times 3 + 5 = 23, 6 \times 5 - 3 = 27, 6 + 3 - 5 = 4$$

Collect in examples, particularly those using brackets incorrectly, and discuss with the class what the errors are. Recall the rules of BODMAS. Repeat if there is time.

Main teaching points

The two main words that need to be explained in this section are 'expression' and 'formulae'. Pupils need to understand that algebra follows the rules of arithmetic, using the same symbols and order of operations. Refer to the seven important rules in the Pupil book, page 144.

Common mistakes

Pupils find it difficult to understand the difference between an expression and a formula.

Differentiation

Questions 1 to 6 are grade F and 7 to 17 are grade E. Higher achieving pupils could begin at question 9. Those who work more slowly could complete the even-numbered questions. Pupils may have difficulty accessing the mathematics if they have poor reading skills.

Plenary

Run through the seven important rules and check that pupils understand them.

● 3 more than $x = x + 3$
● 5 less than (or fewer than) $y = y - 5$ (not $5 - y$) (Make sure pupils understand the difference.)
● 4 multiplied by $z = 4z$
● b divided by $2 = \dfrac{b}{2}$ (not $\dfrac{2}{b}$) (Again, check to make sure pupils understand the difference.)
● $7a = 7 \times a$
● $1 \times c = c$ (not $1c$)
● $t \times t = t^2$ (Again, discuss the difference between this and $2t$.)

Incorporating exercises:	7B, 7C	**Key words**
Homework:	7.2a, 7.2b	like terms
Example:	7.2	simplify
Resources:	7.2a, 7.2b	

Learning objective(s)

- simplify algebraic expressions by multiplying terms
- simplify algebraic expressions by collecting like terms

Prior knowledge

None required.

Starter

- Show pupils the algebra pyramids (Resource 7.2a). Ask them to complete each pyramid by first adding and then multiplying the expressions in adjacent boxes, writing the answer in the appropriate box in the row above. The answers are, (adding) $6 + 2m$ and $6 + 4u$, (multiplying) $9m^2$ and $12u^3$.

- Show pupils the array of algebraic expressions (Resource 7.2b). Ask them to match up the expressions, for example linking $2x + x$ with $3x$. They can do this individually, in groups or as a class.

Main teaching points

When simplifying expressions there are conventions that must be followed. Numbers come before letters and letters are written in alphabetical order. This must be emphasised so that, when there are powers in a term, there is no confusion.

When working with powers, pupils must know that they can only combine the same letters. They must add indices when they are multiplying powers of the same base and subtract when they are dividing.

Common mistakes

Pupils will multiply the indices as well as the numbers, or add the numbers as well as the powers.

Differentiation

Questions 1 to 20 of Exercise 7B are grade E, questions 21 to 40 are grade D. You may wish to begin asking for answers orally and then let pupils write down their answers from question 15 onwards. Lower achieving pupils may have trouble with questions 33 to 36 as they involve negative numbers.

Plenary

Check pupils' understanding by asking them questions such as, "Give me two expressions that could add to $3x^2$." "Give me two expressions that multiply to give $4n^3$."

Incorporating exercises:	7D, 7E	Key words	
Homework:	7.3a, 7.3b	expand	multiply out
Examples:	7.3	expand and simplify	simplify

Learning objective(s)

- expand brackets such as $2(x - 3)$
- expand and simplify brackets

Prior knowledge

Pupils need to remember the order in which to carry out operations, following BODMAS.

Starter

Tell pupils you are thinking of a number. When you multiply by two and add seven, you get the answer 17. Ask, "What was the number I was thinking of?" (5)

Repeat, but this time add six and then multiply the result by three, and give the answer as 30. Ask, "What was the number I started with this time?" (4)

Talk about the methods pupils use to get the answers.

Main teaching points

Go through the reason for using brackets, emphasising that everything inside the brackets is multiplied by the number outside and that the multiplication sign is left out. Point out that a negative sign outside the brackets changes the signs of the terms inside.

Work carefully through one of the examples 8, 9 or 10. Emphasise how important it is not to take any short cuts and to write working out in full. In particular explain the need for care with minus signs, as in the second bracket in Example 9. In an examination, one error is usually allowed and, providing no further mistakes are made, only one mark is lost, but examiners need to see where the mistake was made.

Common mistakes

The most common error pupils make is to multiply only the first part of the expression inside the brackets and ignore the rest. Pupils also get confused when there are negative signs.

Differentiation

In Exercise 7D the first 24 questions are grade E and 25 to 42 are grade D. Higher achieving pupils should be able to complete only selective examples from questions 1 to 24. Pupils who work more slowly could attempt the even-numbered questions. In Exercise 7E question 1 is grade E, questions 2 to 4 are grade D and questions 5 and 6 grade C.

Plenary

Put the following on the board:

$$2(x + 3) + 4(x - 1) = 3(2x + 1) + 2(x - 1)$$

Ask for one difference between this and what we have seen so far. These will be met later, but challenge the pupils to find the value of x that makes the equation true. They should suggest expanding. This has an equals sign and is an equation.

Expanding and simplifying both sides gives $6x + 2 = 8x + 1$. Pupils may be able to guess (if given a clue that the answer is a fraction) that the solution is $x = \frac{1}{2}$.

Incorporating exercise:	7F	**Key words**
Homework:	7.4	factor
Examples:	7.4	factorisation

Learning objective(s)

- 'reverse' the process of expanding brackets by taking out a common factor from each term in an expression

Prior knowledge

Pupils need to understand what is meant by the term 'factor'. They also need to know the times tables up to 10×10.

Starter

Ask the class for factors of 12. List them on the board. Ask for factors of 21. List these. Make sure pupils understand that it is not the size of the number that decides how many factors it has.

Challenge the class to find the number under 100 that has the most factors. (96)

Main teaching points

Explain that factorising is reversing the process of expanding brackets. To do this, they take out the highest common factor or factors from each of the terms in the expression. This is written outside the brackets. What is left goes inside. There may be common factors in both the letters and the numbers. All the factors have to be taken out. The HCF may be a 'compound' factor that includes numbers and letters.

Common mistakes

Pupils may not take out all of the common factors. Some may not realise that f means $1 \times f$.

In a question such as $4a - 12ab$, pupils may put the $4a$ outside the brackets but not put a 1 inside, or put 0 inside the bracket.

Differentiation

Questions 1 to 16 of Exercise 7F are grade D, questions 17 to 39 are grade C. Lower achieving pupils will find all of this difficult and should concentrate on understanding and completing the questions with a single common factor (questions 1 to 9). Higher achieving pupils should attempt all the questions.

Plenary

Put the following on the board:

$$16 \times 18 - 6 \times 18$$

Ask pupils if they can work this out easily without a calculator.
They will probably find the multiplications difficult and, even if they find these correctly, may get the subtraction wrong.
Ask if they can see anything in common with each part of the calculation.
Taking out the common factor of $\times 18$ means we can rewrite the calculation as $(16 - 6) \times 18$. They should be able to do this easily.
Repeat with: $17 \times 15 - 7 \times 15$, $23 \times 32 - 3 \times 32$, etc.

Incorporating exercise:	7G
Homework:	7.5
Examples:	7.5

Key words

quadratic expansion   quadratic expression

Learning objective(s)

● expand the product of two linear expressions to obtain a quadratic expression

Prior knowledge

Pupils need to know how to multiply out single brackets.

Starter

Revise the process of multiplying out expressions with single brackets.

Main teaching points

Explain that a quadratic expression is one in which the highest power of its terms is 2, for example x^2 or $x^2 + 3x$ or $4x^2 + 6$. When two linear expressions are multiplied together the result is a quadratic expression. Remind pupils that when they are dealing with brackets they must multiply everything inside the first set of brackets by everything inside the second set. Therefore, if they have two sets of brackets each with two parts inside, then there must be four multiplications. In addition to the method of multiplying out the brackets shown in the text, two other methods are commonly used (see Worked examples 7.5). Pupils who struggle with one method may have success with another. The box method is the most commonly used.

Common mistakes

Pupils have problems with negative signs when they are expanding brackets.

Plenary

Using FOIL expand a pair of brackets, for example $(x + 3)(x + 4)$:

$$(x + 3)(x + 4)$$

Decorate it to make a funny face. Pupils will find this amusing and it may help some to remember the method.

Incorporating exercises:	7H, 7I
Homework:	7.6
Examples:	7.6
Resource:	7.6

Key words

brackets	formula
calculator	substitution

Learning objective(s)

- substitute numbers for letters in formulae and evaluate the resulting numerical expression
- use a calculator to evaluate numerical expressions

Prior knowledge

Pupils must have a working knowledge of BODMAS in order to complete this section successfully. They must also be able to work with negative numbers. They need to be familiar with how the calculator they are using works (scientific, non-scientific, DAL).

Starter

Show or give pupils a copy of the puzzle, supplied on Resource 7.6. Ask them to work out values of A, B, C and D that make the puzzle work.

Repeat with a puzzle of your own, or ask the pupils to make one up.

Main teaching points

It is important for pupils to understand the concept of a formula (as a general rule) and where they are used in everyday life. Have examples of these formulae ready to give pupils, but ask them for suggestions first. Common formulae include conversions between metric units, metric and imperial units and temperatures.

There are also formulae that pupils will meet in science lessons. These involve speed, distance, time, mass, volume and density. Formulae are also used to calculate simple interest and household bills such as those for gas, electric and telephone, as well as areas and volumes. Area formulae are good starting points, as diagrams are often helpful.

Before starting the second section, "Using a calculator", make sure both you and the pupils are familiar with the calculators being used. Pupils need to know when to put in brackets. Refer them to Example 7.6.

Common mistakes

Common mistakes occur when operations are ordered incorrectly and when there is a negative before a bracketed expression. Examples used when teaching substitution should include and reinforce the correct method of working.

For the section about working with calculators, the most common mistake is likely to be leaving out brackets where they are needed.

Differentiation

As this section includes grade D work, lower achieving pupils will find it all difficult. They will need extra help with expressions that need brackets and when negative numbers are involved. They may need to be reminded of how to use brackets on a calculator. They will find the last part of the exercises especially challenging. Higher achieving pupils should attempt all the exercises.

Plenaries

- Check pupils' understanding of simplifying, and that they can recognise what can and what cannot be simplified.
- Check that pupils can expand brackets and factorise simple expressions.
- Make sure pupils understand BODMAS and the impact of the negative sign on an expression.

Overview

8.1 Long multiplication
8.2 Long division
8.3 Solving real-life problems
8.4 Arithmetic with decimal numbers
8.5 Arithmetic with fractions
8.6 Multiplying and dividing with negative numbers
8.7 Approximation of calculations

This chapter begins by reminding pupils how to do long multiplication and division. It then moves on to calculating with decimal numbers and interchanging decimals and fractions. Next it looks at multiplying and dividing negative numbers and finally approximating and rounding.

Context

This chapter deals with topics that are useful, not only for passing examinations, but in everyday life. In the 'real world' many people would now use a calculator for long multiplication and division, but it is important to understand which calculation is required in any given situation and to know how to carry out this calculation when a calculator is not available.

The most common uses of decimals are money and measurement. Because of this it is vital that pupils can deal with the arithmetic of decimals, even if they can only approximate an answer.

Edexcel A references

Ma3 Number and algebra: Calculations

8.1, 8.2, 8.3, 8.4	2.3k "use standard column procedures for multiplication of integers …"
	2.3j "use standard column procedures for addition and subtraction of … decimals"
8.5	2.3c "… add and subtract fractions by writing them with a common denominator; perform short division to convert a simple fraction to a decimal"
	2.3l "use efficient methods to calculate with fractions, including cancelling common factors before carrying out the calculation, recognising that, in many cases, only a fraction can express the exact answer"
8.6	2.3a "… multiply and divide integers …"
	2.3i "develop a range of strategies for mental calculation; derive unknown facts from those they know …"
8.7	2.3h "round to the nearest integer and to one significant figure; estimate answers to problems involving decimals"

Ma3 Number and algebra: Using and applying number and algebra

8.3	2.1a "select and use suitable problem-solving strategies and efficient techniques to solve numerical … problems"

Ma3 Number and algebra: Numbers and the number system

8.4	2.2d "use decimal notation and recognise that each terminating decimal is a fraction; …"

Ma3 Number and algebra: Solving numerical problems

8.7	2.4d "give solutions in the context of the problem to an appropriate degree of accuracy …"

Route mapping

Exercise	G	F	E	D	C	B
A		all				
B		all				
C		all				
D		all				
E		all				
F		1–5	6–8			
G			1–2	3–4		
H			1	2		
I			1–2	3		
J				1	2–7	
K				1–8	9–12	13–15
L					all	
M			all			
N				all		
P				1–7	8–12	
Q				1–2		

Answers to diagnostic Check-in test

1

×	5	8	6	9	7
4	20	32	24	36	28
6	30	48	36	54	42
3	15	24	18	27	21
8	40	64	48	72	56
7	35	56	42	63	49

2 a $\frac{3}{5}$ **b** $\frac{2}{3}$ **c** $\frac{1}{4}$ **d** $\frac{1}{4}$

e $\frac{2}{9}$ **f** $\frac{8}{15}$ **g** $\frac{1}{5}$ **h** $\frac{7}{30}$

1 Complete the multiplication grid.

×	5	8	6	9	7
4					
6					
3					
8					
7					

2 Cancel each of these fractions to express them as simply as possible.

a $\dfrac{30}{50}$

b $\dfrac{24}{36}$

c $\dfrac{9}{36}$

d $\dfrac{12}{48}$

e $\dfrac{22}{99}$

f $\dfrac{16}{30}$

g $\dfrac{14}{70}$

h $\dfrac{21}{90}$

Incorporating exercise:	8A	Key words	
Homework:	8.1	carry mark	partition
Example:	8.1	column	

Learning objective(s)

- multiply a three-digit number by a two-digit number using
  - the partition method
  - the traditional method
  - the box method

Prior knowledge

Pupils need to know their times tables up to 10×10. They should also know methods for short multiplication.

Starter

Do some mental tables work. Pupils can write their answers on mini-whiteboards. Start with basic tables, for example 3×7, 7×8, and move on to multiples of 10, for example 20×5, 7×400, 30×400. Recall the rules for dealing with these types of multiplications.

Main teaching points

Pupils will be expected to know an appropriate method for working out short multiplication. Some may already have a method for long multiplication with which they are comfortable; others may not understand how to use any method. The Pupil Book demonstrates three common methods for long multiplication.

Some pupils use a mixture of methods. As a general rule, a pupil who is competent in using one method is better sticking to that method. Encourage pupils to develop the habit of estimating the size of their answer before they start. In this way they might know if they have made a mistake.

Common mistakes

When they are using the traditional method, a common error is for pupils to miss off the zero when multiplying by the 'tens'.

Plenary

Pupils are only expected to do a two-digit by three-digit multiplication without a calculator. Put a three-digit by three-digit calculation on the board, for example 317×286.

Discuss which method would be best for this calculation. If the traditional method is used, two zeros will need to be added to one of the lines. Choose a method and do the calculation. ($317 \times 286 = 90\ 662$)

Incorporating exercise:	8B	**Key words**
Homework:	8.2	long division
Example:	8.2	remainder

Learning objective(s)

● divide, without a calculator, a three- or four-digit number by a two-digit number

Prior knowledge

Pupils need to know their times tables up to 10×10.

Starter

Run through a quick revision of mental division, using times tables up to 10×10. Include some examples where there is a remainder, for example $40 \div 6 = 6$ rem. 4.

Main teaching points

This has traditionally been a difficult topic for pupils to grasp. The Pupil Book shows two methods, the *Italian method* and a 'chunking' method. Example 8.2 shows another example of the 'chunking' method.

If your pupils are comfortable with a particular method then let them stick to that, otherwise a different method may help.

Common mistakes

Pupils do not always line up their answers correctly.

Plenary

Put the following methods on the board, which all show $500 \div 14$.

$$
\begin{array}{r}
35 \\
14\overline{)500} \\
\end{array} \text{rem 10}
\qquad
\begin{array}{r}
35 \\
14\overline{)500} \\
42 \\
\hline
80 \\
70 \\
\hline
10
\end{array}
\qquad
\begin{array}{r}
500 \\
420 \quad \times 30 \\
\hline
80 \\
70 \quad \times 5 \\
\hline
10
\end{array}
$$

Discuss the similarities between the three methods.

Incorporating exercise:	8C	
Homework:	8.3	
Examples:	8.3	

Learning objective(s)

- identify which arithmetical process is required to solve some real-life problems

Prior knowledge

Pupils need to know their times tables up to 10×10. They also need to be able to calculate, using long multiplication and division.

Starter

Tell the pupils that the answer is 30. What is the question?

Initial responses are likely to be fairly easy, for example $15 + 15$ or 3×10. Ask for a division if one isn't given.

Now ask for a real-life problem to which the answer is 30 pupils, £30, 30 kg, etc. Repeat with larger quantities such as 320 km, £625.

Encourage pupils to come up with sensible and realistic problems.

Main teaching points

Examination questions are likely to be set in problem form. Performing the arithmetic will only gain part of the marks. Pupils will also be awarded marks for knowing which calculations to do and showing the method they use. Pupils need to read questions carefully, picking out the important parts and discarding the rest. They then need to decide what method to use, write it down and then work out the answer.

Common mistakes

The most common error is not reading the questions carefully.

Plenary

Ask the class to imagine that all the pupils in Year 10 were being taken to Alton Towers for a day. The head of year needs to know how many coaches to book and how much to charge each pupil. What calculations would need to be made?

Incorporating exercises:	8D, 8E, 8F, 8G, 8H	**Key words**
Homework:	8.4a, 8.4b, 8.4c, 8.4d, 8.4e	decimal fraction
Examples:	8.4	decimal place
Resources:	8.4a, 8.4b	decimal point
		digit

Learning objective(s)

- identify the information that a decimal number shows
- round a decimal number
- identify decimal places
- add and subtract two decimal numbers
- multiply and divide a decimal number by a whole number less than 10
- multiply a decimal number by a two-digit number
- multiply a decimal number by another decimal number

Prior knowledge

Pupils need to be able to recognise a decimal fraction.

Starters

- Go around the class asking pupils to round to the nearest 10, 100, 1000.

- Use the diagram of an alien with six legs, provided as Resource 8.4a. Write a number on its mouth, for example 63.598 346. Ask for volunteers to round the number to five, four, three, two, one and then no decimal places, filling in legs as they go.
  Repeat with other numbers.

- Give pupils prepared copies of Resource 8.4b and allow them 10 minutes to play 'Complete the square'. They play in pairs, taking turns to add a line. The pupil who completes the square gains the number in the square. When they have finished, they both add up their numbers and the pupil with the higher score wins.

- Draw a divisibility clock on the board. Put the divisor in the middle and decimal answers around the clock face.

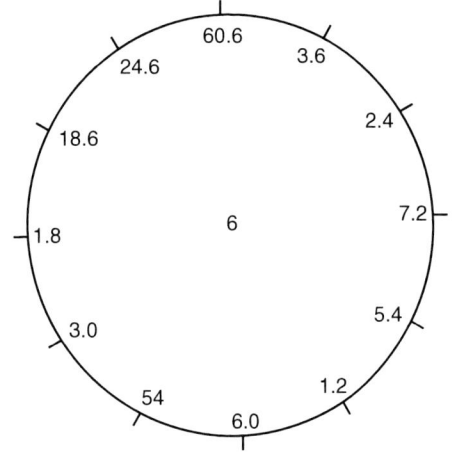

Point to an answer and ask pupils to give the number that can be divided by the number in the centre to give this answer.

- Ask questions such as, 'If 26 × 7 = 182, what is 26 × 70? × 700? × 0.7?' Discuss the answers.

- Write on the board: 0.5 × 0.8. Rewrite this as (5 ÷ 10) × (8 ÷ 10). This becomes 5 × 8 ÷ 100 = 0.4. Discuss this method and investigate it for other numbers.

Main teaching points

Show how the number system extends to include decimal numbers to represent fractions. This is covered on page 172 of the Pupil Book. Pupils must understand that the value of the digits decreases, the further away from the decimal point they occur.

Pupils need to know that the numbers written after the decimal point represent tenths, hundredths, ... The number of decimal places is the number of digits written to the right of the decimal point.

Adding and subtracting decimals is very similar to adding and subtracting integers. The important thing is to make sure the decimal points are lined up with each other. If a number does not have a decimal point it means it is an integer. There is no problem with adding a decimal point and putting zeros after it, if this makes it easier for the pupil to add or subtract.

When multiplying and dividing a decimal by an integer the same rule applies. Line up the decimal points and then multiply or divide as normal.

When multiplying two decimals, first do the calculation as if the decimal points were not there. Count how many digits there are after the decimal points in the numbers in the question and make sure there is the same number after the decimal point in the answer. Remind pupils to include any zeros at the end of the calculated answer, such as in $2.5 \times 1.2 = 3.00$.

Common mistakes

Errors occur when pupils do not line up the decimal points when adding or subtracting decimals.

Pupils may include the integer part of a number when counting decimal places, when multiplying or dividing.

They may forget to insert the decimal point in the final answer to a decimal multiplication.

Differentiation

The questions in each exercise are progressively more difficult.

Plenary

As this is a series of lessons, use a plenary based on the next lesson starter. This provides continuity and gives hints as to the next topic.

Incorporating exercises:	8I, 8J, 8K, 8L
Homework:	8.5a, 8.5b, 8.5c, 8.5d
Examples:	8.5
Resource:	8.5

Key words

decimal	mixed number
denominator	numerator
fraction	

Learning objective(s)

- change a decimal number to a fraction
- change a fraction to a decimal
- add and subtract fractions with different denominators
- multiply a mixed number by a fraction
- divide one fraction by another fraction

Prior knowledge

Pupils need to know how to cancel fractions.

Starters

- Give pupils the target card from Resource 8.5 and ask them to match the fractions with their decimal equivalents.

- Write various unsimplified fractions on the board and ask pupils to rewrite each in its simplest form.

- As a revision, ask pupils to convert improper fractions to the appropriate mixed numbers.

- Ask simple division questions in the form, "How many halves are there in six? How many quarters in 12?" Then move on to examples such as, "How many three-quarters are there in 12?"

Main teaching points

To convert a fraction into a decimal, pupils need to divide the numerator by the denominator.

When converting a decimal into a fraction, the decimal becomes the numerator. The denominator is 1 followed by the same number of zeros as there are decimal places in the decimal. Remind pupils that they should then simplify this fraction if possible.

To add and subtract fractions, pupils must first find the lowest common denominator and change the fractions into equivalent fractions with this denominator. Then they can add or subtract the numerators of these fractions.

To multiply fractions with mixed numbers, pupils must first change the mixed number into a top-heavy fraction. Then they can multiply the numerators together and multiply the denominators together. They should simplify, if possible, and then convert the answer to a mixed number if necessary.

To divide by a fraction, turn the divisor upside down and then multiply.

Common mistakes

When adding fractions pupils sometimes add the denominators as well as the numerators.

Plenary

Link the plenary with the starter for the next lesson. For example, if cancelling fractions is to be the next lesson starter, use this as the plenary.

Incorporating exercise:	8M
Homework:	8.6
Resource:	8.6

Learning objective(s)

- multiply and divide with negative numbers

Prior knowledge

Pupils need to understand what negative numbers are and where they fit on the number line.

Pupils need to know the times tables up to 10×10.

Starter

Give pupils prepared copies of Resource 8.6 and allow them 10 minutes to play 'Complete the square'. They play in pairs. The pupil who completes the square gains the number in the square. When they have finished, they both add up their numbers and the pupil with the higher score wins.

Main teaching points

Make sure that pupils know the rules for multiplying and dividing negative numbers.

- When the signs are the same the answer is positive.
- When the signs are different the answer is negative.

Illustrate these rules with some examples.

Plenary

Ask questions such as, 'What number would you multiply by -4 to get -20?'

Put a calculation, for example $3 - -2$, on the board and ask for the answer. Many will get it wrong. Now say the problem, "Three minus minus two." Many will now appreciate that it is 3 plus 2. Encourage pupils to say calculations to themselves.

Emphasise that marks are often lost in examinations because of errors in calculating with negative numbers.

			Key words
Incorporating exercises:	8N, 8P, 8Q		approximate
Homework:	8.7a, 8.7b, 8.7c		round
Examples:	8.7		significant figure
Resource:	8.7		

Learning objective(s)

- identify significant figures
- round to one significant figure
- approximate the result before multiplying two numbers together
- approximate the result before dividing two numbers
- round a calculation, at the end of a problem, to give what is considered to be a sensible answer

Prior knowledge

Pupils should know how to round to the nearest whole number and to a given number of decimal places.

Starter

Show the three signs from Resource 8.7. Play 'True or false'. If the statement could be true, pupils put their thumbs up; if it is false they put them down. Make statements such as, "There are 632 people living in Westhome. There could be the same number of people living in Westhome and Collinswood."

Main teaching points

Significant figures are often used when it is necessary to approximate a number that has a large number of digits. The rules for rounding are similar to those for decimal places. These are explained in the section 'Rounding to significant figures', on page 187 of the Pupil Book.

It would be useful for pupils to acquire the skill of estimating an answer to a calculation. A sensible way to make an estimate is to start by rounding all the numbers in the calculation to one significant figure.

When completing a calculation it is sensible to round the answer appropriately. For example, when dealing with money, any answer that has more than two places of decimals is nonsensical, since it implies an amount that is less than one penny. Similarly, if pupils are asked to work out how much wallpaper is needed to paper a room, it is only sensible to round to a whole number of rolls. When marking papers, examiners are looking for sensible rounding. If pupils are in doubt about rounding the answer, a general rule is to match the degree of accuracy in the question.

Common mistakes

Pupils may leave out the zeros after rounding.

They may not ignore the zeros on numbers that are less than 1.

They may not round sensibly.

Plenary

Draw a table on the board, similar to that for the homework task. Ask volunteers to fill in spaces on the table. Check for pupils' understanding of approximating by oral questioning.
Talk to pupils about the degrees of accuracy that are sensible for different situations.

Overview

9.1 Ratio
9.2 Speed, time and distance
9.3 Direct proportion problems
9.4 Best buys

In this chapter pupils will learn what a ratio is, how to simplify a ratio and how to express it as a fraction. They will divide amounts according to ratios, and solve problems. Pupils will look at speed, distance and time problems and then study direct proportion. The chapter concludes with a section on 'best buys'.

Context

There are many practical uses of ratio and proportion; this chapter covers the most commonly used. This includes recipes, mixing paints, looking at speed over time and, especially, looking at best buys.

Edexcel A references

Ma2 Number and algebra: Numbers and the number system

9.1   2.2f "use ratio notation, including reduction to its simplest form and its various links to fraction notation"

Ma2 Number and algebra: Calculations

9.1   2.3f "divide a quantity in a given ratio"
9.3, 9.4   2.3n "solve word problems about ratio and proportion, including using informal strategies and the unitary method of solution"

Ma2 Number and algebra: Solving numerical problems

9.2, 9.4   2.4a "draw on their knowledge of operations ... and the relationships between them, ... to solve problems ... involving ratio and proportion ... and compound measures ..."

Route mapping

Exercise	G	F	E	D	C
A			1–2	3–12	
B					all
C					all
D				1–11	12–16
E				all	
F				all	

Answers to diagnostic Check-in test

1 a $\dfrac{1}{2}$ **b** $\dfrac{1}{4}$ **c** $\dfrac{2}{3}$ **d** $\dfrac{5}{7}$

2 a £36   **b** 2.5 cm   **c** 224 litres   **d** 72 kg

3 2.5 hours

1 Simplify these fractions by cancelling.

a $\dfrac{15}{30}$ **b** $\dfrac{18}{72}$ **c** $\dfrac{44}{66}$ **d** $\dfrac{35}{49}$

2 Find the following quantities.

a $\dfrac{3}{4}$ of £48   **b** $\dfrac{1}{8}$ of 20 cm   **c** $\dfrac{2}{3}$ of 336 litres   **d** $\dfrac{4}{5}$ of 90 kg

3 If I am in a car travelling at 60 mph, how long will it take me to drive 150 miles?

Incorporating exercises: 9A, 9B, 9C	**Key words**
Homework: 9.1a, 9.1b, 9.1c	cancel ratio
Examples: 9.1	common unit simplest form
Resource: 9.1	

Learning objective(s)

- simplify a ratio
- express a ratio as a fraction
- divide amounts according to ratios
- complete calculations from a given ratio and partial information

Prior knowledge

Pupils should know their times tables up to 10×10, how to cancel fractions, how to find a fraction of a quantity and how to multiply and divide, both with and without a calculator.

Starters

- Give pupils practice in converting between metric units by asking quick-fire questions around the room.
- Write pairs of fractions on the board with either the numerator or denominator from one fraction missing. Ask pupils to provide the missing number to make the fractions equivalent.

Main teaching points

Pupils need to know that a ratio is a way of comparing the sizes of two or more quantities. The quantities must be in the same units, for example comparing centimetres to centimetres. If the units of the quantities are different then one must be converted before the ratio can be formed and simplified. This is because a ratio does not have units. A ratio can be expressed as a fraction. The denominator of the fraction is obtained by adding the numbers in the ratio.

To divide amounts according to ratios, pupils must first find the total number of shares. Divide by this total and then multiply by the number of shares each receives. For example, to divide 500 in the ratio of 2 : 6, first divide 500 by 8 and then multiply the answer by 2 or 6.

Common mistakes

A common error is to forget to express all quantities in the same unit.

When expressing 3 : 5, for example, as a fraction, pupils may simply write it as $\frac{3}{5}$.

Differentiation

Exercise 9A includes questions from grade E to D. Exercises 9B and 9C are all grade C.

Plenary

Show the pupils a spider diagram as on Resource 9.1. Ask pupils to complete it, giving the correct amount of money for each ratio.

Incorporating exercise:	9D	Key words
Homework:	9.2	average
Examples:	9.2	

Learning objective(s)

- recognise the relationship between speed, distance and time
- calculate average speed from distance and time
- calculate distance travelled from the speed and the time taken
- calculate the time taken on a journey from the speed and the distance

Prior knowledge

Pupils will need to know how to multiply and divide.

Starter

Talk about the different measurements that are used in relation to speed, distance and time. Make sure that pupils are clear about the meaning of mph (miles per hour) and km/h (kilometres per hour, which may also be written as kph).

Make sure pupils know the number of seconds in an hour and the number of metres in a kilometre. Discuss how to convert from km/h to m/s and vice versa.

Main teaching points

The simplest way to explain the relationship between speed, distance and time is to think of miles per hour. Pupils will be familiar with this unit, even if they have not met it formally before. Speed is a measure of how quickly a person or object travels for a given distance over a given time. Speed is therefore distance divided by time. Once they have seen this written as a rule it is easy for pupils to see how to rearrange the rule to find time and distance. Using simple examples that pupils can work out in their heads will help with forming general rules.

$$s = \frac{D}{T} \qquad\qquad D = ST \qquad\qquad T = \frac{D}{S}$$

Explain that the speed that is being calculated is an average for the journey time.

Common mistakes

Pupils may be confused about times, muddling decimal parts of an hour with hours and minutes.

Differentiation

Questions 1–11 of Exercise 9D are grade D and questions 12–16 are grade C.

Plenary

Give pupils a two part journey, for example 100 miles at an average speed of 40 mph followed by 90 miles at an average speed of 60 mph. Go through the process of calculating the average speed of the whole journey.
(190 miles in 4 hours = 47.5 mph)

Incorporating exercise:	9E
Homework:	9.3
Examples:	9.3

Key words

direct	unitary method
proportion	
unit cost	

Learning objective(s)

- recognise and solve problems using direct proportion

Prior knowledge

Pupils should know how to multiply and divide without using a calculator.

Starter

Put the basic diagram below on the board and ask the pupils to give you an answer.

    6   cost   36   How much do   5   cost?

Pupils will have an intuitive idea of this and will answer 30.
Discuss the method then change values to, for example, 9   45   5.

Main teaching points

Two quantities are in direct proportion if their ratio remains constant when the quantities increase or decrease. The easiest way to solve problems involving direct proportion is to use the unitary method. This is where the value of one unit is established, in relation to the other unit, such as the price for one article, in pounds. This is the constant factor that links the two quantities.

Plenary

Write on the board a simple recipe for six people. Ask pupils how much of each ingredient would be needed for one person, two people, 12 people, and so on. Include an item, such as two eggs, which cannot be easily divided. Such a problem would not occur in an examination, but could be met in real life.

Incorporating exercise:	9F		**Key words**
Homework:	9.4		best buy
Example:	9.4		value for money

Learning objective(s)

- find the cost per unit weight
- find the weight per unit cost
- use the above to find which product is the cheaper

Prior knowledge

Pupils need to know how to use a calculator to multiply and divide.

Starter

Draw two jars of different sizes on the board. Label both jars 'jam'. Write 250 g and £0.55 on one and 600 g and £1.20 on the other. Ask pupils if they can tell which jar is the best value for money.
Various methods could be explored, for example:

Find the cost of 50 g (11p and 10p)
Find a common multiple of 250 and 600 (3000), giving $12 \times 55 = 660$ and $5 \times 120 = 600$.

Pupils may still be confused about which is best value.
Emphasise the phrase 'More jam per penny'.
Point out that this is a clue as to how to work out the problem as 'More jam per penny' can be worked out as jam ÷ money, with the word 'per' being replaced with ÷.

Main teaching points

Any pupils who shop in supermarkets will have met 'best buys' before. Most supermarkets now have a unit or 100 g price alongside the total price of a product. Make sure that your pupils have really read the instruction 'find the price per unit weight'. The key to answering these questions is in the wording. 'Per' means divide, so price (or cost) per unit weight means total price (or cost) divided by total weight. Similarly, weight per unit price means weight divided by price. Once pupils understand this, solving these kinds of problem becomes simpler.

The smaller the unit price, the better the value of an item. The greater the weight per unit price, the better value it is.

Common mistakes

Pupils often make mistakes by not making the units the same for each item.

They may not realise which is the best buy once they have completed the calculations.

Plenary

Ask pupils if they think the larger quantities will be proportionally cheaper than the smaller quantities. Why might it not always be the best option to buy the biggest?

Overview

10.1 Lines of symmetry
10.2 Rotational symmetry
10.3 Planes of symmetry

This chapter explores the symmetries of 2-D and 3-D shapes.

Context

Symmetry has applications in architecture and in patterns, such as for textiles, wallpaper and flooring.

Edexcel A references

Ma3 Shape, space and measures: Transformations and coordinates

10.1, 10.2, 10.3   3.3b "recognise and visualise rotations, reflections ... including reflection symmetry of 2-D and 3-D shapes, and rotation symmetry of 2-D shapes..."

Route mapping

Exercise	G	F	E	D	C
A	1	2–7	8–9		
B		1–5	6–7		
C				all	

Answers to diagnostic Check-in test

1 Square, rhombus, rectangle, parallelogram, trapezium, kite, isosceles triangle, equilateral triangle, right-angled triangle

2 Cube, cuboid, square-based pyramid, triangular prism, cylinder (or circular prism), cone, sphere (<u>do not accept</u> ball)

3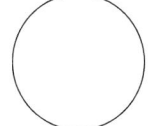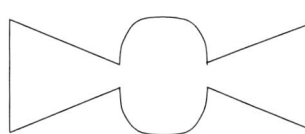

1 Name each of these 2-D shapes.

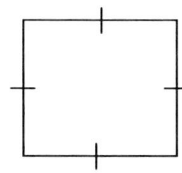   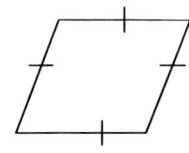   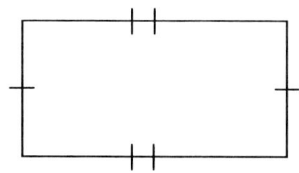

_____   _____   _____

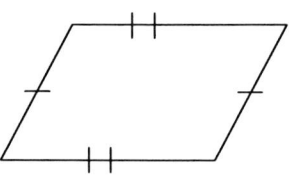   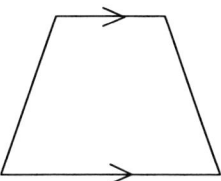   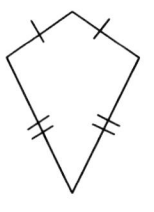

_____   _____   _____

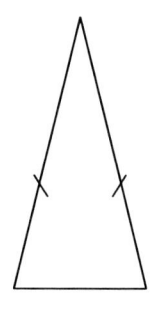   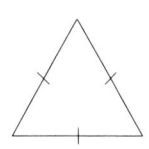   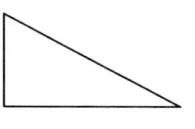

_____   _____   _____

2 Name each of these 3-D shapes.

    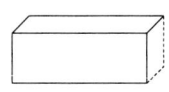   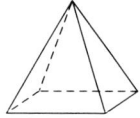   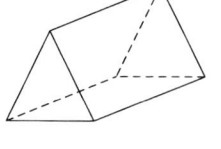

_____   _____   _____   _____

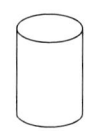      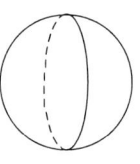

_____   _____   _____

3 A mirror (the dotted line) has been placed next to these shapes. Draw what you would see.

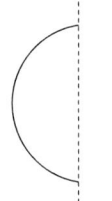 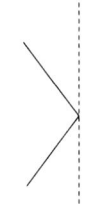   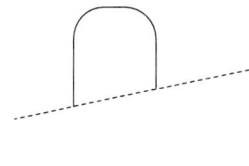   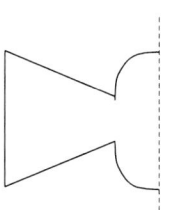

			Key words
Incorporating exercise:	10A		line of symmetry symmetry
Homework:	10.1		mirror line
Examples:	10.1		

Learning objective(s)

- draw the lines of symmetry on a 2-D shape
- recognise shapes with reflective symmetry

Prior knowledge

Knowing the names of common 2-D shapes is an advantage.

Starter

Have some large shapes made out of thin paper, for example a square, a rectangle and a parallelogram. Ask pupils where the lines of symmetry are for each. Fold the shapes along these. For the square, this will give each half exactly covering the other. It is likely that the pupils will designate a diagonal of the rectangle as a line of symmetry. Make sure that they see this does not work, similarly with the parallelogram.

Main teaching points

Tracing paper is allowed in SAT and GCSE examinations for questions on symmetry, so have a good stock to use in class and encourage its use. Mirrors are not allowed in examinations but, if you have them, use them – especially for the lower ability pupils.

Pupils have difficulty seeing lines of symmetry that are not horizontal or vertical. Encourage them to turn the book, so that lines of symmetry become either horizontal or vertical.

Common mistakes

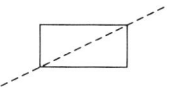

Drawing this as a line of symmetry is by far the most common error, closely followed by not putting in all the lines when dealing with polygons, for example putting only three lines of symmetry on a regular hexagon.

Differentiation

Lower ability pupils benefit from using a mirror initially, especially with rectangles, parallelograms, pentagons and hexagons.

Plenary

How many lines of symmetry are there in this shape?

Discuss the connection between the number of sides of a regular polygon and the number of lines of symmetry.

How many lines of symmetry are there in each of these letters?

O T I S

Incorporating exercise:	10B		Key words
Homework:	10.2		order of rotational symmetry	rotational symmetry
Examples:	10.2			

Learning objective(s)

- find the order of rotational symmetry for a 2-D shape
- recognise shapes with rotational symmetry

Prior knowledge

Pupils need to know the names of the commonly used 2-D shapes.

Starter

Draw a square with a dot in the top right-hand corner:

In your head, turn it once clockwise and draw it:

Do it again: , and again: , and again:

How many different squares are there? (4)

Do the same with a rectangle (2), an equilateral triangle (3) and a hexagon (6).
What about a circle? (∞) Or a right-angled triangle? (0)

Main teaching points

Encourage the use of tracing paper. If a shape has 'no' rotational symmetry, that is, it only fits onto itself once in one complete 360° rotation, then it has order 1.

Common mistakes

Not using tracing paper usually leads to inaccurate answers on the more complicated shapes. Pupils often say a shape has order 0 instead of order 1 for 'no' rotational symmetry.

Plenary

Ask pupils to name any capital letters with line symmetry. List them on the board. (A, B, C, D, E, H, I, M, O, Q, T, U, V, W, X, Y)

Ask pupils to name any letters with rotational symmetry. (H, I, N, O, S, X, Z)

Ask the class what is special about the words:

BED? (line symmetry)
NOON? (rotational symmetry)

Are there any others?

Incorporating exercise:	10C
Homework:	10.3
Example:	10.3

Key words
plane of
  symmetry

Learning objective(s)

- find the number of planes of symmetry for a 3-D shape
- recognise shapes with planes of symmetry

Prior knowledge

Names of the commonly used 3-D shapes are needed.

Starter

This starter is best done with actual shapes made out of Plasticine, or a similar material, which can be cut to show the symmetries.

Sketch a cuboid.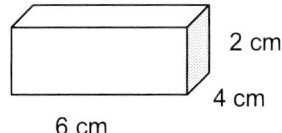
2 cm
4 cm
6 cm

Imagine cutting it in half and draw both halves side by side. There are three different ways.

How many ways are there for this cuboid? (5)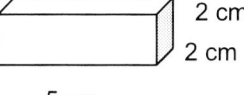
2 cm
2 cm
5 cm

How many ways are there for a cylinder? (∞)

How many ways are there for a cube? (9)

Main teaching points

Keep emphasising that a plane of symmetry divides a shape into two equal halves (mirror images).

Differentiation

Using multilink cubes to make cuboids and then using them to split the cuboid into equal halves will really help lower ability pupils get to grips with the concept of planes of symmetry. (Keep dimensions as even numbers.)

Plenary

What is a plane of symmetry?
How do you recognise a shape with one or more planes of symmetry?
Can a prism have no planes of symmetry? (No, minimum = 1.)
How many planes of symmetry are there in a hexagonal prism? How do you work it out? (Hexagon = 6 lines of symmetry, prism = 1; so 6 + 1 = 7 planes of symmetry.)

Averages

Overview

11.1 The mode
11.2 The median
11.3 The mean
11.4 The range
11.5 Which average to use
11.6 Frequency tables
11.7 Grouped data
11.8 Frequency polygons

This chapter falls into two broad sections. The first four exercises cover the calculation of the different types of averages and the range from listed data. The last three exercises use data that has been organised into frequency tables. There is a linking exercise, 11E, which prompts a little more thought into the nature of the different summary measurements.

Context

Averages are used in a huge variety of everyday situations, from schools (test marks, attendance figures) and shops (daily/weekly takings, annual turnovers, profit margins) to finance (planning and making forecasts) and politics (voter analysis, focus groups), along with sport (batting averages, attendance figures) and pop (top 40).

Edexcel A references

Ma4 Handling data: Processing and representing data

11.1, 11.2, 11.3, 11.4	4.4b "calculate mean, range and median of small data sets with discrete then continuous data; identify the modal class for grouped data" 4.4j "use relevant statistical functions on a calculator ..."
11.6, 11.7	4.4g "find the median for large data sets and calculate an estimate of the mean for large data sets with grouped data"
11.8	4.4a "draw and produce ... diagrams for continuous data, including ... frequency diagrams..."

Ma4 Handling data: Interpreting and discussing results

11.5	4.5a "relate summarised data to the initial questions" 4.5d "compare distributions and make inferences, using ... measures of average and range" 4.5j "discuss implications of findings in the context of the problem"

Route mapping

Exercise	G	F	E	D	C
A	1–3	4–5		6–7	
B	1–2	3–6	7–9	10–11	
C		1–7			8
D	1	2–3	4–5		
E		1	2–5	6–9	10–11
F				all	
G					all
H				1–2	3–5

Answers to diagnostic Check-in test

1 **a** 8, 17, 25, 32, 100
b 3.9, 5.7, 5.7, 8.1, 10.2
c −4, −1, 2, 3, 5

2 **a** 4.7
b 3.1
c 4.2
d 0.6
e 29.5
f 17.0
g 35.0

3 1, 5, 5, 6, 4, 3, 2, 0, 1

4 18, 18, 18, 19, 19, 19, 19, 19, 20, 20, 22

5 **a** 49
b Spain
c 18
d 9

1 Put each of these sets of numbers in order, from lowest to highest.

   a 17, 25, 8, 32, 100

   b 5.7, 3.9, 8.1, 5.7, 10.2

   c 2, −1, −4, 5, 3

2 Round each of these numbers to 1 decimal place.

   a 4.66

   b 3.09

   c 4.205

   d 0.551

   e 29.52

   f 16.97

   g 35.018

3 Complete the table to show how many times each number appears in the following list.

   3, 5, 2, 3, 3, 6, 1, 4, 4, 2, 1, 1, 6, 5, 3, 2, 1, 0, 8, 4, 4, 3, 2, 1, 5, 2, 3

Number	Tally	Frequency
0		
1		
2		
3		
4		
5		
6		
7		
8		

4 Use the information in the following table to write out the complete list of numbers that produced the table.

Number	Frequency
18	3
19	5
20	2
21	0
22	1

5 In a survey, people were asked where they had been on their most recent holiday. The responses were used to make a bar chart. Use the bar chart to answer the following questions.

Holiday destinations

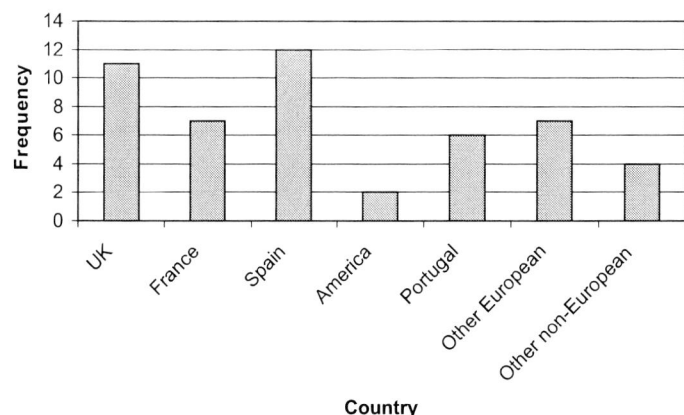

a How many people were interviewed in the survey?

b To which destination did the largest number of people go?

c How many people altogether went to either Spain or Portugal?

d How many more people stayed in the UK than went to America?

Incorporating exercise:	11A	**Key words**
Homework:	11.1	frequency
Examples:	11.1	modal value
		mode

Learning objective(s)

- find the mode from lists of data and from frequency tables

Prior knowledge

Pupils must be familiar with the work in Chapter 6 on frequency tables and statistical diagrams. They must be able to extract information from either of these sources.

Starter

Go round the class and ask pupils for their shoe size. Record these on the board, keeping boys' and girls' results separate. Ask pupils to suggest the best value to represent the average shoe size of the class. This may lead to discussions of the most common, calculating a mean, etc.
Discuss whether data should be split into boys and girls.

Main teaching points

Pupils should understand that the 'most common' or 'most popular' is a quick and easy piece of information that is often used in familiar situations. It is important that they know they will be looking at other methods of summarising collections of data and they need to make sure they can find ways of linking the words 'mode' and 'modal' with the idea of highest frequency. They should also appreciate that this is the only average that can be used if the data is qualitative. They will need to understand this point in order to answer question 6 of Exercise 11A.

It is important to look at situations in which there is one mode (where a single data value occurs with the highest frequency), more than one mode (where more than one data value occurs with the highest frequency) and no mode (where all the data values occur with the same frequency).

Common mistakes

Pupils might easily confuse highest *value* with highest *frequency*.

When finding the mode from a frequency table, a common mistake is to look for the number that occurs most often in the frequency column. Pupils should be reminded that the mode (if there is one) is always one of the data values.

Differentiation

As this exercise is aimed principally at grades G and F, many pupils will find it easy and will finish it quickly.
A useful exercise for these pupils would be to review the diagrams drawn in Exercise 6C and ask them to decide in which cases it would be appropriate to use the mode and in which it would not. In the latter cases, they should try to explain clearly why it is not appropriate.

Low achieving pupils might find it easier to appreciate what the mode is from a frequency table if they are instructed to list out all the data values first.

Plenary

Ask the class for some common, everyday modes. For example, modal gender in class, modal record in charts, modal name in class, modal way of getting to school, modal pet of class, etc.

Incorporating exercise:	11B
Homework:	11.2
Examples:	11.2

Key words
median
middle value

Learning objective(s)

- find the median from a list of data, a table of data and a stem-and-leaf diagram

Prior knowledge

Pupils must be able to order numbers, including decimals and directed numbers. They must be able to read information from tables and bar charts.

Starter

Use pairs of numbers and ask pupils which is higher and which lower. Use a variety of types of numbers, including some more difficult decimals, with some negative. Move on to three numbers, to be arranged in order, and so on.

Use pairs of numbers and ask pupils for the number that is halfway between them. Start with simple pairs (2 and 4, 9 and 11, etc.) and then use increasingly difficult pairs (3 and 6, 22 and 50, −9 and 5, 2.1 and 8.7, etc.). Try to develop a method for finding the midpoint.

Main teaching points

Pupils should understand that the median is the data value that separates the entire ordered collection into two equal-sized sections.

Three situations are covered here. Firstly, finding the median from a list. Secondly, finding the median from a frequency table. Thirdly, finding the median from a stem-and-leaf diagram.

The method for locating the *position* of the median should be taught, that is, for n items the position is $(n + 1) \div 2$. Pupils should be shown the difference between an even number of data points and an odd number and, in particular, how to handle the even case.

Common mistakes

Pupils often forget to order listed data before locating the median.

Pupils often forget to add one to the number of data items before halving to find the central one.

When reading a median from a stem-and-leaf diagram, pupils often forget to include the stem.

When using a frequency table, a common error is to use the central class from the table, instead of the central data value.

Differentiation

Low achieving pupils will have difficulty finding the median from a frequency table. It may make it easier to understand if they list out all the data items first.

Low achieving pupils will have difficulty getting the correct information from stem-and-leaf diagrams. It may prove useful to spend some time reviewing the work done in Exercise 6E before they attempt questions 8, 9 and 11 of Exercise 11B.

Plenary

Give a median and ask for examples of lists of three numbers that would give this median.
Give another median and ask for examples of lists of four numbers that would give this median.
Give a number and ask for two numbers that are the same distance from it.
Ask for a definition of the median and a method for remembering it.

Incorporating exercise:	11C	Key words
Homework:	11.3	average
Examples:	11.3	mean

Learning objective(s)

- calculate the mean of a set of data

Prior knowledge

Some questions in Exercise 11C require the pupils to be able to change the units of some measurements, for example from hours and minutes or fractions of hours into minutes, and from pounds and ounces into ounces.

Starter

Pick some pairs of consecutive even numbers. Ask pupils to add them and divide the answer by 2, and then to comment on the result. Do the same for pairs of consecutive odd numbers. Pick pairs of non-consecutive even numbers and non-consecutive odd numbers and repeat.

Pick some sets of three consecutive numbers. Ask pupils to add them and divide the answer by 3, and then to comment on the result. Repeat the process with four consecutive numbers and dividing by 4, then 5, and so on as far as possible.

Select a small group (4 or 5) of participants and give each of them some cards (or similar), ensuring that the cards are not distributed equally. Ask them to share the cards fairly or equally. Ask them how they could work out how many each person should get.

Main teaching points

Pupils should understand that calculating the mean is a two-stage process and they should be encouraged to show their working out at each stage, whether they are using a calculator or not. First, the total of all the data values must be calculated and this total should be shown. The total should then be divided by the number of data items and the answer rounded if necessary.

Pupils should understand that this is the most commonly used measure of average and that its benefit is that it takes all the data into account. It may be helpful to show them that the effect of the mean is the same as taking the total of the data and sharing it equally among members of the group, as illustrated in the starter.

Higher achieving pupils will need to understand the effect of a single new member in a data group (in the case where the new value is equal to the original mean, and in the case where it is different), and the effect of a shift of the same amount to all of the data values.

Common mistakes

The most common mistake when using a calculator to find the mean is to try to do the calculation in one step, without finding the total first. This will not affect the answer on a simple calculator, but it will on a scientific one. Pupils should be encouraged to do the two stages separately, whatever type of calculator they are using.

Differentiation

Low achieving pupils may find question 8 difficult. Higher achieving pupils should be encouraged to think about question 5 from a range of different view-points. The answer to **d** may depend on what the average is going to be used for, and who is going to use it.

Plenary

Ask for summaries of the three different types of average, and for ways of remembering which is which.

Give a number that is the mean of two numbers and ask for suggestions for what the two original numbers might have been. Do the same for sets of three or more numbers.

Incorporating exercise:	11D
Homework:	11.4
Examples:	11.4

Key words

consistency　　　spread

range

Learning objective(s)

● find the range of a set of data and compare different sets of data using the mean and the range

Prior knowledge

Pupils must be able to carry out subtraction with decimal numbers and with negative numbers.

Starter

Pick some pairs of numbers and ask for the difference between them.

Pick some differences and ask for possible pairs of numbers.

Pick some pairs of numbers that have the same mean and ask for the mean of each pair. Ask for suggestions about how the different pairs of numbers could be compared with each other if their means are the same.

Main teaching points

The key words are particularly important here. The method is straightforward but the purpose behind it is not generally well understood. Pupils should be given plenty of examples of situations where consistency is an important issue. Pupils should understand that the range is the answer to the subtraction of the lowest data value from the highest data value. Before embarking on the exercise, ensure that pupils are comfortable subtracting with decimal numbers and with negative numbers. If this is difficult, a number line could be used to illustrate it.

An important point in this exercise is the use of mean and range to make comparisons, using the ideas of 'location of data' and 'dispersion of data'. So, for example, two sets of data might have the same mean, but very different ranges. In this case a high range might be 'good' or 'bad' depending on the circumstances. It should be pointed out to pupils that some questions might not have 'right or wrong' answers in this exercise, as the answers depend on people's opinions, and on the situation under consideration.

Common mistakes

Pupils sometimes use the first and last data values in a list, instead of checking to see if the list is ordered first. Stress that they should be using the *highest* and *lowest*.

Pupils often give the answer as, for example, 9 to 13, instead of 13 − 9 = 4. Stress that the range is the answer to the subtraction.

Differentiation

Questions in this exercise are aimed at grades G, F and E. Higher achieving pupils will find this exercise quite straightforward and may finish it quite quickly. They should be instructed to give full and clear explanations in their answers to **4c** and **5c**. If there is time, this might be a good point to introduce a practical activity, such as the one suggested in the Pupil Book.

Plenary

Ask for a definition of the range.

Discuss situations in which consistency might be an important element. Try to elicit real situations which the pupils have experienced, such as sporting situations, preparation for exams, part-time jobs they may have experience of, etc.

Incorporating exercise:	11E	Key words
Homework:	11.5	appropriate representative
Examples:	11.5	extreme values

Learning objective(s)

• understand the advantages and disadvantages of each type of average and decide which one to use in different situations

Prior knowledge

Pupils should know how to calculate all three types of average and how to find the range of a set of data.

Starter

Put this list of numbers on the board: 1, 2, 4, 9, 9.

Tell the pupils that the mode is 9, the median is 4 and the mean is 5. Ask which of the three averages best represents the data.

The mode can easily be eliminated as it is an extreme value. There is not much to choose between median and mean.

Now add a sixth value, 71. The mode is 9, the median is 6.5 and the mean is now 16. Discuss which is the best average now. The mean can be eliminated as it is affected by an extreme value. There is not much to choose between mode and median this time.

Main teaching points

This exercise requires the pupils to think and make decisions for themselves. It is not simply teaching them a method for working something out. It is important that they understand the concept of 'representative'. The table is useful to help them eliminate an average that would be inappropriate and it should be pointed out to them as something that they can refer to as they work through the exercise. It might also be useful to consider cases in which different people might want to use different measures of average for the same data, as their reasons might be served better by one than another. Question 8 addresses this issue.

Common mistakes

Mistakes here generally come from a lack of thought about the situation, or a lack of clarity in the understanding of how to use the table.

Differentiation

Questions 1 to 5 are relatively straightforward questions that just require the application of a method. From question 6 onwards, more thought is required and low achieving pupils may struggle with some of these questions. Questions 10 and 11 are aimed at grade C pupils, who should be encouraged to try to find a method for solving the problems. A 'trial and improvement' method could be used for those who find this too difficult.

Plenary

Give the following data about average pocket money for a class:

   Mode = £6   Median = £8   Mean = £12

Which would be the best average to use if:

   You were the head teacher wanting to work out if a vending machine will be profitable?
   You were a pupil after a rise in pocket money?
   You were a parent trying to resist giving a rise in pocket money?

Incorporating exercise:	11F		Key words
Homework:	11.6		frequency table
Examples:	11.6		

Learning objective(s)

- revise finding the mode and median from a frequency table
- calculate the mean from a frequency table

Prior knowledge

How to find the mode and median from a frequency table (see exercises 11A and 11B).

Starter

Ask for definitions of each of the three types of average, and ways of remembering which is which.

Choose some small sets of numbers and ask for all the averages of them.

Select a set of straightforward numbers, with some repeated numbers (for example, 2, 2, 3, 3, 5), and ask pupils to calculate the mean. Do this with a few similar sets, leaving each set and each answer visible, then put each set into table form and ask for a quick method.

Main teaching points

The finding of modes and medians from a frequency table is essentially revision, as it has been covered in exercises 11A and 11B.

The new work here is finding the mean from a frequency table. The method is fairly long, and needs to be shown in detail. Pupils should understand why an extra column is needed on the frequency table and, unless the reasons behind the method are clearly explained, it will mean very little to them.

The use of a scientific calculator in statistical mode will depend on whether pupils have them available, and which type they have. If this can be done successfully, it will usually save some time, but they need to be very sure about what they are doing! It is not recommended to use a statistical calculator in the examination. If pupils press the wrong button it will result in zero marks, but a wrong calculation in a table will only lose them one mark.

Common mistakes

The most common mistake is simply adding up the numbers in the frequency column (or the data class column) and then dividing by the number of rows in the column. This often leads to a mean that is well outside the range of data values and is, therefore, clearly nonsense. An example of this should be shown to the pupils, so that they can appreciate why it is nonsense.

When using a calculator, there are two common mistakes. Firstly, pupils often forget that, if they make a mistake and start again, they must be very sure that they have cleared the calculator's memory before re-entering any data. Secondly, they must be sure which way round *their* calculator accepts the data value and frequency inputs.

Differentiation

Low achieving pupils will find this work difficult, or at least difficult to remember accurately. They may be more successful if the data is taken out of tabular form and listed in full before any calculations are attempted.

Plenary

Show the pupils some frequency tables and ask them to estimate the mean of each. Ensure that pupils understand that the mean must be somewhere between the lowest and highest data value in the table.

Incorporating exercise: 11G	**Key words**
Homework: 11.7	estimated mean modal class
Example: 11.7	grouped data

Learning objective(s)

●   identify the modal class
●   calculate an estimate of the mean from a grouped table

Prior knowledge

Pupils should be familiar with using grouped frequency tables (see Exercise 6A). They will also need to be able to use inequality symbols.

Starter

Give pupils some inequalities and ask them to suggest numbers that are included in them. Make sure that some of the inequalities are inclusive and that some of the suggestions are the extreme values.

Use a non-inclusive inequality, such as $t < 5$, and ask for the largest possible number that could be included. This may need some discussion.

Use an inequality such as $5 \le x < 10$ and/or $10 < x \le 20$. Discuss what this means.

Main teaching points

Pupils should not have any difficulty with the first point in this section, that is finding the modal class from a grouped frequency table, as this is no different from the method seen previously for a frequency table (see Exercise 11A and 11F). A reminder that the mode concerns the data value with the highest frequency should be sufficient, and pointing out that here the answer will be a range of values, rather than a single value.

Pupils should have it clearly explained that, when calculating the mean, the best that can be done is an estimate and that is what the method leads to. They should appreciate that all the individual values of each group are being represented by a single value, assumed to be the midpoint of the group, and this is why the answer will be an estimate. Otherwise, the method is the same as that for a frequency table (see Exercise 11F).

The method for calculating the midpoint of a group should be clearly explained.

Pupils should be reminded about the quick checks that can be done to see if answers are roughly correct.

Common mistakes

The most common mistake here is that pupils misunderstand the phrase 'find an estimate for the mean', which they understand as being 'guess the mean'.

Pupils often make mistakes finding the midpoints of the groups.

Differentiation

As this is a grade C topic, low achieving pupils will find it difficult. It may be made easier if they draw up an entirely new table, replacing each grouped class with a single midpoint value, so that the method becomes exactly the same as that experienced in Exercise 11F.

Plenary

Give pupils some pairs of numbers and ask them for the midpoint of each pair.

Incorporating exercise:	11H
Homework:	11.8
Examples:	11.8

Key words

| continuous data | frequency |
| discrete data | polygon |

Learning objective(s)

- draw frequency polygons for discrete and continuous data

Prior knowledge

Pupils must know how to plot coordinates.

Starter

Draw x- and y-axes and a coordinate grid. Plot some points and ask pupils for the coordinates of each point. Give the pupils some coordinates and ask them to plot the points.

Main teaching points

It is important that pupils are clear about where to plot the points. The height of each point is straightforward, as it just represents the frequency, but the horizontal position is more complex.

For ungrouped data, the position is directly above the data value. For grouped data, pupils should understand that they need to find the midpoint of each group, as if they were going to calculate the mean, and then use this as the horizontal position to plot. It generally helps if pupils get into the habit of adding a midpoint column onto all their grouped frequency tables, regardless of what they are going to be using them for.

Horizontal axes should always be drawn with a continuous scale, regardless of whether grouped or ungrouped data is being used.

Common mistakes

The most common mistake here is the use of 'grouped labels' on data axes, rather than continuous scales. (For example, labelling a whole section of the axes '5 to 10' instead of a clear 5 at one mark and 10 at the next mark, with consistently sized gaps between the marks.)

Differentiation

The principal differentiation here is with the type of data used. Drawing frequency polygons for ungrouped data is a grade D topic, whereas, if the data is grouped, it becomes a grade C topic.

Plenary

Sketch two different frequency polygons on the same axes. For example, age distribution at a local sports club compared to age distribution of the Women's Institute. Make sure they are distinctly different (one could have a mode at one extreme, the other could be fairly consistent). Discuss the differences and how these can be identified from the distributions.

Overview

12.1 Equivalent percentages, fractions and decimals
12.2 Calculating a percentage of a quantity
12.3 Calculating a percentage increase or decrease
12.4 Expressing one quantity as a percentage of another

This chapter begins by looking at what 'percentage' means. It moves onto calculations that involve percentages. This includes how to use a calculator to work out percentages, using a multiplier, and finally working out one quantity as a percentage of another.

Context

Pupils will meet percentages continually, throughout their lives. In school, their examination marks are often given as percentages. They will pay a percentage of their wages in income tax; shops increase and decrease their prices according to percentages; estate agents charge commission as a percentage; politicians measure the amount of support they get at elections in terms of a percentage. It is therefore essential that pupils understand what a percentage is and how to calculate with percentages.

Edexcel A references

Ma2 Number and algebra: Numbers and the number system

12.1 2.2e "understand that 'percentage' means 'number of parts per 100' and ... interpret percentage as the operator 'so many hundredths of'; use percentage in real-life situations"
12.3 2.2e "... use this [understanding of percentages] to compare proportions ..."

Ma2 Number and algebra: Calculations

12.1 2.3e "convert simple fractions of a whole to percentages of the whole and vice versa ..."
12.2 2.3e "... understand the multiplicative nature of percentages as operators"
12.3 2.3m "solve simple percentage problems, including increase and decrease"
12.4 2.3m "solve simple percentage problems ..."

Route mapping

Exercise	G	F	E	D	C
A	all				
B			all		
C				all	
D				1–11	12
E				1–4	5–9
F	1		2	3–5	6–7

Answers to diagnostic Check-in test

1 a 780   **b** 90 500   **c** 0.69   **d** 0.095   **e** 0.0084

2 a $\frac{1}{5}$ **b** $\frac{3}{4}$ **c** $\frac{12}{25}$

3 a 54   **b** 41

1 Work these out.

a 7.8×100

b 905×100

c $69 \div 100$

d $9.5 \div 100$

e $0.84 \div 100$

2 Simplify these fractions.

a $\dfrac{12}{60}$

b $\dfrac{9}{12}$

c $\dfrac{48}{100}$

3 Work these out.

a $\dfrac{3}{4} \times 72$

b $\dfrac{1}{3} \times 123$

Incorporating exercise:	12A
Homework:	12.1
Examples:	12.1
Resource:	12.1

Key words

decimal   fraction
decimal   percentage
  equivalents

Learning objective(s)

● convert percentages to fractions and decimals and vice versa

Prior knowledge

Pupils should know how to cancel fractions and how to calculate with fractions. They must be able to multiply and divide decimals by 100.

Starter

Give pupils a copy of the equivalence sheet, Resource 12.1. Ask them to fill in the fraction, decimal and percentage equivalents that they know. This can become a useful tool for revision as these are the basic equivalences that pupils need.

Main teaching points

'Per cent' means 'out of 100', so 34% means '34 out of 100'. Written as a fraction this is $\frac{34}{100}$, which simplifies to $\frac{17}{50}$.

Any percentage can be written as a decimal by dividing it by 100: 34% is 0.34.

Similarly, to express a decimal as a percentage you multiply it by 100: 0.67 is equivalent to 67%.

Plenary

Go quickly around the class, asking pupils for common equivalents.

Incorporating exercise:	12B
Homework:	12.2
Examples:	12.2
Resource:	12.2

Key words
multiplier

Learning objective(s)

- calculate a percentage of a quantity

Prior knowledge

Pupils need to understand that 'per cent' means 'out of 100'.

Starter

Use the target board, Resource 12.2, to allow pupils to practise converting fractions to percentages, and to link equivalent fractions, decimals and percentages. Ask pupils to explain the methods they are using to find the equivalents.

Main teaching points

To calculate a percentage of a quantity you multiply the quantity by the percentage. Before multiplying you need to convert the percentage to either a fraction or a decimal. For non-calculator paper questions, it is usually easier to use fractions and to base these on 10% (dividing by 10) or 1% (dividing by 100).

When using a calculator, it is easier to convert the percentage into a decimal. This is called a *percentage multiplier*. For example, 12% is equivalent to a multiplier of 0.12 and this is what you would multiply by ($12 \div 100 = 0.12$).

Plenary

Go round the class asking for the equivalent percentage multiplier for various percentages, for example 45% = 0.45, 62% = 0.62. Include some that often cause difficulty, for example 3% = 0.03 but is often given as 0.3.

Incorporating exercise:	12C, 12D
Homework:	12.3
Example:	12.3

Key words
multiplier

Learning objective(s)

- calculate percentage increases and decreases

Prior knowledge

Pupils need to know how to use a percentage multiplier.

Starter

Revise the use of percentage multipliers by asking pupils questions such as, "What is two per cent as a multiplier?" Include some of the more difficult questions, such as, "What is 0.8% as a multiplier? What is 3.4% as a multiplier?"

Main teaching points

There are two methods for finding a percentage increase. Firstly, you can find the increase and then add this onto the original amount. Alternatively, you can use a multiplier. An increase of 9% is equivalent to a multiplier of 1.09 (the original 100% plus the increase of 9%).

Likewise, there are two methods for finding a percentage decrease. Firstly, you can find the decrease and subtract it from the original. Alternatively, you can use the multiplier method. A decrease of 12% is 12% less than the original 100% so this needs to be subtracted. You are left with 88%, which is equivalent to a multiplier of 0.88.

Common mistakes

The most common mistake made by pupils is not reading the question carefully and giving as the answer the actual increase or decrease.

Plenary

Go round the class asking for the equivalent percentage multiplier for various percentage increases or decreases. For example, an increase of 5% = 1.05, a decrease of 8% = 0.92.
Include some that often cause difficulty, for example an increase of 3% = 1.03 but is often given as 1.3.

Incorporating exercises:	12E, 12F
Homework:	12.4
Examples:	12.4

Learning objective(s)

● express one quantity as a percentage of another

Prior knowledge

Pupils need to know how to use a percentage multiplier.

Starter

Ask quick-fire questions about converting between units. Ask pupils to make some simple conversions.

Main teaching points

To express one quantity as a percentage of another, pupils first need to make sure they are working in the same units. They then simply express the first quantity as a fraction of the second and then multiply the result by 100.

Common mistakes

Pupils frequently forget to make sure the units are the same.

Plenary

Check pupils' understanding of the different types of problem by going through Exercise 12F and identifying whether they are a percentage increase, percentage decrease, or one quantity as a percentage of another. If there is time, set up a couple of calculations for pupils to do.

Equations and inequalities

Overview

13.1 Solving simple linear equations
13.2 Solving equations with brackets
13.3 Equations with the letter on both sides
13.4 Setting up equations
13.5 Trial and improvement
13.6 Rearranging formulae
13.7 Solving linear inequalities

This chapter begins with work on solving linear equations, where the variable appears on one side only, by various methods. It then moves onto solving linear equations where the variable appears on both sides. It shows pupils how to set up and solve equations and how to use trial and improvement to solve equations. After work on rearranging simple formulae, there is a final section on solving linear inequalities.

Context

Although pupils, especially at foundation level, are unlikely to actually use symbolic algebra in real life, they will meet situations where it is implied. Examples include cooking times, household bills and phone charges.

Edexcel A references

Ma2 Number and algebra: Equations, formulae and identities

13.1, 13.2, 13.3	2.5f "solve linear equations, with integer coefficients, in which the unknown appears on either side …"
	2.5f "solve linear equations, with integer coefficients, in which the unknown appears on either side or on both sides of the equation; solve linear equations that require prior simplification of brackets, including those that have negative signs occurring anywhere in the equation, and those with a negative solution"
13.4	2.5e "set up simple equations; solve simple equations by using inverse operations or by transforming both sides in the same way"
13.5	2.5m "use systematic trial and improvement to find approximate solutions of equations where there is no simple analytical method of solving them"
13.6	2.5g "… change its subject"
13.7	2.5d "solve simple linear inequalities in one variable, and represent the solution set on a number line"

Route mapping

Exercise	G	F	E	D	C
A		all			
B			all		
C			all		
D			1–15	16–21	
E				all	
F				1–8	9–14
G				1–4	5–9
H					all
I					all
J					all
K					all

Answers to diagnostic Check-in test

1 $6x$

2 a $35x - 21$ **b** $2x^2 + x$

3 $19x - 1$

4 a 7   **b** 3.5   **c** 21

1 Simplify this expression.

$7x + 3x - 4x$

2 Expand the brackets.

a $7(5x - 3)$

b $x(2x + 1)$

3 Expand the brackets and simplify this expression.

$5(x + 4) + 7(2x - 3)$

4 Put in the missing number to make each mathematical statement correct.

a $8 + \boxed{} = 15$

b $6 \times \boxed{} = 21$

c $\boxed{} - 6 = 15$

Incorporating exercises:	13A, 13B, 13C, 13D
Homework:	13.1a, 13.1b, 13.1c
Examples:	13.1
Resource:	13.1

Key words

do the same to both sides	inverse operations
equation	rearrangement
inverse flow diagram	solution
	variable

Learning objective(s)

- solve a variety of simple linear equations, such as $3x - 1 = 11$, where the variable only appears on one side
- use inverse operations and inverse flowcharts
- solve equations by doing the same on both sides
- deal with negative numbers
- solve equations by rearrangement

Prior knowledge

Pupils should be familiar with the basic language of algebra and know how to collect like terms. They should also understand that addition is the opposite (inverse) operation to subtraction (and vice versa), and that multiplication is the opposite (inverse) operation to division (and vice versa).

Starters

- Play "Think of a number." Say, "I am thinking of a number. I multiply it by 6 and subtract 2. My answer is 46. What was my number?" (8) Repeat with different starting numbers and operations.
- Ask ten quick-fire questions that will require pupils to use BODMAS.
- Use the algebra grid, Resource 13.1, to practise simplifying expressions by adding the expressions in the columns and the rows. Make up some of your own grids.

Main teaching points

There are three ways to solve linear equations. Pupils are shown all three ways but should be encouraged to use the way that suits them best. Whichever method they choose, they should always check that their answers work. The first method, inverse operations, is a good method when the variable only appears on one side of the equation. The second method, doing the same to both sides, is efficient but long-winded. Pupils often miss out numbers or get confused with signs. The most efficient method is solving by rearrangement. If pupils can manage to do this they will be able to solve more complicated equations. As usual, they must take care when dealing with negative numbers. It is sometimes useful, especially if there are unknowns on both sides, to use arrows to show what is happening. This is a visual way to show that "when you change the side, you change the sign".

Common mistakes

Many pupils make the mistake of not changing signs as they rearrange the equations.

Differentiation

Questions in this section range from grade F in Exercise 13A, E in Exercises 13B and 13C to E- and D-graded questions in Exercise 13D. Questions in each exercise in this section are also progressively more difficult. Lower achieving pupils may need help with the questions that involve negative numbers or fractions, or both. Higher achieving pupils could tackle the second half of each exercise.

Plenary

Write an example on the board and encourage pupils to use the different methods to solve it.

Incorporating exercise:	13E
Homework:	13.2
Example:	13.2

Learning objective(s)

● solve equations that include brackets

Prior knowledge

Pupils should know how to expand expressions that include brackets.

Starter

Write on the board:

$31 + 32 + 33 = 96$
$96 \div 3 = 32$

Repeat with three more consecutive numbers. Ask, "Is the sum of three consecutive numbers always divisible by 3?" Let pupils try to prove this, using algebra. Then ask them to try to prove that the sum of five consecutive numbers is always divisible by 5.

Main teaching points

Before they can solve this type of equation, pupils must multiply out the brackets. Stress that everything inside the brackets must be multiplied by what is outside. Special care must be taken when dealing with negative numbers. Once they have removed the brackets, pupils can solve the equations as before.

Common mistakes

Pupils often go wrong by multiplying only the first part of the expression inside the brackets by the term outside.

Plenary

Practise factorisation with the class. For example:
$4x + 8 = 4(\ldots)$
$x^2 + 3x = x(\ldots)$
$6x + 14 = \ldots$

Do some more examples with just a single number or single letter as the common factor.

Incorporating exercise:	13F
Homework:	13.3
Example:	13.3
Resource:	13.3

Learning objective(s)

- solve equations where the variable appears on both sides of the equation

Prior knowledge

Pupils should know how to expand an expression that includes brackets.

Starter

Set pupils to solve the algebra pyramid, Resource 13.3, by adding together the numbers in the bricks on the bottom row to get the middle row. The top row is the solution to the equation, formed by the expressions in the middle row. Solve to find the value of x.

Main teaching points

When solving these equations, it is easiest to use the 'do the same to both sides' method. The variable should be 'collected' to one side of the equation and the constant to the other side. It is usual to manoeuvre the variable to the left-hand side but when this means pupils will end up with a negative variable it is more sensible to turn the equation round, or collect the variable on the right-hand side.

Common mistakes

Pupils often get the wrong answer by not changing the signs when rearranging. They do not always appreciate that the sign relates to the number that follows it. Pupils should be encouraged to be logical and to rearrange before simplifying and not try to do both at the same time.

Differentiation

Questions 1 to 8 are grade D, 9 to 14 are grade C. The latter questions involve multiplying out brackets before simplifying. Lower achieving pupils will find the last two questions really difficult, but the more able will enjoy the challenge.

Plenary

Give pupils a 'think of a number' problem, for example "I am thinking of a number. I double it and add 5. The result is 8 more than the number I originally thought of." (3)

Whether they solve it mentally or not, set up the equation $2x + 3 = x + 8$ and solve it.

Repeat with similar examples.

Incorporating exercise:	13G
Homework:	13.4
Example:	13.4

Learning objective(s)

○ set up equations from given information and then use the methods already seen to solve them

Prior knowledge

Pupils should know how to solve simple equations.

Starter

Ask pupils to formulate equations for simple word problems such as, "If you cut m centimetres from 2 metres of ribbon, how much is left?" and, "The side of a square is c metres long. What is its area?"

Ask pupils to give you any simple formulae they know. They may give these in words. Then, as a class, convert them into algebra.

Main teaching points

This section covers the use of equations to solve problems in real life. Pupils need to focus on what is important mathematically in solving these problems. It is often simplest to use letters that relate to the questions, such as 'b' for the number of bottles in the example. Stress that the letter stands for a number and not an item – in the example about the milkman, b is the number of bottles in the crate. Pupils should check their answers and take care with units.

Differentiation

Questions 1 to 4 are grade D, 5 to 9 are grade C. There is also a lot of reading involved and this may affect the ability of pupils to do the mathematics. Higher achieving pupils could pair up with those who have problems with the reading to help them to understand what is required.

Plenary

Ask pupils to give you simple problems, for example:

Mary goes to the shops with ten pounds and spends x pounds. She then has three pounds left. How much did she spend?

Set up the equation to solve it.

Encourage pupils to invent problems that use multiplication and division.

Incorporating exercise:	13H	Key words	
Homework:	13.5	comment	trial and
Example:	13.5	decimal place	improvement
		guess	

Learning objective(s)

● use the method of trial and improvement to estimate the answer to equations that do not have exact solutions

Prior knowledge

Pupils should understand approximation and estimation.

Starter

Put pupils into pairs. One thinks of a number between 1 and 100 and writes it down without the other seeing it. The partner has 10 guesses to find the number. Then they reverse roles. The winner is the one who guessed the number in the fewest tries.

Main teaching points

Not all equations can be solved exactly and so a method is required to find an approximate solution. Trial and improvement is a way of doing this. Emphasise that it is trial and improvement, *not* trial and error. Questions of this type appear on the calculator paper, so pupils need to understand that they must show their working and their solutions in order to gain the method marks.

Emphasise that once two one-decimal place numbers that bracket the answer have been found, the middle value must be tested to see which of them is nearer to the real answer. This can be demonstrated with a diagram like the one on page 288 of the Pupil Book.

Common mistakes

Pupils may put as their answer the value of the equation instead of the value of the variable.

Plenary

Draw a cuboid on the board. Tell pupils that the lengths of the sides have a total of 12 cm, so two possible sets of dimensions are:

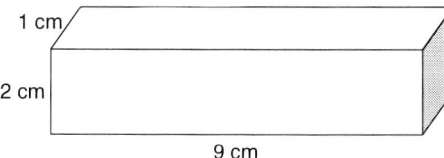
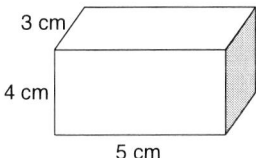

Ask pupils to work out the volumes (18 cm³ and 60 cm³ respectively).
Now ask them to find the set of dimensions that gives the greatest volume (4, 4, 4).

Incorporating exercise:	13l
Homework:	13.6
Example:	13.6

Key words

expression	transpose
rearrange	variable
subject	

Learning objective(s)

- rearrange formulae, using the same methods as for solving equations

Prior knowledge

Pupils should know how to solve equations.

Starter

Give pupils a mathematical statement, for example "y is three more than x", and ask them to give the relationship of x to y (x is three less than y).

Other examples would be "y is twice x", "y is 6 less than x", "y is a quarter of x", etc.

Main teaching points

Pupils need to understand that the subject of a formula is the variable that stands on its own. To change the subject means to rearrange the formula so that a different variable is on its own. Explain that pupils will have already been rearranging formulae when they were solving equations; the only difference is that an equation gives a numerical answer and a formula an algebraic one. Using the method of inverse operations is useful here and pupils should be reminded of the rule, "Change the side, change the sign."

Common mistakes

Pupils do seem to find this a difficult topic, perhaps because it is so abstract. They make the usual mistakes with signs.

Plenary

Look at simple mathematical formulae with which pupils will be familiar, such as the area of plane shapes, speed, distance, time. Ask pupils to say how to find, for example, the length of a rectangle when they know the area and width.

Write down the formula for some of these, for example $l = A \div w$.

Incorporating exercises:	13J, 13K
Homework:	13.7
Examples:	13.7
Resource:	13.7

Key words

integer	number line
linear inequality	

Learning objective(s)

- solve a simple linear inequality

Prior knowledge

Pupils should know how to solve equations.

Starter

Give pupils sheets of cards, Resource 13.7. Pupils, working in pairs, cut out the cards, solve the equations and then put the cards in order, according to the solution for x.

Main teaching points

Pupils need to know the four inequality signs that are used in solving inequalities. They also need to realise that inequalities behave in the same way as equations and so the same rules can be used to solve them. The only difference is that the equals sign is replaced by an inequality sign. Stress the difference between $<$ and $\leq$. At foundation level, pupils are only expected to deal with linear inequalities.

When using a number line, make sure pupils are clear about when to use the open circle (less than or greater than) and when to use the filled circle (less than or equal to, or greater than or equal to).

Common mistakes

Many pupils solve these as equations and do not put the inequality back in for the answer. It is best to encourage pupils to keep the inequality in the solution at each step.

Plenary

Check understanding by drawing some number lines and then writing up some inequalities. Ask pupils to volunteer to draw these inequalities on the number lines. Vary the degree of difficulty to suit the class.

Graphs

Overview

14.1 Conversion graphs
14.2 Travel graphs
14.3 Flow diagrams and graphs
14.4 Linear graphs

The work in this chapter will show pupils how to read information from conversion and travel graphs. It then moves on to using flow diagrams or function machines to plot coordinates, and then finally shows pupils how to draw linear graphs from equations, with coordinates in all four quadrants.

Context

Graphs are a useful and diagrammatic method of showing information in a way that is easy to understand. They are used in a wide variety of contexts in our everyday lives, ranging from changes in political popularity, to plotting car journeys, through to recording changes in temperature and blood pressure in hospital patients. It is important that pupils can read from graphs and understand the information they are showing.

Edexcel A references

Ma2 Number and algebra: Sequences, functions and graphs

14.1, 14.2 2.6c "... discuss and interpret graphs modelling real situations; ..."
14.3, 14.4 2.6b "use the conventions for coordinates in the plane; plot points in all four quadrants; recognise (when values are given for m and c) that equations of the form $y = mx + c$ correspond to straight-line graphs in the coordinate plane; plot graphs of functions in which y is given explicitly in terms of x, or implicitly"

Route mapping

Exercise	G	F	E	D	C
A		1–8	9–10		
B				all	
C			1–7	8	
D				all	
E					all
F					all

Answers to diagnostic Check-in test

1 Rectangle   **2 a** 165 miles   **b** 10 hours   **3** $A = 40$

1 Draw a set of axes on graph paper and label them x and y. Mark each axis from 0 to 8.

Plot the points (1, 3), (1, 7), (3, 7) and (3, 3). Join them in order.

What shape does this make?

2 A car is travelling at an average speed of 55 mph.

a How far does it travel in 3 hours?

b How long will it take to travel 550 miles at this speed?

3 If $A = 3s + t$, find the value of A when $s = 12$ and $t = 4$.

Incorporating exercise:	14A	**Key words**
Homework:	14.1	conversion
Example:	14.1	graph

Learning objective(s)

● convert from one unit to another unit by using a graph

Prior knowledge

Pupils should know how to plot coordinates.

Starter

Draw these two graphs on the board:

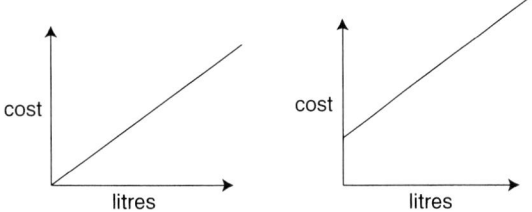

Explain that the first graph shows the relationship between cost of petrol and number of litres, and that the second graph shows the cost of delivering litres of oil.

Discuss what each graph shows. For example, the first graph shows that 0 litres costs £0. Why does the second graph start someway up the cost axis?

Establish the idea of a standing charge and a linear relationship between amounts and costs.

Main teaching points

The scale of the axes on conversion graphs is important. Pupils must understand what each scale shows. They should understand that conversion graphs do not necessarily start at zero (temperature), and that to read from a graph they need to find a value on one axis and follow it through to the other axis.

It does not matter which axis is used for which unit when converting between units, but for graphs such as those used to show electricity consumption and prices charged, the convention is that the money goes on the vertical axis.

Common mistakes

Pupils miss out units when giving answers.

Differentiation

Questions 1 to 8 of Exercise 14A are grade F, questions 9 and 10 are grade E. A higher achieving group could answer the first eight questions orally. All pupils should attempt questions 9 and 10.

Plenary

Tell the pupils that a gas bill for 100 units is £20. Can they use this information to work out the cost of 1 unit of gas? They may say 20p, but others should say, rightly, that there could be a fixed charge.

Now tell them that a different bill for 80 units was £17. Can pupils work out the cost per unit now?

Hopefully they can work out that a unit costs 15p and the fixed charge is £5.

			Key words	
Incorporating exercise:	14B		average speed	travel graph
Homework:	14.2		distance–time	
Example:	14.2		graph	

Learning objective(s)

- read information from a travel graph
- find an average speed from a travel graph

Prior knowledge

Pupils should know how to read from a conversion graph.

Starter

Ask pupils about expressing time in terms of fractions and decimals. Ask questions such as, "What is each of these numbers as a fraction/decimal of an hour: 15 minutes, 40 minutes, 5 hours 30 minutes, 1 hour 6 minutes, 45 minutes, 4 hours 12 minutes?" Vary the difficulty of the questions according to the ability of the pupils.

Main teaching points

Travel graphs are particular types of conversion graph. Pupils must be taught how to find speed from a distance–time graph.

Care must be taken with the scales on travel graphs, particularly with time, as pupils can easily become confused with parts of an hour. Usually in examinations time scales are marked in divisions of six, each of which represents 10 minutes, or divisions of four, each of which represents 15 minutes.

It is important to explain how to show the subject of a graph returning to the place of origin. Time continues to go forward but coordinates for distance can go back to zero. This is because they indicate the distance from the starting point.

Common mistakes

Pupils may read point five of an hour as 50 minutes, rather than 30 minutes. They may also show the subject of the graph going back to the start time of a journey, rather than the starting distance for a graph that represents a return journey or round trip.

Plenary

Check pupils' understanding by asking some quick-fire questions about calculating speed. Questions might include, "How fast would you be travelling if you covered 60 miles in 2 hours? 3 kilometres in 30 minutes?" 10 kilometres in 15 minutes? 210 miles in 3 hours?"

Incorporating exercise:	14C
Homework:	14.3
Example:	14.3

Key words

equation of a line	negative coordinates
flow diagram	output value
function	x-value
input value	y-value

Learning objective(s)

- find the equations of horizontal and vertical lines
- use flow diagrams to draw graphs

Prior knowledge

Pupils need to know how to plot coordinates in the first quadrant.

Starter

Play 'Make me say…'. Ask a pupil to give you a number. Apply a rule to the number and tell the class the result or write it on the board. For example, if the rule is add 2 and a pupil gives you the number 5, you say 7 or write (5, 7) on the board. Repeat with more numbers. The idea is for them to spot the rule and make you say a particular number, for example 25. So a pupil should eventually give you the number 23, making you say 25.

Repeat with other numbers and more complicated rules, such as times by 2 and add 3.

Main teaching points

Use Example 4 on page 311 of the Pupil Book to teach coordinates in four quadrants. Tell pupils that the equation of the x-axis is $y = 0$ and the equation of the y-axis is $x = 0$.

Show pupils how they can calculate pairs of coordinates by using simple flow diagrams. The input values are the x-coordinates and the output values are the corresponding y-coordinates. The function is the equation the pupils need to plot.

Most functions have more than one operation and, as always, the order of working is important.

Usually, in an examination pupils are given the x-values and are only asked to calculate the y-values. They should do this before drawing axes. The axes may also be drawn for them in their examination answer booklet.

Differentiation

Questions 1 to 7 in Exercise 14C are grade E, question 8 is grade D. Pupils are given the function machine, the blank table and the axes, so most should be able to complete this exercise, although it may be necessary to demonstrate, using the first question. All pupils should attempt questions 1 to 6 and the higher achievers should be able to do questions 7 and 8.

Plenary

Write (x, y) on the board. Ask pupils for a number. Take this as x. Apply a rule to it to get y, for example $y = 2x - 1$. Underneath the (x, y) write the coordinate pair resulting from the pupil's number.

Ask pupils to give the rule as a statement connecting x and y. So, for the example above you may get (5, 9), (3, 5), (10, 19), etc. Encourage pupils to be methodical so that they give you starting numbers of 1, 2, 3, etc. and make the rule easier to see.

Repeat with other numbers. Include some divisions but, if dividing by 3 for example, insist that the pupils give you multiples of 3.

Incorporating exercise:	14D, 14E, 14F
Homework:	14.4
Example:	14.4

Key words

coefficient   linear graphs
constant term   slope
gradient
gradient
   intercept

Learning objective(s)

- draw linear graphs without using flow diagrams
- find the gradient of a straight line
- use the gradient to draw a straight line
- use the gradient-intercept method to draw a linear graph

Prior knowledge

Pupils need to know how to plot coordinates in all four quadrants and how to use flow diagrams to calculate coordinates. They should also know how to substitute numbers into formulae.

Starter

Repeat the plenary from the previous lesson as a starter.

Write (x, y) on the board. Ask pupils for a number. Take this as x. Apply a rule to it to get y, for example $y = 2x - 1$. Underneath the (x, y) write the coordinate pair resulting from the pupil's number.

Ask pupils to give the rule as a statement connecting x and y. So, for the example above you may get (5, 9), (3, 5), (10, 19), etc. Encourage pupils to be methodical so that they give you starting numbers of 1, 2, 3, etc. and make the rule easier to see.

Repeat with other numbers. Include some divisions but, if dividing by 3 for example, insist that the pupils give you multiples of 3.

Main teaching points

Make sure that pupils learn how to draw graphs without using flow diagrams. They need to know how to complete a table of values as this often comes up in exams.

Pupils need to be able to interpret descriptions of how to label the axes. They must understand that the two forms, "label the axis from 0 to 5" and "$0 \le x \le 5$" both mean the same.

They must always label the graph with its equation, especially if they are required to draw more than one graph on a set of axes.

Pupils need to be taught that, when choosing values for x, it is sensible to choose two values at each end of the range of x and a value in the middle. One of these values should always be zero is possible.

Plenary

Ask pupils to look at the graphs they have drawn in the lesson and their equations (their graphs should be labelled). Can they see any connections?

They should spot that the y-intercept is the constant term. Point out that this always happens. They may not see that the coefficient of x is relevant, but given enough prompting they may see that the larger the coefficient, the steeper the line. Gradient can be mentioned if the class are able, otherwise it is not a concept required at Foundation level.

Angles

Overview

15.1 Measuring and drawing angles
15.2 Angle facts
15.3 Angles in a triangle
15.4 Angles in a polygon
15.5 Regular polygons
15.6 Parallel lines
15.7 Special quadrilaterals
15.8 Bearings

This chapter consists of the measuring and drawing of angles, interior and exterior angles in polygons, properties of angles in parallel lines and a short introduction to bearings.

Context

Angles in polygons give more complete information on simple shapes and so are a fundamental part of mathematics. Bearings are more usefully applied to the real world as they provide a *consistent* approach to describing the position of one object relative to the other (using the north line). The most common examples of these offered are those of travelling boats or aeroplanes.

Edexcel A references

Ma3 Shape, space and measures: Geometrical reasoning

15.1, 15.2   3.2a "recall and use properties of angles at a point, angles on a straight line (including right angles), perpendicular lines, and opposite angles at a vertex"

15.3, 15.6   3.2c "…use parallel lines, alternate angles and corresponding angles; understand the consequent properties of parallelograms and a proof that the angle sum of a triangle is 180 degrees; understand a proof that the exterior angle of a triangle is equal to the sum of the interior angles at the other two vertices"

15.4, 15.5, 15.7   3.2d "use angle properties of equilateral, isosceles and right-angled triangles; understand congruence; explain why the angle sum of a quadrilateral is 360 degrees"
3.2f "recall the essential properties … of special types of quadrilateral, including square, rectangle, parallelogram, trapezium and rhombus; classify quadrilaterals by their geometric properties"
3.2g "calculate and use the sums of the interior and exterior angles of quadrilaterals, pentagons and hexagons; calculate and use the angles of regular polygons"

Ma3 Shape, space and measures: Measures and construction

15.8   3.4b "understand angle measure using the associated language"

Route mapping

Exercise	G	F	E	D	C
A		1–3	4		
B		1–22	23–5		
C			1–7	8	
D			1–4	5	
E					all
F				1–6	7–9
G				all	
H				all	

Answers to diagnostic Check-in test

1 a 23° **b** 134°

2 a 90 **b** 90, 180 **c** 180, 360 **d** 90 **e** 90

3 a $x = 60$ **b** $x = 15$ **c** $x = 36$ **d** $y = 12$ **e** $x = 75$

1 Measure the following angles with a protractor (to the nearest degree).

a

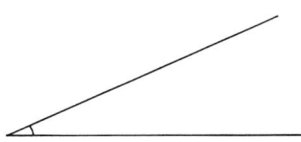

Angle is _____ degrees.

b

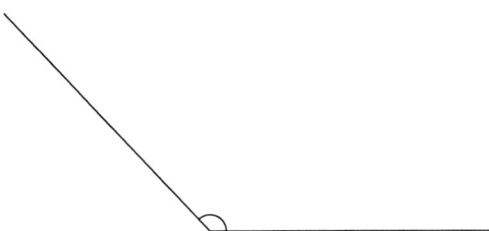

Angle is _____ degrees.

2 Fill in the gaps.

    a An acute angle is less than _____ degrees.

    b An obtuse angle is an angle greater than _____ degrees but less than _____ degrees.

    c A reflex angle is an angle greater than _____ degrees but less than _____ degrees.

    d A right angle is an angle measuring _____ degrees.

    e Perpendicular lines intersect at an angle of _____ degrees.

3 Solve the following equations.

    a $3x = 180$

    b $4x + 60 = 120$

    c $3x + 2x = 180$

    d $4y + 3y + 8y = 180$

    e $2x + 30 = 180$

			Key words	
Incorporating exercise:	15A		acute angle	protractor
Homework:	15.1		obtuse angle	reflex angle
Example:	15.1			

Learning objective(s)

- measure and draw an angle of any size

Prior knowledge

Pupils need to be able to measure acute angles and obtuse angles using a semicircular protractor.

Starter

Draw some angles on the board between 0 and 360 degrees. Mark the angles with an arc. Ask pupils to estimate the size of each angle and say if it is acute, obtuse or reflex. Check by measuring.

Main teaching points

Pupils are often confused as to which scale to 'read off' on their protractor. Emphasise acute, obtuse and reflex angles before commencing this section. Before pupils measure any angles, encourage them to look at the diagrams and see what type of angle they are expecting. If they are expecting an obtuse angle, for example, it should then become clear which of the two scales on the protractor they should be using.

Common mistakes

Reading the incorrect scale on the protractor as described above.

Plenary

Ask each pupil to draw one acute, one obtuse and one reflex angle. Ask them to measure their angles, swap their diagrams with a neighbour, measure their neighbours' angles and check each others' answers.

			Key words	
Incorporating exercise:	15B		angles around a	angles on a
Homework:	15.2		point	straight line
Examples:	15.2			

Learning objective(s)

● calculate angles on a straight line and angles around a point

Prior knowledge

Pupils need to be able to solve simple linear equations.

Starter

Ask pupils to do some mental arithmetic on complements of 90, 180 and 360.
For example, give a value, such as 35, and ask for the complement to 90 (55), 180 (145) and 360 (325).

Main teaching points

'Angles at a point' are sometimes referred to as 'angles in a circle'. The setting up of the equations is likely to be relatively easy. The weaker pupils will inevitably again struggle with the formalisation of solving simple linear equations. Chapter 13, therefore, needs to have been covered thoroughly.

Plenary

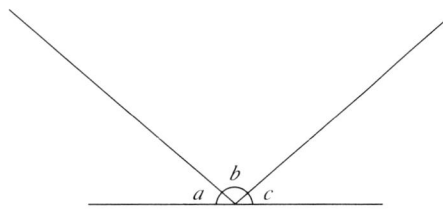

● If $a = 70°$ and $b = 110°$, calculate c.
● If $a = x$, $b = 2x$ and $c = 3x$, calculate x.
● If $a = b = c$, find a.

			Key words	
Incorporating exercise:	15C		angles in a	exterior angle
Homework:	15.3		triangle	interior angle
Example:	15.3		equilateral	isosceles
			triangle	triangle

Learning objective(s)

●   calculate the size of angles in a triangle

Prior knowledge

Pupils need to be able to solve simple linear equations.

Starter

Ask pupils, "What types of triangle are there?", "What can we say about the angles in a triangle?"
Many should be able to recollect most of the information this section requires themselves.

Main teaching points

The interior angles of a triangle add up to 180°.

An equilateral triangle is a triangle with all its sides equal and all its angles equal.
An isosceles triangle is a triangle with two of its sides equal and two of its angles equal.
A scalene triangle has no equal sides and no equal angles.
A right-angled triangle has one angle of 90°. The other two therefore have a sum of 90°.

Proof that the exterior angle in a triangle is equal to the sum of the interior angles at the other two vertices is required. Consider the following diagram:

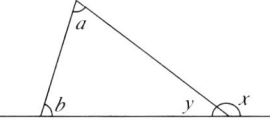

The angles in a triangle add up to 180°, so $a + b + y = 180°$.

Also, the angles on a straight line add to 180°, so $x + y = 180°$.

Comparing the two equations directly gives us $a + b = x$.

Plenary

Ask pupils what they understand by a right-angled triangle.
What do they think is meant by an 'acute-angled triangle'? (A triangle such that each angle is less than 90°.)
What do they think is meant by an 'obtuse-angled triangle'? (A triangle such that one angle is greater than 90°.)
Can they draw an acute-angled isosceles triangle?
Can they draw an obtuse-angled isosceles triangle?

Incorporating exercise:	15D
Homework:	15.4
Example:	15.4

Key words

decagon	octagon
heptagon	pentagon
hexagon	polygon
interior angle	quadrilateral
nonagon	

Learning objective(s)

● calculate the sum of the interior angles in a polygon

Prior knowledge

Pupils need to be able to solve simple linear equations and know that the angles in a triangle add up to 180°.

Starter

Use the introduction to the activity on page 338 of the Pupil Book. For example, draw a triangle, establish the angle sum, draw a quadrilateral, split it into two triangles, find the angle sum, etc.
Establish the rule or let pupils continue with the activity to find the rule for themselves.

Main teaching points

Each polygon of n sides can be split into $n - 2$ triangles. The sum of the interior angles of a polygon of n sides is therefore given as $180(n - 2)$.

Note that this result is true for both convex and concave polygons. (A polygon is concave if and only if at least one of its internal angles is greater than 180°, so a concave polygon must have at least four sides). Although pupils are not expected to differentiate between convex and concave polygons, it may be worth checking that the results in the 'activity table' still hold, for instance, by examining the interior angles of a concave pentagon.

That the angles in a quadrilateral add up to 360° is a common result and should be emphasised.

While pupils will inevitably refer to the 'activity table' during the course of this chapter, it is important to emphasise that they will have to learn the formula $180(n - 2)$ for when they come across similar questions in an examination setting.

Common mistakes

There may be misuse of the expression $180(n - 2)$. For example, it might be misinterpreted as $180n - 2$. So, this requires care in the first few examples.

Plenary

Ask pupils to give the names of n-sided shapes, starting with triangle and going as far as decagon (triangle, quadrilateral, pentagon, hexagon, heptagon, octagon, nonagon, decagon).

An 11-sided shape is called a hendecagon and a 12-sided shape is a dodecagon. Without them referring to the table at the start of section 15.4 in the Pupil Book, ask pupils to work out the sum of the interior angles for each polygon.

Incorporating exercise:	15E
Homework:	15.5
Example:	15.5

Key words

exterior angle   regular polygon
interior angle

Learning objective(s)

- calculate the exterior angles and the interior angles of a regular polygon

Prior knowledge

Pupils should know how to calculate the sum of the interior angles of a polygon, as covered in section 15.4.

Starter

You could use this alternative approach to finding the size of each exterior angle.

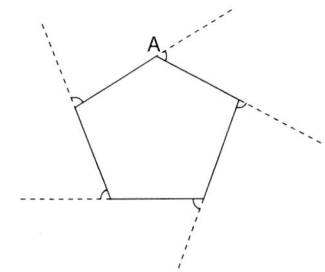

Draw a regular pentagon and use this to explain what is meant by an 'exterior angle'.
Now starting at A, for example, and walking round the pentagon clockwise, you would finally turn round one complete revolution before returning to A. Therefore, since there are five identical exterior angles, each of these must be $360° \div 5 = 72°$.

Main teaching points

Pupils need not know the formula, but should have an intuitive grasp of the idea.

For a regular polygon of n sides, the size of each exterior angle is $\dfrac{360°}{n}$.

The interior angle and exterior angle of a polygon add to 180°.

The size of each interior angle is, therefore, $180° - \dfrac{360°}{n}$.

When calculating the size of an interior angle of a regular polygon, it is usually easiest to find the size of the exterior angle to begin with (see Worked examples 15.5).

Common mistakes

A common error is to treat the exterior angle as 360° – (the interior angle).

Plenary

Draw a regular pentagon on the board. Establish the interior and exterior angles.
Draw lines from each vertex to the centre. Establish the angles in each triangle. Discuss the connections.

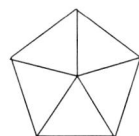

Repeat with a hexagon to show that the connections are true for all regular polygons.

			Key words	
Incorporating exercise:	15F		allied angles	vertically
Homework:	15.6		alternate angles	opposite
Example:	15.6		corresponding	angles
			angles	

Learning objective(s)

- find angles in parallel lines

Prior knowledge

Pupils should know how to calculate angles on a straight line and angles at a point, as covered in section 15.2.

Starter

Use the introduction to the activity on page 344 of the Pupil Book. Ask pupils to draw two parallel lines and a transversal and establish (possibly using tracing paper) which angles are equal.
Establish the equivalences or let pupils continue with the activity to find the equivalences for themselves.

Main teaching points

Corresponding, alternate, vertically opposite and allied angles, as described in the activity in the Pupil Book.

Angles that add up to 180° are called supplementary angles. Therefore, allied angles are supplementary.
Allied angles are sometimes referred to as co-interior angles.
A line intersecting two parallel lines is called a transversal.

Pupils often score highly on these kinds of diagrammatical questions when trying to find an angle, but noticeably less so when they have to give a reason for their answers. It is, therefore, important that they become familiar with the mathematical terminology (corresponding angles, alternate angles, etc.), rather than the F-angles, Z-angles which are often seen, but which do not count as *a reason*.

As part of the National Curriculum Ma3 2c, a proof that the angles of a triangle add up to 180° should be known. This can be seen as follows. Simply draw a line parallel to one of the sides of the triangle:

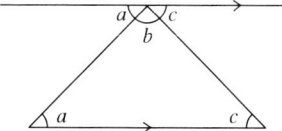

Now angles marked *a* are the same, as are angles marked *c*. If the remaining angle is *b*, then $a + b + c = 180°$ (since angles in a straight line add to 180°). But *a*, *b* and *c* are precisely the angles in a triangle. So the proof is complete. It should be noted that this requires knowledge of alternate angles, which are covered in this section.

Common mistakes

Any mistakes are often due to pupils guessing at the size of the angles. This will be apparent if they do not thoroughly understand the main definitions that include corresponding angles, alternate angles, etc.

Plenary

Draw this diagram on the board:

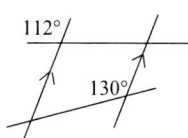

Establish all 14 missing angles, asking for reasons for each (angles are 112°, 68°, 130°, 50°).

Incorporating exercise:	15G	**Key words**	
Homework:	15.7	kite	rhombus
Example:	15.7	parallelogram	trapezium

Learning objective(s)

● use angle properties in quadrilaterals

Prior knowledge

Pupils should now have covered the angle properties of a triangle, Section 15.3, and the material on angles and parallel lines, Section 15.6.

Starter

Ask pupils to give the names of some special quadrilaterals. For each one offered, ask them to describe precisely what defines their quadrilateral, for example a rhombus is a parallelogram with four equal sides.
Draw a parallelogram on the board. Ask, "Which angles are equal and why?" Insist on reasons being given, as in Section 15.6. Repeat for the trapezium.

Main teaching points

The main aspects of this section are to understand the shapes and properties of the four quadrilaterals: the parallelogram, the rhombus, the kite and the trapezium. These are given in detail in the Pupil Book.

Pupils should be able to calculate missing angles using the properties of the quadrilaterals in question, along with the material on parallel lines covered in Section 15.6. Careful consideration might be given to the kite and rhombus, as these are rarely seen elsewhere at GCSE, whereas, for example, the formulae for the areas of trapezia and parallelograms have been covered previously in Chapter 5.

Plenary

Give a definition, for example "Diagonals intersect at right angles." Ask pupils which quadrilaterals obey this definition (square, rhombus, kite).
Repeat with other definitions, for example "All four angles are 90°." (Square, rectangle) "Opposite sides equal." (Rectangle, parallelogram)

Incorporating exercise:	15H
Homework:	15.8
Example:	15.8

Key words
bearing
three-figure
bearing

Learning objective(s)

● use a bearing to specify a direction

Prior knowledge

Pupils should know how to use a protractor to measure and draw angles.

Starter

Draw a compass rose on the board.
Starting from North as 0° and working clockwise, establish that the angles at E, S and W are
90°, 180° and 270°. Mark these on the diagram.
Angles for NE, SE, SW and NW could also be given.
Now draw some lines from the centre of the rose and ask pupils to estimate the angle measured
clockwise from North.

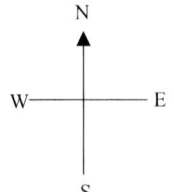

Main teaching points

Bearings seem to instil fear and dread in most pupils, despite their being only a form of 'dressed-up' angles. Clearly
identify the three properties of bearings to the pupils and ensure they are learnt.

● Bearings are angles measured from a north line.
● Bearings are measured in a clockwise direction.
● Bearings are written using three digits in the form of a three-figure bearing.

Common mistakes

Make sure to identify clearly where the north line (and hence the bearing) is to be drawn by emphasising the word
'from'. Consider Exercise 15H, question 1a, that is, 'Totley is on a bearing of 110° *from* Dore.' So, to illustrate this,
pupils need to begin by drawing a north line at Dore. The most common error pupils make is to draw the north line
at Totley, thus confusing Totley with Dore.

Plenary

Ask pupils, "If B is on a bearing of 060° from A, what is the bearing of A from B?" (240°) Illustrate this with a
diagram.
Repeat, replacing 060° with 290°, 045°, 090°, etc.
If there is time, list the two values in each case and see if pupils can spot the connection (the difference between
the two is 180°).

Circles

The section on drawing circles can be done in isolation. Sections 16.2 and 16.3 should be done consecutively to give an all-round appreciation of the circle skills required. These two sections are brought together neatly in Section 16.4, while developing the skill of leaving an answer in terms of π.

Context

Uses of circles and circle formulae are found in the following contexts: lines of longitude and latitude, craters made by meteorites, playing time on CDs and DVDs, strength and flow rate in pipes, lenses, optical illusions, crop circles and design.

Edexcel A references

Ma3 Shape, space and measures: Geometrical reasoning

16.1   3.2i "recall the definition of a circle and the meaning of related terms, including centre, radius, chord, diameter, circumference, tangent, arc, sector and segment; ..."

Ma3 Shape, space and measures: Measures and construction

16.2, 16.3, 16.4   3.4h "find circumferences of circles and areas enclosed by circles, recalling relevant formulae"

Route mapping

Exercise	G	F	E	D	C
A	1–2	3–6			
B				1–7	8–13
C				1–6	7–10
D				1–3	4–9

Answers to diagnostic Check-in test

1 Circle of radius 4 cm
2 Circle of radius 3 cm
3

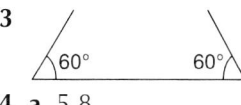

4 a 5.8   **b** 16.1   **c** 132.7
5 a 5.76   **b** 16.13   **c** 1.33
6 81
7 3

1 Using a pair of compasses, draw a circle with a diameter of 8 cm.

2 Using a pair of compasses, draw a circle with radius 3 cm.

3 Use a protractor to draw an angle of 60° at each end of this line.

_____

4 Round the following numbers to one decimal place.
   a 5.79   **b** 16.1267   **c** 132.65

5 Round the following numbers to two decimal places.
   a 5.763   **b** 16.1267   **c** 1.3265

6 What is 9 squared?

7 What is the square root of 9?

Incorporating exercise:	16A
Homework:	16.1
Examples:	16.1

Key words

arc	radius
centre	sector
chord	segment
circumference	tangent
diameter	

Learning objective(s)

- draw accurate circles
- draw diagrams made from circles

Prior knowledge

Pupils should be able to use a pair of compasses and be familiar with the words diameter, radius and circumference (and perhaps other circle related words).

Starter

This set of instructions will help develop the dexterity and accuracy needed for future drawings.
1. Draw a circle, radius 3 cm, in the centre of the page.
2. Do *not* change the compasses setting (keep at 3 cm).
3. Put the point on the edge of the circle and draw another circle.
4. Move the point around the circumference of the original circle and put it at the intersection of the two circles. Draw another circle. Move the point to the next intersection, draw the next circle and so on.
5. If you are accurate, you will get this pattern:

Main teaching points

Many pupils need to practise drawing a neat circle with a pair of compasses. Some will really struggle with this. Drawing concentric circles is good practice, with $r = 7$ cm, 6 cm, 5 cm, and so on. Show them how leaning the compasses slightly forward helps with smoothness of operation. Tell pupils that drawings of semicircles and quadrants still require the radius of the circle to be accurate.

Common mistakes

These are mainly because of blunt pencils, floppy compasses and poor ruler use.

Differentiation

Some pupils will require a lot of practice to master drawings, especially squares around circles and neat semicircles.

Plenary

Draw a circle of radius 4 cm:

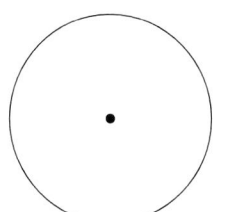

Measure and mark off as shown here:

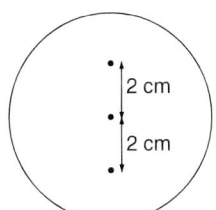

Use compasses to draw two semicircles from the marked points:

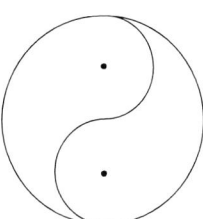

This is the Yin Yang symbol.
Check vocabulary of the circle.

Incorporating exercise:	16B
Homework:	16.2
Examples:	16.2

Key words
circumference
diameter
π (pronounced pi)
radius

Learning objective(s)

● calculate the circumference of a circle

Prior knowledge

Pupils should be able to round off to a given number of decimal places to give sensible answers.

Starter

Do the activity 'Round and round' on page 359 of the Pupil Book.

Main teaching points

Say the formulae for circumference, $C = \pi d$ and $C = 2\pi r$, as often as possible during the lesson and also continually interrupt the lesson to ask pupils for the formulae. Having heard, $C = \pi d$ and $C = 2\pi r$, twenty or thirty times in one lesson does have its rewards later.

Common mistakes

Pupils often confuse r with d and consequently use $C = \pi r$ or $C = 2\pi d$. Later, the main problem will be confusing the formulae for circumference with the formula for area $(A = \pi r^2)$.

Plenary

Ask pupils for the formulae for circumference.
Get the pupils to work out a few circumferences mentally using $\pi = 3$. For example, cup $r = 4$ cm, egg $d = 4$ cm, football $r = 12$ cm, head $r = 9$ cm, big head $d = 22$ cm, oil drum $r = 40$ cm, gas storage tank $r = 10$ m, pencil $d = 8$ mm).

			Key words	
Incorporating exercise:	16C		area	π
Homework:	16.3		diameter	radius
Examples:	16.3			

Learning objective(s)

⬤ calculate the area of a circle

Prior knowledge

Pupils should be able to round to a given number of decimal places to give sensible answers. They also need to be able to take squares and square roots using their calculators.

Starter

Ask the class for the answers to 1^2, 2^2, 3^2, ... ,15^2, all mentally, then ask for 27.41^2 (they should use a calculator). Discuss how the π number is 3 for mental calculations, 3.14 for written calculations and the π button on a calculator for real accuracy.
Show pupils that a good way of learning the value of π to 7 or 8 decimal places is by counting the letters in the words of this phrase:

How	•	I	wish	I	could	calculate	pi	quickly
3	•	1	4	1	5	9	2	7

For eight decimal places, they should change 'quickly' to 'really quick'.

Main teaching points

Say the formula for area, $A = \pi r^2$, as often as possible during the lesson and also continually interrupt the lesson to ask pupils the formula. As with calculating the circumference, give the full answer, then round off.

Common mistakes

Confusing r with d and confusing the formulae for area and circumference. Pupils also work out πr^2 as $(\pi r)^2$.

Differentiation

Lower achieving pupils will need reminding of the circle formulae each lesson for three or four lessons at least.

Plenary

Ask pupils to work out a few areas mentally using $\pi = 3$. For example, pond $r = 3$ m, window $d = 20$ cm, etc.

Emphasise that radius must be used in the calculation, so if a diameter is given in the question it must be divided by two.

Incorporating exercise:	16D	Key words	
Homework:	16.4	area	π
Examples:	16.4	circumference	radius
		diameter	

Learning objective(s)

- give answers for circle calculations in terms of π

Prior knowledge

Pupils should know and be able to use the formulae for the circumference and area of a circle.

Starter

Ask pupils, "In your head, work out the circumference of a circle with a radius of 10 cm.
– Did you do $2 \times 10 = 20$, then 20×3 ($\pi \approx 3$ for mental calculations) $= 60$?
– So, $20 \times$ pi is the answer?
– So, (write on board) 20π is the answer?
– Use your calculator to find the actual answer.
– Which is easier to write, 20π cm or 62.831 853 07 cm?
Repeat with the circumference for a diameter of 10 m.
Repeat with the area for a radius of 10 cm.

Main teaching points

These have been covered in the work for the starter.

Plenary

Ask pupils to work out some variations of the starter calculations, including semicircles.

This chapter covers the reading of various scales (for example, weighing scales) and making sensible estimates of height, weight, etc. of various objects. It also covers some aspects of drawing: scale drawing, drawing accurate nets and using isometric paper to give a 2-D representation of 3-D objects.

Context

Being able to read scales accurately has obvious advantages in real life, for example measuring height and weight, and cooking from recipes. Similarly making sensible estimates has wide applications: "Will it fit? Can it reach? How high? How deep? How many of those? How far? How much?" When fitting a new kitchen or new furniture, doing a scale drawing checks it will fit. All architects and designers have to be able to draw to scale. Package design needs nets and isometric drawing is fun and looks good.

Edexcel A references

Ma3 Shape, space and measures: Measures and construction

17.1   3.4a "interpret scales on a range of measuring instruments, including those for time and mass ..."

Ma3 Shape, space and measures: Transformations and coordinates

17.2, 17.3   3.3d "... use and interpret maps and scale drawings; ..."

Ma3 Shape, space and measures: Geometrical reasoning

17.4, 17.5   3.2k "use 2-D representations of 3-D shapes and analyse 3-D shapes through 2-D projections and cross-sections, including plan and elevation; ..."

Route mapping

Exercise	G	F	E	D	C
A	1–2	3–4	5		
B	1	2–5			
C		all			
D		1–2	3–6		
E			1	2–7	

Answers to diagnostic Check-in test

1 6 kg   **2** 6 kg   **3** 15 g   **4** 2 m
5 100 g (50 g–150 g)   **6** 4–6 mm typically **7** 6   **8** triangle
9 6   **10**

1 To what weight does arrow A point?

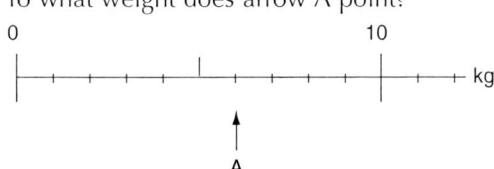

2 To what weight does arrow B point?

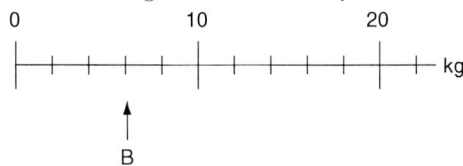

3 To what weight does arrow C point?

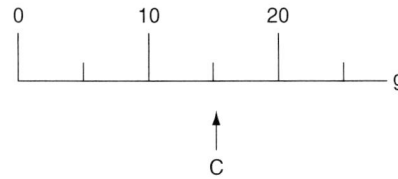

4 Roughly how high is your classroom door?

5 Roughly how heavy is an apple?

6 Roughly how long is an average eyelash?

7 How many faces (flat surfaces) does a cube have?

8 What shape is the side of a pyramid?

9 How many cubes are there in this shape?

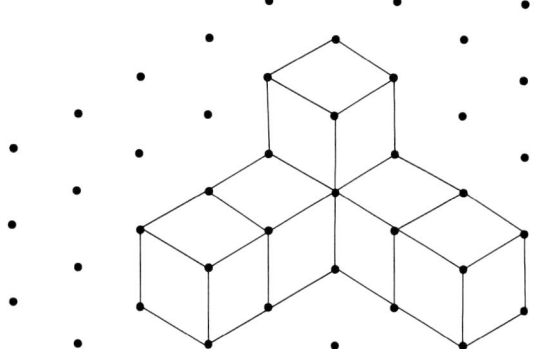

10 Draw the shape in question **9** as it would look from directly above.

Incorporating exercise:	17A
Homework:	17.1
Examples:	17.1

Key words

divisions　　　units
scales

Learning objective(s)

- read and interpret scales

Prior knowledge

Pupils should realise that, on a thermometer, below zero is negative. They should also appreciate the decimal number line between two whole numbers.

Starter

Ask, "What is halfway between: **a** 100 and 200 **b** 20 and 30 **c** 15 and 16 **d** 8.6 and 8.7?"

Using a number stick, where one end is 100 and the other 200, get pupils to say what the value is at different divisions. Use the same method for **b, c** and **d** above.

Main teaching points

Most scales do not go up in 1s. Pupils should always work out what each division is 'worth' and *then* answer the question.

Common mistakes

Pupils often assume that each division is 1, 5, 10 but do not actually check.

Plenary

Repeat the use of the number stick, as shown in the starter.
Draw a few scales with divisions of 1, 2, $2\frac{1}{2}$, 4, 5, 20, 25 and 50 for pupils to practise working out the value of each division.

Incorporating exercise:	17B		**Key word**
Homework:	17.2		estimate
Examples:	17.2		

Learning objective(s)

● make sensible estimates using standard measures

Prior knowledge

The pupils will need some 'reference points' for this skill. Some useful ones are: distance around a running track = 400 m, door = 2 m, man = 1.7 or 1.8 m, ballpoint pen = 15 cm, eye lash = 5 mm, small car = 1 tonne, bag of sugar = 1 kg, apple = 100 g.

Starter

Learn the reference points given above.
Use these to give estimates of everyday objects. Start off with things you can actually see around you, for example desks, chairs, windows, white board, room, corridor and packs of books. Remember to use length, width, height and weight.

Main teaching points

Ask, "If a pen is about 15 cm, roughly how wide is your desk?" This exercise almost always gets the pupils using the pen as a length measure, counting how many pens 'make' a desk and multiplying by 15. This is exactly the skill they will need for this type of GCSE question. For length and height questions, it is usually easiest to use a piece of paper to mark off a given length, see how many times this length is required and then multiply (as with the pen earlier). For weight questions, multiplication and division (and some logic) will be the usual methods for solving these (see Pupil Book Exercise 17B, questions 3 and 5), unless you have to estimate a weight where no reference is given, then pupils will need to rely on the prior knowledge learnt.

Note: Look at pupils' answers for question 7 of the homework. If it is anything other than 1 kg, they are 'doing' and not actually thinking. Pupils who have written 1.4 kg will need to have a series of questions set (from the Pupil Book) in a random order, to make them read and *understand* the process, not just follow a series of steps that worked for the last few questions.

Common mistakes

Pupils often use incorrect units, for example a man weighs 72 g (should be kg) or a dog's height is 50 m (should be cm).

Plenary

Draw a large rectangle on the board. Ask pupils to estimate the perimeter.
Set the following questions. Warn pupils that they will need to use their imaginations.
● Your little finger is 1.5 m long. How long is your page?
● The nail on your index finger is 20 m wide. How long/wide is your pen?
● If 2 (or 4, 5, 10, 20, 50) pencils weigh the same as a bag of sugar, how much does 1 pencil weigh?
● The four chairs over there weigh the same as two small cars! How much does each chair weigh? (About 500 kg)

Incorporating exercise:	17C	Key words	
Homework:	17.3	measurement	scale drawing
Examples:	17.3	ratio	scale factor

Learning objective(s)

● read scales and draw scale drawings

Prior knowledge

Pupils must be able to use a pencil and ruler accurately to draw a straight line. They should be able to convert, for example, 1.5 km into 1500 m (multiplying by 1000) into 150 000 cm (multiplying by 100) and to do the inverse, for example, 2 000 000 cm into 20 000 m (dividing by 100) into 20 km (dividing by 1000).

Starter

Get each pupil to draw a straight line between 5 cm and 15 cm, and write down how long their line is on another page. Ask them to swap books, measure the line and write down the length of the line. Compare the answers. If there is more than a 2 mm error, they will lose a mark in the GCSE examination, as 2 mm is the tolerance allowed for line drawing.

Give instructions such as, "Pretend 1 cm is worth 20 m. Draw a line 80 m long."

Ask, "How many centimetres are there in a metre? How many metres in a kilometre? How many centimetres are there in a kilometre? In 5 km? In 2.5 km?"

Main teaching points

The scale is given as a ratio. If the units for each part are different they will be given, for example, 1 cm : 10 m. Usually the scale has no units, for example 1 : 1000, so pupils can use 1 cm : 1000 cm or 1 m : 1000 m, that is, 1 anything : 1000 anythings. It is important to emphasise that a scale drawing is a bit like a photocopy in so far as the size may change but all of the angles will remain unchanged.

Common mistakes

Pupils may not be able to work out how many kilometres there are in, for example, 3 000 000 cm or how many centimetres there are in, for example, 0.5 km.

Differentiation

For lower achieving pupils, initially only use questions with given units, for example 1 cm : 20 km. Remember that the very low ability pupil will require a great deal of practice with the 1 : 20 000 type question to be able to change it into 200 m or 0.2 km. You could use the 'drip feed' method and give one question (for example, change 1 000 000 cm to metres and kilometres) each lesson as an extra starter.

Plenary

Ask, "How many centimetres are there in: 1 km, 2 km, 10 km, 0.5 km, 1.5 km?"
Ask, "How many metres are there in: 2000 cm, 10 000 cm, 15 000 cm, 4 000 000 cm?"
Ask, "How many kilometres are there in: 4 000 000 cm, 15 000 cm, 10 000 cm, 2 000 cm?"

Incorporating exercise:	17D	Key words
Homework:	17.4	3-D shape
Examples:	17.4	net

Learning objective(s)

- draw and recognise shapes from their nets

Prior knowledge

Almost all cardboard packaging is made from a net, that is, made from one piece of cardboard. The pupils should know the names of 3-D shapes (cube, cuboid, pyramid and prism) as well as the 2-D shapes such as square, rectangle and triangle (equilateral, isosceles and right-angled).

Starter

Using squared paper, ask pupils how many different shapes can be made with three squares (2). Make sure pupils understand what is meant by 'different'.

Now ask how many shapes can be made with four squares (5).

Main teaching points

Always emphasise the need for accuracy in the drawings: examiners allow tolerances of 2 mm and 2°. It tends to be easier for pupils if they draw a rough shape first with all the measurements written on it, and then draw the net accurately. Encourage the use of compasses for the drawing of triangles (see Chapter 20).

Common mistakes

A common mistake is to draw the two sides that should join in the 3-D shape as different lengths. Pupils are often outside the maximum 2 mm error allowed.

Differentiation

Lower ability pupils will find drawing the triangles challenging and may require help when using compasses to draw accurate sides.

Plenary

Ask the class how many different shapes can be made with five squares.

There are 13, but pupils may not find them all. This is revisited in the activity on page 390 of the Pupil Book.

How many of these can be folded to make an open cube?

Incorporating exercise:	17E	**Key words**	
Homework:	17.5	elevation	plan
Examples:	17.5	isometric grid	

Learning objective(s)

- read from and draw on isometric grids
- interpret diagrams to find plans and elevations

Prior knowledge

Pupils need to know that the 'plan view' means the view from directly above, which has no 3-D aspect at all. The plan view is sometimes called the 'birds-eye view'. The side elevation is the view from one side, which also has no 3-D aspect at all.

Starter

Ask pupils to draw a 3-D view of a cube, or copy your sketch:

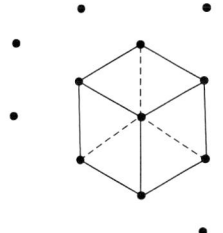

Explain that the dotted lines show hidden edges.

Pupils find this technique difficult so they could draw two squares and then join up the vertices.

If pupils drew their own 3-D view of a cube at the start of this activity, ask them to copy your sketch.

Main teaching points

Questions on plans and elevations will include squares and rectangles only. Pupils' isometric drawings are not scale drawings, but they should be able to take the true measurements straight from their drawings. You will probably be using triangular dot paper – this must be orientated as portrait. Pupils who use it in landscape will have their hands up for help.

Common mistakes

Pupils use paper in landscape and not portrait in class. In examinations the most common mistakes are: drawing 'see-through' cubes; vertices not being accurately drawn to the dots (or intersection of lines); not using measurements that are given.

Differentiation

The grade D questions that ask for plans and elevations from an isometric drawing, or the isometric drawing from a plan and elevations, are very difficult for many pupils – not necessarily those of low mathematical ability. Give them cubes to make the shapes. The more able will also enjoy using the cubes to make a more complex shape before drawing it.

Plenary

Using multi-link cubes, ask how many different shapes can be made with three cubes (2). If multi-link cubes are not available, ask for sketches on isometric paper.

Repeat with four cubes (eight different shapes are possible).

Probability

Overview

18.1 Probability scale
18.2 Calculating probabilities
18.3 Probability that an outcome of an event will not happen
18.4 Addition rule for outcomes
18.5 Experimental probability
18.6 Combined events
18.7 Expectation
18.8 Two-way tables

This chapter covers all the probability material in the Foundation specification, including the language of probability and the scale of likelihood, identifying theoretical probabilities in simple 'one-event' cases and calculating probabilities in more complex situations, such as the 'not' and 'or' cases for single events and probabilities associated with combined events. Clear links are made with the comparison between theoretical probability and the actual outcomes of an experiment, and the method for determining a probability from experimental data is covered.

Context

The subject of probability is one which pupils can readily link to their own experiences in life. With the recent increase in games of chance, such as the National Lottery, pupils are likely to have experiences which they can relate to the theory covered in this chapter.

It is helpful throughout the study of probability to use the language of chance and prediction, so that pupils are reminded that probabilities do not predict results in an exact way, only the likelihood of particular results.

Edexcel A references

Ma4 Handling data: Processing and representing data

18.1	4.4c "understand and use the probability scale"
18.2	4.4d "understand and use estimates or measures of probability from theoretical models (including equally likely outcomes) ..."
18.3, 18.4	4.4f "identify different mutually exclusive outcomes and know that the sum of the probabilities of all these outcomes is 1"
18.5	4.4d "understand and use estimates or measures of probability from ... relative frequency"
18.6, 18.8	4.4e "list all outcomes ... for two successive events, in a systematic way"

Ma4 Handling data: Interpreting and discussing results

18.1	4.5g "use the vocabulary of probability to interpret results involving uncertainty and prediction"
18.5	4.5i "understand that if they repeat an experiment, they may – and usually will – get different outcomes, and that increasing sample size generally leads to better estimates of probability and population characteristics"
18.7	4.5h "compare experimental data and theoretical probabilities"

Route mapping

Exercise	G	F	E	D	C
A	all				
B		1–9	10–15		
C			all		
D				1–4	5–8
E				1	2–7
F			all		
G					all
H	1		2–4	5–9	10

Answers to diagnostic Check-in test

1 a 30% **b** 77% **c** 94% **d** 9%

2 a $\frac{1}{3}$ **b** $\frac{5}{8}$ **c** 0.6

d 0.82 **e** $\frac{7}{12}$

3 a $\frac{3}{4}$ **b** $\frac{7}{10}$ **c** $\frac{5}{6}$ **d** 0.91

e 0.68 **f** 0.39

4 a $\frac{18}{125}$ **b** 20% **c** $\frac{8}{25}$ **d** 500

5 a 24 **b** 50 **c** 135 **d** 112

1 For each of these percentages, work out how much must be added to reach 100%.

    a 70% _____   **b** 23% _____   **c** 6% _____   **d** 91% _____

2 For each fraction or decimal, work out how much must be added to reach 1.

    a $\dfrac{2}{3}$ _____   **b** $\dfrac{3}{8}$ _____   **c** 0.4 _____   **d** 0.18 _____   **e** $\dfrac{5}{12}$ _____

3 Work out each of these, simplifying your fraction answers wherever possible.

    a $\dfrac{1}{8} + \dfrac{5}{8} =$ _____

    b $\dfrac{3}{10} + \dfrac{2}{5} =$ _____

    c $\dfrac{2}{3} + \dfrac{1}{6} =$ _____

    d 0.32 + 0.59 = _____

    e 0.28 + 0.4 = _____

    f 0.3 + 0.09 = _____

4 The travellers on a ferry were asked the reason for their journey. The results were put into this table.

Reason for journey	Holiday	Business	Shopping	Family visit	Other
Frequency	40	25	20	18	22

    a What fraction of the travellers were visiting family? _____

    b What percentage were on business? _____

    c What fraction were on holiday? _____

    d If 2500 people use the ferry in a month, how many, based on these results, would you expect to be travelling on business?

5 Work out each of these.

    a $\dfrac{1}{4}$ of 96 _____

    b $\dfrac{2}{3}$ of 75 _____

    c $\dfrac{3}{5}$ of 225 _____

    d $\dfrac{7}{8}$ of 128 _____

Incorporating exercise:	18A
Homework:	18.1
Examples:	18.1

Key words

certain	outcome
chance	probability
event	probability scale
impossible	unlikely
likely	

Learning objective(s)

- use the probability scale and the basic language of probability

Prior knowledge

Very little mathematical knowledge is required for this exercise, as it simply involves judgement of how likely it is that a variety of different events will happen. There are some events which require some more specific knowledge, for example throughout this chapter pupils will need to know in some detail the make-up of a deck of cards.

Starter

Ask the pupils to suggest events which they consider to be impossible. Probe to check that they really should be considered impossible and not just very unlikely. Do the same for events which they consider certain.
Suggest a list of events and ask the pupils to rank them in order of likeliness. It is useful to have a numbered list of the events and a line on which the relevant numbers can be placed in order.

Main teaching points

Pupils should understand the use of the five main words or phrases associated with likeliness: impossible, unlikely, even chance, likely and certain. These can be subdivided as necessary, for example 'very unlikely' or 'fairly likely'.

The use of a scale or line to order events provides a route through to the use of numbers to quantify the likelihood of events, which will be used in the following section.

Common mistakes

It is quite common for pupils to see some events as having an even chance, using the erroneous reasoning that 'it could either happen or not happen'. If this arises, discussion is useful to compare more and less likely events.

Differentiation

Question 3 of Exercise 18A provides the opportunity for pupils to use their imagination. More able pupils should be questioned about their choice of events, to ensure that they have really considered the true likelihood of each one, particularly for those that they have classified as impossible and certain.

Plenary

Ask pupils to summarise the main words associated with probability and chance.
Ask for examples of events which could be described as 'impossible', 'unlikely', 'even chance', 'likely' and 'certain'.

Incorporating exercise:	18B
Homework:	18.2
Examples:	18.2

Key words

equally likely	probability
event	fraction
outcome	random

Learning objective(s)

- calculate the probability of outcomes of events

Prior knowledge

Pupils must know how to express one number as a fraction of another, how to simplify fractions and how to add together fractions with the same denominator.

Starter

Prepare a bag containing a number of different coloured balls, or similar. Ask pupils to select one without looking and put it back. Have a pupil collect the data as it is generated. At different stages, ask for suggestions about what is in the bag. Ensure that pupils give reasons for their suggestions.

Main teaching points

Pupils should understand the method for calculating theoretical probabilities. They need to identify all the possible outcomes for an event. The number of possible outcomes becomes the bottom of the fraction. The number of events that fit the description of the outcome under consideration becomes the top of the fraction. This is most easily described in words, for example the probability of obtaining a number greater than 4 on the roll of a dice is 'two out of six', since there are six possible outcomes and two of them fit the description 'greater than 4'. This gives the probability $\frac{2}{6}$, which simplifies to $\frac{1}{3}$.

It should be carefully pointed out to pupils that a description of an outcome which contains the word 'or' means that both of the options described must be included.

The shorthand notation should be introduced to pupils, so that they understand that P(blue) means 'the probability of getting blue'.

Common mistakes

When dealing with dice probabilities, it is common for pupils to use the required number as the top of the fraction, instead of the number of ways that this outcome can be obtained. For example, the probability of obtaining a 5 is often given as $\frac{5}{6}$ instead of $\frac{1}{6}$.

When dealing with an outcome which contains the word 'or', it is common for pupils to list both the probabilities of the individual outcomes, instead of including both outcomes as acceptable. For example, the probability of obtaining a 2 or 3 on a dice is often given as '$\frac{1}{6}$ or $\frac{1}{6}$' instead of $\frac{1}{3}$.

Differentiation

Questions 1 to 9 are aimed at grade F, while questions 10 to 15 are aimed at grade E. In particular, question 10 requires more careful thought and pupils should be instructed to be particularly organised about the layout of their answers to this question.

Plenary

Use a target board with whole numbers on it and ask for probabilities of different outcomes of picking a number at random, for example P(prime number), P(less than 10) or P(multiple of 4). Your choice of outcomes will depend on your target board. Try to make sure you choose some outcomes which are impossible.

Incorporating exercise:	18C	Key words
Homework:	18.3	outcome
Examples:	18.3	

Learning objective(s)

- calculate the probability of an outcome of an event not happening when you know the probability of the outcome happening

Prior knowledge

Pupils must know how to find the probability of an event, such as those covered in Exercise 18B.

Starter

Practise complements to one, for example ask pupils what is $1 - \frac{4}{5}$, etc.

This was a plenary in a previous lesson so they may recall the rule. If not, ask them if they can see an easy way to work these problems out.

Main teaching points

Pupils should understand that the total probability of all the possible outcomes to an event is 1 and that the probabilities of mutually exclusive and exhaustive events can, therefore, sometimes be found more easily by subtracting from 1.

It should be made clear to pupils that they must ensure that they have catered for all the possible outcomes. It should also be made clear that the outcomes must be mutually exclusive. It is advisable to avoid the use of these words, but give pupils plenty of examples to illustrate the concept. For example, it may be helpful to discuss why the probability of it raining tomorrow could be $\frac{3}{5}$ and, at the same time, the probability of the sun shining tomorrow could be $\frac{1}{2}$, yet the total of these two probabilities is greater than 1.

Common mistakes

It is most common for pupils not to take sufficient care in identifying mutual exclusivity of events. For example, the events 'picking a prime number' and 'picking an even number' are not mutually exclusive.

Another common mistake is not to take sufficient care in identifying the exhaustiveness of events. For example, the events 'scoring less than 2' and 'scoring more than 2' when rolling a dice are not exhaustive.

Differentiation

While all of the questions in this exercise are aimed at grade E, the final parts of questions 2 and 3 are significantly more difficult than the rest of the exercise. It may be worth pointing out to lower achieving pupils that they will need to use the previous answers to be able to answer the final part of each question.

Plenary

Use a target board with whole numbers on it. Ask a variety of 'not' probability questions, for example P(not a multiple of 3), P(not less than 8) and P(not more than 1 digit).

Incorporating exercise:	18D	**Key words**
Homework:	18.4	mutually
Examples:	18.4	exclusive
		outcome

Learning objective(s)

● work out the probability of two outcomes such as P(outcome A) or P(outcome B)

Prior knowledge

Pupils must know how to find the probability of an event, such as those covered in Exercise 18B.

Pupils must know how to add fractions with the same or with different denominators.

Starter

Display the fractions $\frac{1}{2}$, $\frac{1}{3}$, $\frac{1}{4}$, $\frac{1}{6}$ and $\frac{1}{12}$. Ask pupils to choose a pair to add. Then ask pupils to choose any three to add, then any four to add, and finally to add all five.

Main teaching points

Pupils should understand that the probability of either of two (or more) mutually exclusive outcomes can be found by adding together the probabilities of each of the individual outcomes. The concept of mutual exclusivity should be carefully explained (the terminology is not expected but the concept is crucial) with plenty of examples of outcomes that are, and are not, mutually exclusive to illustrate the difference.

Pupils should understand why probabilities of 'either one outcome or another outcome' are bigger than each individual probability and why probabilities of 'one outcome and then another outcome' are smaller than each individual probability. They should also understand why it is not appropriate to add together probabilities of outcomes which are not mutually exclusive.

Common mistakes

Pupils often make mistakes in adding together probability fractions.

Pupils often learn how to add together probabilities but do not understand when it is appropriate to do so and when it is not. Question 8 of this exercise is particularly useful in illustrating occasions when it is not appropriate to do so.

Differentiation

Lower achieving pupils will find the C grade questions quite difficult. It may help them to access the ideas on probability if they are helped to identify some crucial information. For example, in question 5, that 0.4 is the same as $\frac{2}{5}$. Some discussion may be helpful for question 8, to help them put reasons into words.

Plenary

Display a target board with whole numbers on it. Ask for probabilities of events such as 'picking a multiple of 4 or 6', 'picking a prime number or a factor of 100' or 'picking a number which is a factor of 40 or 60'. The choice of questions will depend on the numbers you have displayed.

Incorporating exercise:	18E
Homework:	18.5
Examples:	18.5

Key words

bias	historical data
equally likely	relative
experimental	frequency
data	trials
experimental	
probability	

Learning objective(s)

- calculate experimental probabilities and relative frequencies from experiments
- recognise different methods for estimating probabilities

Prior knowledge

Pupils must know how to find the probability of an event, such as those covered in Exercise 18B.

Pupils must know how to express one number as a fraction of another.

Starter

Prepare a bag or box containing a number of different coloured balls, or similar. Ask pupils to select one without looking and put it back. Have a pupil collect the data as it is generated. At different stages, for example after four selections and again after ten, ask for suggestions about what is in the bag. Ensure that pupils give reasons for their suggestions.

Main teaching points

Pupils should understand that there are three different methods for finding probabilities: equally likely outcomes, experiment or survey, and use of historical data. They should understand which method to use in any given situation.

Pupils should understand that experimental probability increases in accuracy with increasing numbers of trials.

At this stage it is worth reminding pupils that probabilities may be expressed as fractions, decimals or percentages. Whilst fractions may be the most convenient way to express the probabilities in some exercises, it is often more useful to use one of the other representations for experimental probabilities as they are easier to compare as the number of trials of the experiment increases.

Common mistakes

When data is presented in tabular form, pupils often have difficulty in identifying the correct information. It should be made clear to them that they need to use 'number of correct results' and 'number of trials' in all cases but they need to be able to interpret the table correctly to find these values. In some tables the values will be cumulative frequencies of the required outcome and in others they will be frequencies of all the results.

Differentiation

There are two activities suggested in the Pupil Book, which lower achieving pupils may find particularly helpful in understanding the principles underlying this section. These are question 5 of the exercise and the activity 'Biased spinner'.

Plenary

Ask the pupils to pick a number between zero and nine, inclusive, and write it down.
Ask the class how many zeros, ones, twos, etc. they would expect to get. Pupils will understand that, for a class of 30 for example, there should be about three of each.

Now collate the results. Are they as expected? It is unlikely, as seven tends to get chosen more than any other number. Discuss why the actual results did not meet expected results, or why they did.

Incorporating exercise:	18F
Homework:	18.6
Example:	18.6

Key words

probability	sample space
space	diagram
diagram	

Learning objective(s)

● work out the probabilities for two outcomes occurring at the same time

Prior knowledge

Pupils must know how to find the probability of an event, such as those covered in Exercise 18B.

Starter

Split the class into pairs. Provide each pair with two dice. With a time limit of 2 minutes, ask each pair to roll the dice, add the scores for each roll and record each total score. While they are doing this, prepare a tally chart on the board and then collate all the results from the class when they have finished. Ask for the relative frequencies, or experimental probabilities, for each score.

Main teaching points

Pupils should understand what is meant by 'combined events'.

They should understand how to construct a sample space diagram for combined events, and that this is simply a method for easily identifying all the possible equally likely outcomes. From this knowledge, the method for finding a theoretical probability is now just the same as that described and experienced in Section 18.2, that is: number of ways an event can occur ÷ total number of possible outcomes.

Pupils should understand that all the other techniques learned in this chapter can be applied to combined events as well (for example, the addition rule, experimental probability, probability that an event will not happen).

Common mistakes

The most common mistake with this type of problem is that pupils are careless about reading the instructions thoroughly. It should be made clear to them that a sample space diagram can either record two separate results in each 'cell' or an outcome from both results, such as adding them or finding the difference between them, or whatever is required by the particular question. Pupils should make the decision about what to record themselves.

Differentiation

This technique can be extended to more complex situations. For example, there could be two spinners, one numbered 8, 9, 10, 12, 15 and the other numbered 4, 6, 14, 18, 24, and outcomes such as highest common factor or lowest common multiple could be considered. Alternatively, the idea of a game of chance could be introduced and, for example, a charge for playing the game, a winning score and a prize amount for a winning score could be considered.

Plenary

Compare the results from the starter activity with the theoretical probabilities that have been calculated in question 1 of Exercise 18F. Discuss any differences.

Incorporating exercise:	18G	**Key words**
Homework:	18.7	expect
Examples:	18.7	

Learning objective(s)

● predict the likely number of successful events given the number of trials and the probability of any one outcome

Prior knowledge

Pupils must know how to find the probability of an event, such as those covered in Exercise 18B.

Pupils must know how to calculate a fraction of a quantity.

Starter

Recap, or ask a pupil to explain, how to find a fraction of a quantity.
Display the number 240 and ask pupils to choose a fraction of this number to find. It may be more appropriate to limit the choice of fractions to be used, for example half, thirds, quarters, fifths, sixths, eighths, tenths, twelfths.

Main teaching points

Pupils should understand that probabilities are a measure of the proportion of trials that are expected to conclude in the outcome under consideration. It is important that they understand that reality rarely follows exactly what is expected in theory but that, as the number of trials increases, the proportion should become closer to the expected or predicted proportion.

It is worth putting this in context and giving pupils examples of where this theory is used in daily practice. For example, as suggested in the Pupil Book, the National Lottery relies entirely on expectations. Also, games of chance, such as fairground games, would not operate if the owners could not be confident, in the long run, of making a profit out of them. The calculation of expected profit from these games, and from any game of chance, relies entirely on a large number of participants ensuring that the proportion of winners to losers is very close to what the theoretical probability suggests.

Common mistakes

Mistakes are likely to be confined to one of two kinds: (1) working out the required probability incorrectly, or (2) working out the fraction of the number of trials incorrectly.

Differentiation

Question 8 of this exercise will stretch all but the most able pupils as it requires a little more creativity of thought, rather than just following a prescribed method to find an answer.

Plenary

Display a sample space diagram of total scores from the roll of two dice. Ask the pupils how many times they would expect to get different scores from 360 rolls of the dice. (Examples could be 4, 12, 5, less than 4 and so on.) Ask them which score they would expect to get most often. Ask them why you picked 360 rolls.

Incorporating exercise:	18H		Key word
Homework:	18.8		two-way table
Example:	18.8		

Learning objective(s)

● read a two-way table and use them to do probability and other mathematics

Prior knowledge

Pupils must be able to retrieve information presented in tabular form.

Pupils must know how to find the probability of an event, such as those covered in Exercise 18B.

Pupils must be able to find the expected number of results from the total number of trials and the probability of the event in question.

Starter

Construct a table with column headings 'Male' and 'Female', and row headings, for example, of four popular artists or groups, or four football teams or sports. Collect the data from the class, and tally the results into the table. Ask the class to provide probabilities of selecting different classes of people (for example, a girl who supports Man Utd or a boy whose favourite sport is golf). Choose a relatively straightforward multiple of the number of pupils in the class and ask how many out of this total would be expected in each category in the table.

Main teaching points

Pupils should understand that a two-way table is a means of classifying or categorising a population into sub-sections. They will need to understand that the size of the population can be found simply by adding all the entries in the table together. The probability associated with each category in the table is the fraction that each category represents of the total population.

Pupils should understand that these probabilities can be used to find the expected numbers of other populations, provided that the two populations represent similar characteristics.

Common mistakes

Most mistakes will come from misunderstandings in how to read the data from a two-way table. As many examples as possible, with as much discussion as possible, will assist understanding of how to interpret these tables.

Differentiation

The questions in this exercise cover a wide range of grades and, therefore, abilities. More able pupils should find question 1 easy and questions 2 to 4 quite easy. Less able pupils will find questions 5 to 9 difficult and question 10 very difficult.

Plenary

Revisit the starter but tweak the numbers so that totals are out of a multiple of 10, or some values are easy percentages of the column, row or table totals.

Ask pupils to calculate some percentages such as 'Percentage of class that like Man Utd.', 'Percentage of boys that like Oasis.', so that pupils know which two values to pick from the table to calculate with.

Overview

19.1 Congruent shapes
19.2 Tessellations
19.3 Translations
19.4 Reflections
19.5 Rotations
19.6 Enlargements

This chapter is broadly broken into two topics. Sections 1 and 2 cover congruency and tessellations, and Sections 3 to 6 cover all aspects of transformations.

Context

Vectors are used in navigation, and congruency and tessellations are used in tile patterns and flooring.

Edexcel A references

Ma3 Shape, space and measures: Geometrical reasoning

19.1, 19.2   3.2d "... understand congruence ..."

Ma3 Shape, space and measures: Transformations and coordinates

19.3   3.3a "... understand that translations are specified by a distance and direction (or a vector ...)"
3.3f "understand and use vector notation for translations"
19.4   3.3a "... understand that reflections are specified by a mirror line ..."
19.5   3.3a "understand that rotations are specified by a centre and an (anticlockwise) angle; rotate a shape about ... simple fractions of a turn ..."
19.6   3.3a "... understand that ... enlargements [are specified] by a centre and positive scale factor"

Route mapping

Exercise	G	F	E	D	C
A	1–3		4–7		
B			1–3	4	
C				1–2	3–6
D			1–5	6–8	9–10
E				1–5	6–7
F				1–4	5–7

1 a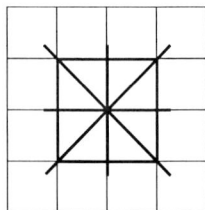

b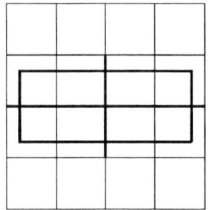

c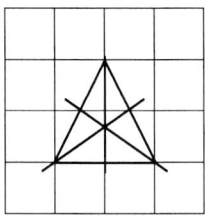

d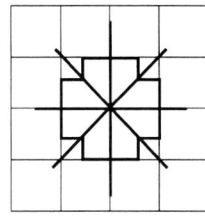

e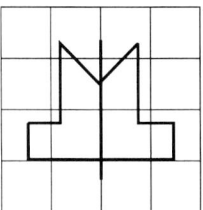

f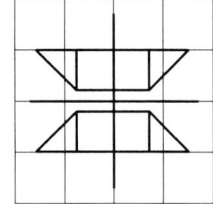

g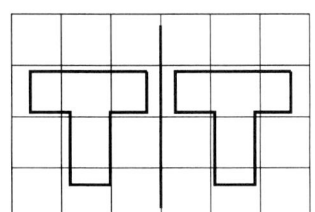

h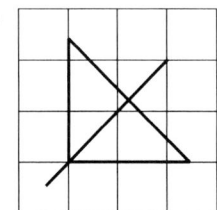

2 a 4   **b** 2   **c** 3   **d** 4
  e 2   **f** 4   **g** 2

3 a $y = 3$ **b** $x = -2$ **c** $x = y$ **d** $x = -y$

1 Draw the lines of symmetry on each of the following shapes.

a

b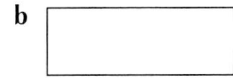

c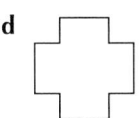

d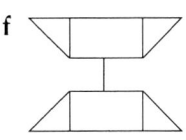

e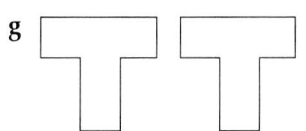

f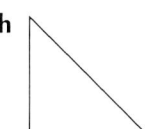

g

h

2 Give the order of rotational symmetry of each of the following shapes.

a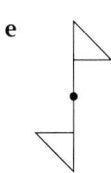

b

c

d

e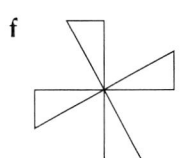

f

g

3 Write down the equation of each of the lines drawn on the grid.

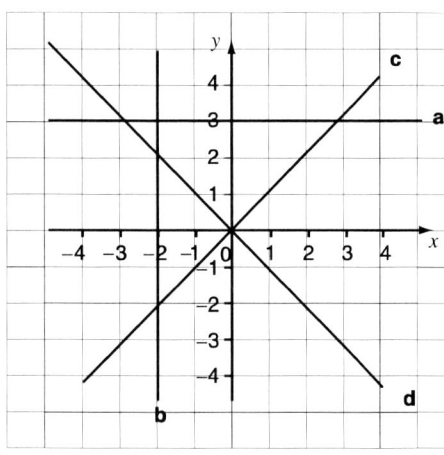

a _____

b _____

c _____

d _____

Incorporating exercise:	19A
Homework:	19.1
Examples:	19.1

Key word
congruent

Learning objective(s)

● recognise congruent shapes

Prior knowledge

No prior knowledge is needed.

Starter

Using squared paper, ask pupils to draw a shape using four squares that must touch edge to edge. There are five different shapes possible.

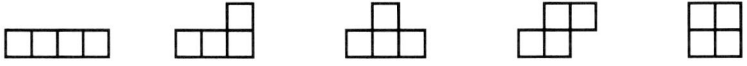

Go round the class and collect examples. It is likely that pupils will have the same shape but in different orientations. Show examples of these. Make sure that pupils have an intuitive idea of congruency.

Main teaching points

Emphasise that congruent shapes are identical in shape *and* size. Tell pupils that shapes that are the same shape but of a different size are 'similar'.

Common mistakes

Mistakes are made when pupils do not use tracing paper for complicated shapes. Pupils often do not recognise that identical shapes can be rotated and still be congruent.

Differentiation

Ensure that you give enough time for the lower achieving pupils to use tracing paper on all but the most obviously congruent shapes.

Plenary

Revisit the starter. Ask different groups to take one of the shapes made with four squares and add an extra square in different places to make shapes with five squares.

If there is time, collect in examples. There are 13 different possibilities, but many more alternative orientations. Discuss which are congruent.

Incorporating exercise:	19B
Homework:	19.2
Example:	19.2

Key words
tessellate
tessellation

Learning objective(s)

● tessellate a 2-D shape

Prior knowledge

No prior knowledge is needed.

Starter

Ask pupils to follow these instructions:
● Draw a square of side length 1 cm (for example). Draw congruent squares all round the first one (you will need eight extra). If you are accurate, you will have no gaps.
● Draw a rectangle that is 1 cm by 2 cm. Draw congruent rectangles all round the first one (you will need eight extra). If you are accurate, you will have no gaps.
● Sketch a hexagon. Draw congruent hexagons all round the first one (you will need six extra). If you are accurate, you will have no gaps.
● Draw a circle. Draw congruent circles all round the first one. This time you will have gaps.

Discuss tessellations in terms of 'gaps' and 'no gaps' in the diagrams just drawn.

Main teaching points

When drawing tessellations use appropriate paper – usually square grid paper but occasionally isometric paper. This will help accuracy. Another method, if you have time, is to use card and make a template of the first shape, then draw around it for the tessellation.

Common mistakes

Mistakes arise when pupils do not draw accurately.

Differentiation

None – low ability pupils often do well at this topic.

Plenary

Ask a pupil to draw an irregular quadrilateral on the board. Show how this will tessellate.

Repeat with another quadrilateral, for example a trapezium.

Establish that all quadrilaterals will tessellate.

Incorporating exercise:	19C	**Key words**	
Homework:	19.3	image	translate
Examples:	19.3	object	translation
		transformation	vector

Learning objective(s)

- translate a 2-D shape

Prior knowledge

Pupils need to understand and be able to use coordinates in the first quadrant.

Starter

Draw a set of axes from 0 to 6 on x- and y-axes.

Plot a point and ask pupils for the coordinate, for example (3, 2).

Plot another point and ask pupils for the coordinate, for example (5, 3).

Ask pupils how to get from the first point to the second. They will probably say 2 across, 1 up. Suggest that this could be simply expressed as (2, 1).

Now give a move of, for example, (1, 3) from the first point and ask the pupils where it moves to.

Repeat with other moves, including some negative moves.

Discuss the advantages (easy to understand) and disadvantages (confused with coordinates) of this notation.

Main teaching points

When a shape is translated, its position is changed but its shape and orientation are not. Pupils are familiar with coordinates (x, y); show them that a vector $\begin{pmatrix} x \\ y \end{pmatrix}$ is similar, but reinforce the fact that a vector is *not* a coordinate.

Keep reminding pupils that positive numbers in the vector are 'up' and 'right' and that negative numbers are 'down' and 'left'.

Common mistakes

Pupils use coordinate notation instead of vector notation, that is, (x, y) instead of $\begin{pmatrix} x \\ y \end{pmatrix}$.

Pupils use $\begin{pmatrix} x \\ y \end{pmatrix}$ and turn the vector into a fraction.

The most common mistake is that pupils use the vector given as a coordinate and draw the shape from that coordinate rather than translating the shape using the vector.

Plenary

Draw a 2 × 2 grid. Put a dot in the centre.

Ask pupils to give the vectors that take the central dot to each of the other points on the grid.

If there is time, increase the size of the grid and repeat.

Incorporating exercise:	19D
Homework:	19.4
Examples:	19.4

Key words

image	reflect
mirror line	reflection
object	

Learning objective(s)

- reflect a 2-D shape in a mirror line

Prior knowledge

Pupils should be able to find the lines of symmetry of a 2-D shape (see Chapter 10). For grade C work, pupils should also be able to draw the lines $y = x$ and $y = -x$, as well as lines such as $y = 3$ and $x = -2$.

Starter

Draw a set of axes from -5 to $+5$ for x- and y-axes.

Draw some horizontal and vertical lines and ask pupils for their equations.

Make sure they understand that x lines are vertical and y lines are horizontal.

Finish with $y = x$ and $y = -x$.

Main teaching points

Each vertex is reflected at $90°$ to the mirror line and the image vertex is the same distance from it as the object vertex.

If a question has a diagonal mirror line, turn the page so that the line is vertical – the question is the same, but looks easier.

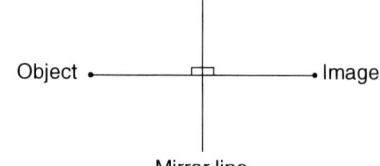

Common mistakes

Pupils often draw the image at a different distance from the mirror line than the object.
They also draw   instead of   .

Differentiation

Low achieving pupils will require help and guidance when using diagonal and multiple mirror lines.

Plenary

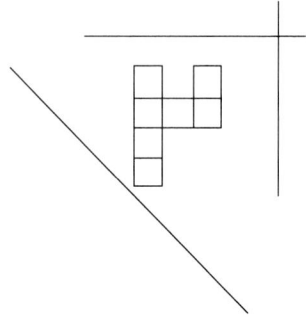

Ask pupils to draw the diagram on grid paper and to reflect the shape in each mirror line.

			Key words	
Incorporating exercise:	19E		angle of rotation	image
Homework:	19.5		anticlockwise	object
Example:	19.5		centre of	rotate
			rotation	rotation
			clockwise	

Learning objective(s)

◉ rotate a 2-D shape about a point

Prior knowledge

Pupils should be able to find the order of rotational symmetry of a 2-D shape (see Chapter 10). They should know what is meant by clockwise and anticlockwise.

Starter

Ask pupils to draw a T-shape.

They should then draw another T-shape to add to the first to make a shape with rotational symmetry of order 2. Ask: "How many had a shape like this?

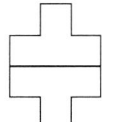 OR 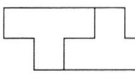 OR

Ask pupils what the difference is between the diagrams.

Establish the concept of the centre of rotation. Mark the centre on the diagrams.

Main teaching points

Tracing paper is allowed in the examination, so encourage its use for all but the most simple rotations. Check that pupils use the centre of rotation correctly – putting a pencil point on it as they rotate the tracing paper is usually enough. The angles of rotation required are 90°, 180°, 270°.

Common mistakes

Common mistakes are ignoring the centre of rotation if it is away from the shape, not using tracing paper and turning in the wrong direction.

Plenary

Draw this diagram on the board:

Ask pupils to describe any transformations that take square A to square B. These could be a translation, a reflection or three rotations.

Incorporating exercise:	19F
Homework:	19.6
Examples:	19.6

Key words

centre of	image
enlargement	object
enlarge	scale factor
enlargement	

Learning objective(s)

●   enlarge a 2-D shape by a scale factor

Prior knowledge

Pupils need to know where the origin is on a set of axes.

Starter

Draw a square of side length 1 cm.
Draw another square of side length 2 cm a few centimetres to the right of the first square.
Draw the lines as shown; they should all meet at one point.

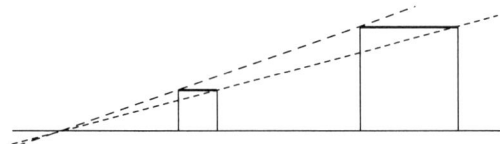

Ask, "What are the perimeters?" (4 cm and 8 cm) Explain that the side lengths are doubled, so the perimeter of the second square is double the first.
Ask, "What is the area of the first square?" (1 cm^2) "The second?" (4 cm^2) "The side lengths are doubled, but the area is four times as big – why?"
Repeat with a square of side length 1 cm and a square of side length 3 cm.

Main teaching points

Pupils should be very careful to make sure the lines from the centre of enlargement to the shapes are as accurate as possible. They can use the grid to help if there is one.

Emphasise that an enlargement with a fractional scale factor is possible.

Common mistakes

Pupils do not use the centre of enlargement that is given. They also draw inaccurate construction lines from the centre of enlargement to the shape, and between shapes, or do not draw them all in.

Plenary

Put 'A' on a small square and 'B' on a larger square.

Ask the following questions:
●   How do you get from square B to square A?
●   What is the scale factor?
●   What is the centre of enlargement?
●   What is the ratio of the perimeters?
●   What is the ratio of the areas?

Constructions

Overview

20.1 Constructing triangles
20.2 Bisectors
20.3 Loci

This chapter covers the construction of triangles (grade C) and bisecting lines and angles, as well as loci (all at grade C).

Context

Accurate drawing is required when designing and building structures involving triangles, such as bridges and roofs. An understanding of loci is important in locating the following: TV, radio and telephone masts, radar stations, water-sprinkler systems for golf courses, movement sensors on security lighting.

Edexcel A references

Ma3 Shape, space and measures: Measures and construction

20.1, 20.2 3.4e "use straight edge and compasses to do standard constructions, including … the midpoint and perpendicular bisector of a line segment, … and the bisector of an angle"
20.3 3.4j "find loci …"

Route mapping

Exercise	G	F	E	D	C
A				all	
B					all
C					all
D					all

Answers to diagnostic Check-in test

1 Lines of **a** 8.4 cm and **b** 67 mm (±2 mm is maximum error permitted)

2

— 3 cm ± 2 mm
± 2°
60°

3 Circle of radius 2 cm drawn (±2 mm)
4 Arcs drawn accurately (±2 mm)
5

3 cm ± 2 mm —
± 2°
100°

1 Draw a line for each length below.

    a 8.4 cm   **b** 67 mm

2 Use a protractor to draw an angle of 60° on the line below. Draw it from the left-hand side of the line. Make the line you draw 3 cm long.

_____

3 Draw a circle of radius 2 cm. Use the centre of the cross as the centre of your circle.

×

4 Copy the diagram below by drawing the arcs with your compasses set at 3 cm.

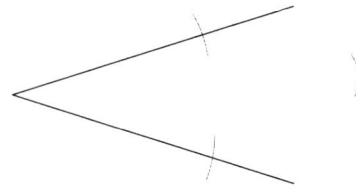 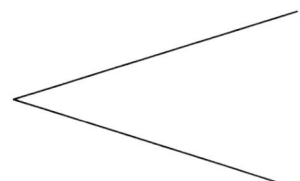

5 Use a protractor to draw an angle of 100°. Draw it from the right-hand side of the line given. Make the line you draw 3 cm long.

_____

			Key words	
Incorporating exercise:	20A		angle	construct
Homework:	20.1		compasses	side
Examples:	20.1			

Learning objective(s)

- construct triangles using compasses, a protractor and a straight edge

Prior knowledge

Pupils must have the skills of drawing and measuring a straight line, of using a protractor accurately and of opening a pair of compasses to a set size and drawing an arc from a set point.

Starter

Pupils will have seen this activity before, but it gives good practice at using compasses.

Ask the pupils to draw a circle and, keeping the radius unchanged, start anywhere and mark off six points around the circumference, drawing arcs within the circle. This gives a nice flower pattern. If drawn accurately the petals will have sharp points.

Main teaching points

The emphasis is on accuracy. Pupils are allowed 2 mm and 2° error either side of the correct size and they must *not* rub out their construction lines.

When drawing triangles, start by drawing the longest known length (accurately) as the base.

The 'included angle' is the angle between the two sides given.

Tell them: "Poor equipment + carelessness = no marks for a (usually) gift of a GCSE question."

Plenary

Ask pupils to draw a line about 5 cm long and set their compasses with the point at one end of the line and the pencil point at the other end.

Tell them to draw arcs from both ends.

They should then join up the ends of the line and the point of intersection of the arcs.

What type of triangle is this? Measure the angles and sides to check.

Incorporating exercise:	20B
Homework:	20.2
Examples:	20.2

Key words

angle bisector   perpendicular
bisect   bisector
line bisector

Learning objective(s)

● construct the bisector of lines and angles

Prior knowledge

Pupils should be able to use a pair of compasses.

Starter

Ask pupils what 'bisect' means.

Ask for any other words that start with 'bi' (bicycle, bifocal, etc.). Emphasise that it means to cut in two.

Ask pupils what perpendicular means. Emphasise that it means 'at right angles'.

Ask for examples of lines in the room that are perpendicular.

Main teaching points

Pupils need to know that bisect means to cut into two *equal* parts. When a line is bisected, a perpendicular bisector is drawn (that is, the line that bisects is at 90° to the one that has been bisected).

Go through the constructions, making sure the pupils follow each step. Check by measuring with rulers and protractors for accuracy. As with any construction question, lack of accuracy means lack of marks.

Common mistakes

Pupils just measure and do not construct. Examiners have a saying, "Arcs means marks".

Plenary

You will need a board pen with a piece of string (at least 50 cm long) tied to it.

● Ask a 'volunteer' to bisect a 120° angle with the pen and the string, a second 'volunteer' to bisect one of the resulting 60° angles, a third to bisect one of the 30° angles, and a fourth to check the size of the 15° angle with a board protractor.
● Draw a horizontal line, 40 or 50 cm in length, on the board. Give another 'volunteer' the pen and the string and ask them to bisect the line. Ask the last 'volunteer' to bisect one of the two halves.

Incorporating exercises:	20C, 20D	Key words
Homework:	20.3	loci
Examples:	20.3	locus

Learning objective(s)

- draw loci

Prior knowledge

Pupils should be able to draw a circle with a pair of compasses and know that from the centre of the circle to any point on the edge is the same distance (that is, the radius).

Starter

Pick a point in the classroom (or go outside if space is limited). Ask a pupil to move so that she/he is always 2 metres from the point. Discuss the shape of the path traced out.

Now choose two points. Ask a pupil to move so that she/he is always the same distance from the two points. Discuss the shape of the path traced out.

Now choose three points, call them A, B and C. Ask a pupil to move so that she/he is the same distance from the lines AB and AC. Discuss the shape of the path traced out.

Main teaching points

Most loci questions at this level involve staying the same distance from a point (a circle), staying the same distance from two points (perpendicular bisector) or staying the same distance from two lines (angle bisector). Other situations are combinations of these, for example overlapping radio transmitter ranges. Before tackling the questions in the exercise it may be a good idea to discuss them.

Emphasise that the mathematics only models the real situation.

Common mistakes

Pupils can confuse the distance from a point with the distance from a line. Lack of accuracy is often a problem.

Differentiation

This is a grade C topic so lower achieving pupils will find it difficult. The more practical and less abstract you can make it the better.

Plenary

Ask pupils to imagine a bird tied by a tether 1 metre long to a point on a perch. What is the locus of the possible area of the bird's flight? (A sphere.)

Now imagine the same bird tied to a perch 3 metres long by a tether 1 metre long. This time the tether is on a ring that can slide along the perch. What is the locus of the possible area the bird can fly this time? (A sausage shape with hemispherical ends.)

Overview

21.1 Systems of measurement
21.2 Metric units
21.3 Imperial units
21.4 Conversion factors

The first section is designed to get pupils to decide upon which units are required when measuring different objects. The second, third and fourth sections are about manipulating metric and imperial units, and converting between the two.

Context

Look around you – just about everything you see probably had to be measured at some time.

Edexcel A references

Ma3 Shape, space and measures: Measures and construction

21.1, 21.2, 21.3, 21.4   3.4a "…convert measurements from one unit to another; know rough metric equivalents of pounds, feet, miles, pints and gallons…"

Route mapping

Exercise	G	F	E	D	C
A	1–15	16–25			
B		all			
C		all			
D		1–13	14–18	19–21	22

Answers to diagnostic Check-in test

1 100 cm, 1 km, 1000 g, 1000 kg
2 lines between: 0.1 cm and 1 mm, 10 mm and 1 cm, 100 cm and 1 m, 1000 m and 1 km
3 a 1000   **b** 1   **c** 1000

1 Circle the correct answer.

| 1 m | = | 0.1 cm | 10 cm | 100 cm | 1000 cm |

| 1000 m | = | 10 mm | 10 cm | 1 mile | 1 km |

| 1 kg | = | 0.001 g | 10 g | 1000 g | 1 tonne |

| 1 tonne | = | 1000 g | 1000 m | 1000 kg | 1000 KW |

2 Draw a line between equal pairs.

| 0.1 cm | 1 cm |

| 10 mm | 1 km |

| 100 cm | 1 m |

| 1000 m | 1 mm |

3 Fill in the empty spaces for units of volume.

a 1 litre = _____ millilitres

b 1 millilitre = _____ cm^3

c _____ litres = 1 m^3

Incorporating exercise:	21A
Homework:	21.1
Examples:	21.1

Key words

capacity	metric
imperial	volume
length	weight

Learning objective(s)

● decide which units to use when measuring length, weight and capacity

Prior knowledge

Pupils should be familiar with the basic metric units (millimetre, centimetre, metre, kilometre, tonne, millilitre, litre) and imperial units (inch, foot, yard, mile, ounce, pound, stone, ton, pint, gallon) and, more importantly, should have a rough idea, at least, of the size of each unit.

Starter

Multiply various numbers by 10, 100, 1000. Divide various numbers by 10, 100, 1000.
Multiply and divide numbers by 8 (pints and gallons).
Multiply and divide numbers by 12 (inches and feet).
Multiply and divide numbers by 3 (feet and yards).

Main teaching points

If pupils appreciate the idea of each unit in relation to a common object (for example, door = 2 m, apple = 100 g), they will be much more successful at this topic.

Common mistakes

Pupils often assume that 1 m is 1 mile. Also, there is a general confusion regarding what a measurement measures, for example whether centimetres are the units for length or volume or weight.

Differentiation

Lower achieving pupils will require that initially you keep to one type of measurement, for example just weight, until that type is understood and used correctly.

Plenary

Go over the links between millimetre, centimetre, metre, kilometre, millilitre, litre, milligram, gram, kilogram and tonne. Try to link them to everyday objects, for example a bag of sugar weighs 1 kg.

Incorporating exercise:	21B
Homework:	21.2
Example:	21.2

Key words

millimetre (mm)	kilogram (kg)
centimetre (cm)	tonne (t)
metre (m)	millilitre (ml)
kilometre (m)	centilitre (cl)
gram (g)	litre (l)

Learning objective(s)

● convert from one metric unit to another

Prior knowledge

Pupils should know (or have written down) the links between the metric units for:
    length: 10 mm = 1 cm, 100 cm = 1 m, 1000 m = 1 km
    weight: 1000 g = 1 kg, 1000 kg = 1 tonne
    capacity/volume: 10 ml = 1 cl, 1000 ml = 100 cl = 1 l, 1 ml = 1 cm^3, 1000 l = 1 m^3

Starter

Do some mental divisions, by 3, 8 and 12, that have remainders. For example, 20 ÷ 3 = 6 rem. 2, 20 ÷ 8 = 2 rem. 4, 20 ÷ 12 = 1 rem. 8.

Main teaching points

Emphasise the words that help:
    kilo   1000 (for example, 1 kilogram = 1000 g)
    milli   1000th (for example, 1 millimetre = 1000th of a metre, so 1000 mm = 1 m)
    centi   100th (for example, 1 centilitre = 100th of a litre, so 100 cl = 1 litre)

Common mistakes

Mistakes occur when pupils multiply and divide by the incorrect number, for example, 1000 instead of 100.

Differentiation

Lower achieving pupils will require that initially you keep to one type of measurement, for example just weight, until that type is understood and used correctly.

Plenary

Play the Metric Quiz.
    Put the class into 2, 3 or 4 teams.
    Give questions to each team, such as "How many metres is 175 cm?"
    If a team member can give an instant answer, award 2 points. If they need to refer to notes or use a calculator, they get 1 point.

Incorporating exercise:	21C
Homework:	21.3
Example:	21.3

Key words

inch (in)	pound (lb)
foot (ft)	stone (st)
yard (yd)	ton (T)
mile (m)	pint (pt)
ounce (oz)	gallon (gal)

Learning objective(s)

- convert one imperial unit to another

Prior knowledge

Pupils should know (or have written down) the links between the imperial units for:
    length: 12 inches = 1 foot, 3 feet = 1 yard, 1760 yards = 1 mile
    weight: 16 ounces = 1 pound, 14 pounds = 1 stone, 2240 pounds = 1 ton
    capacity/volume: 8 pints = 1 gallon

Starter

Do some mental divisions, by 3, 8 and 12, that have remainders. For example, $20 \div 3 = 6$ rem. 2, $20 \div 8 = 2$ rem. 4, $20 \div 12 = 1$ rem. 8.

Main teaching points

Unlike metric, there is no easy way to convert between imperial units – old fashioned rote learning by continually telling and asking for the conversions throughout the lesson will help the pupils remember them.

Plenary

Tell the pupils that many very strange units were in use in olden days. For example, 8 furlongs = 1 mile, 20 hundredweight (112 lb) = 1 ton, 10 chains (22 yds) = 1 furlong.

Many of these are still in use. Furlongs appear in horse racing distances. A chain is the length of a cricket pitch. Ask pupils to research some old units on the Internet.

Incorporating exercise:	21D
Homework:	21.4
Example:	21.4

Key words

conversion	imperial
factor	metric

Learning objective(s)

● use the approximate conversion factors between imperial units and metric units

Prior knowledge

If pupils have now got an idea of the relative 'size' of each unit, then they should be able to tell you what units are going to be converted into what. For example, ask what metric unit an inch will be converted into and hopefully you will get the reply 'centimetres'.

Starter

Ask pupils to recall as many imperial units and their conversions as they can. For example, 12 inches = 1 foot. If pupils were asked to research old units in the previous plenary, ask for any strange ones they may have found.

Main teaching points

The emphasis is on pupils familiarising themselves with which unit converts to which, and the factors involved. The factor alone will not help – if a pupil remembers 2.5 for converting between centimetres and inches, they still have to know which is larger.

For the GCSE exam, pupils are expected to know that 2.2 lb ≈ 1 kg, 5 miles ≈ 8 km, 1 foot ≈ 30 cm, 1 gallon ≈ 4.5 litres and that 1.75 pints ≈ 1 litre. 1 inch ≈ 2.5 centimetres is another useful conversion to know.

Common mistakes

Pupils may not remember the conversion factors, or divide when they should be multiplying and vice versa.

Differentiation

Concentrate on the following as these are the examination requirements: inches ↔ centimetres, miles ↔ kilometres, pounds ↔ kilograms, gallons ↔ litres. Only include hard questions (for example, "How many centimetres are there in 42 yards?") for the most able.

Plenary

Put the five conversions that the pupils should know on the board. Allow them to study the conversions for a minute or two and then rub them out.

Do some approximations such as, "About how many pounds is 10 kilograms?" "About how many litres is 5 gallons?"

22.1 Pie charts
22.2 Scatter diagrams
22.3 Surveys
22.4 Social statistics

This chapter falls into two parts. The first part, Sections 22.1 and 22.2, covers the remaining methods of data representation. Section 22.3 is concerned with appropriate methods of collecting data. This is followed by a brief look at social statistics.

Context

The usefulness of this topic should be evident from the nature of the exercises and questions. Of the two representational techniques covered here, pie charts are widely used and pupils will be familiar with them from general use and also from use in other subjects. Scatter diagrams are rather more specialised and pupils are likely to need more demonstration to appreciate their usefulness.

The latter part of the chapter introduces ideas aimed at avoiding problems that can occur in the collection of data and looks at the everyday use of social statistics.

Edexcel A references

Ma4 Handling data: Processing and representing data

22.1, 22.2   4.4a "draw and produce ... pie charts for categorical data, and diagrams for continuous data, including ... scatter graphs..."

22.2   4.4h "draw lines of best fit..."

Ma4 Handling data: Collecting data

22.3   4.3a "design and use data-collection sheets ... collect data using various methods, including ... data logging, questionnaires and surveys"

Ma4 Handling data: Specifying the problem and planning

22.3   4.2e "design an experiment or survey; decide what primary and secondary data to use"

Route mapping

Exercise	G	F	E	D	C
A		1	2–6		
B			1	2	3–6
C				1–4	5
D				1–2	3–5
E				1–4	5

Answers to diagnostic Check-in test

1 a 36   **b** 60   **c** 45   **d** 24

2 a 90   **b** 240   **c** 150   **d** 54   **e** 50

3 a 51°   **b** 71°   **c** 148°

4 Check points plotted correctly

5 a $\frac{7}{40}$ **b** $\frac{3}{10}$ **c** $\frac{2}{5}$ **d** $\frac{1}{8}$

1 Work out the following divisions.

   a 360 ÷ 10

   b 360 ÷ 6

   c 360 ÷ 8

   d 360 ÷ 15

2 Find the answers to these calculations.

   a $\frac{1}{4}$ of 360

   b $\frac{2}{3}$ of 360

   c $\frac{5}{12}$ of 360

   d $\frac{3}{4}$ of 72

   e $\frac{2}{5}$ of 125

3 Measure each of these angles.

   a 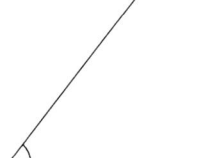   **b** 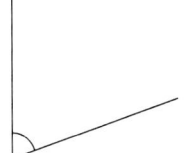   **c**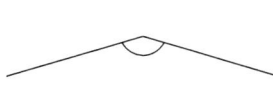

4 Plot these coordinates on the grid.

   a (5, 2)

   b (12, 8)

   c (1, 7)

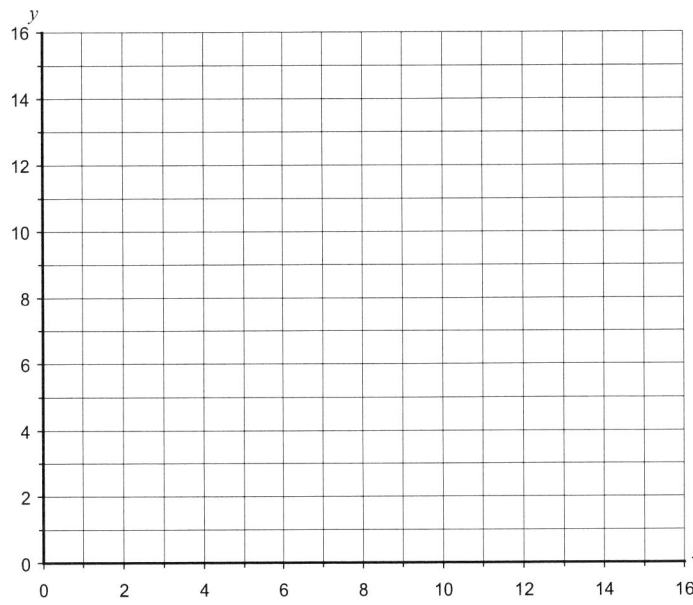

5 Forty children were asked their favourite hobbies. The results were put into the following table.

Favourite hobby	Frequency
Sport	12
Computer games	16
Reading	5
Music	7

For each of the following questions, simplify your answer as far as possible.

   a What fraction of the children chose music?

   b What fraction of the children chose sport?

   c What fraction of the children chose computer games?

   d What fraction of the children chose reading?

Incorporating exercise:	22A	Key words
Homework:	22.1	angle
Example:	22.1	pie chart
		sector

Learning objective(s)

● draw pie charts

Prior knowledge

Pupils must know how to express one number as a fraction of another and how to calculate a fraction of a number.

Pupils must know how to draw and measure angles.

Starter

Ask the pupils to find all the factor pairs of 360. These will be needed in the exercise so it is worth pupils writing them in their exercise books.

Main teaching points

It is important for pupils to understand that a pie chart shows each class or category as a fraction or proportion of the whole set of data. For this reason, the frequencies cannot be read directly from a pie chart. It should be pointed out to pupils that, when comparing results from two pie charts, the frequencies of the categories cannot be compared, only the proportions of each category.

Pupils should be shown how to draw a pie chart, by expressing each frequency as a fraction of the total and then finding the required size of the angle for each sector by calculating the corresponding fraction of 360 degrees.

Pupils should also be shown how to find the frequency of each category when the total is known, by expressing the size of the corresponding angle as a fraction of 360 degrees and then calculating this fraction of the total.

Sectors of pie charts should always be labelled.

Common mistakes

The most common mistake when drawing a pie chart is to measure each angle from the same starting point. A demonstration should be given to pupils, with particular emphasis on starting the measurement of each angle at the end of the previous sector.

Differentiation

Higher achieving pupils will be able to find short cuts for finding the required angle of a pie chart, through their understanding of proportions. This should be encouraged but it should also be emphasised that the full method may be required when the numbers being handled are less obvious.

Plenary

Draw a pie chart with sectors of 90°, 120° and 45°. Ask pupils what fraction of 360° these sectors represent. Give a value for the number represented by the chart, for example 240. Ask how much each sector represents. Reverse the process. For example, tell them that the 45° sector represents nine people and ask them how many people are represented by the whole chart.

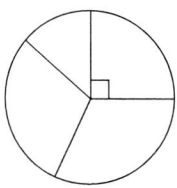

Incorporating exercise:	22B		Key words
Homework:	22.2		correlation positive
Example:	22.2		line of best fit correlation
			negative scatter diagram
			correlation variable
			no correlation

Learning objective(s)

● draw, interpret and use scatter diagrams

Prior knowledge

Pupils must be able to plot points using coordinates.

Pupils must be able to use appropriate scales on axes and interpret intermediate positions on them.

Starter

Draw a coordinate grid and ask pupils to plot points of your choice on it.
Show pupils sections of number lines that are marked off with different scales and ask for intermediate values on them.
Draw a coordinate grid with a straight line graph on it. Ask pupils to find the value of one variable that corresponds with your choice of the other.

Main teaching points

There are two main elements to this section. Firstly, pupils should be shown how to construct a scatter diagram and draw a line of best fit. Pupils should understand that two corresponding data values are required for each point to be plotted and that these two values are used as one pair of coordinates. Pupils should also understand that the line of best fit should be representative of the underlying trend of all the data points. It should be a single straight line, which should extend just beyond the plotted points.

Secondly, pupils should understand how to interpret and use a scatter diagram. The concept of correlation should be discussed at some length, to reinforce the idea of whether two variables have any connection or influence on each other and, if so, whether it is positive or negative. Pupils should also understand how to use the line of best fit to find an approximate corresponding value.

Common mistakes

The greatest difficulty that pupils have is drawing the line of best fit appropriately. Pupils often try to join all the plotted points, as in a line graph. They also try to make the line of best fit pass through the origin.

Differentiation

Higher achieving pupils should be directed to focus on questions 3 to 6 of Exercise 22B, as these are grade C questions. These require the greatest amount of interpretation of the scatter diagrams and the greatest understanding of the underlying concepts. The activity is also a useful exercise, providing practice for Data handling coursework.

Plenary

Ask for examples of variables which would give the different types of correlation.

Incorporating exercises:	22C, 22D	**Key words**	
Homework:	22.3	leading question	response
Example:	22.3	primary data	secondary data
		questionnaire	survey

Learning objective(s)

- conduct surveys
- ask good questions in order to collect reliable and valid data

Prior knowledge

Pupils must be able to construct and use tables. Pupils should know how to use a tallying procedure accurately and effectively.

Starter

Ask the pupils to think of an amount of money between £0 and £20. Give them a (deliberately poor) choice of possible responses, for example, (i) between £0 and £1 (ii) between £1 and £5 and (iii) between £5 and £10. Collect up their responses by tallying on the board. When you have finished, ask for any comments. Points to look for include: (a) Why not just ask exactly how much everybody has? (b) What do you do if you have, for example, exactly £5? (c) How many people thought of an amount above £10 and were not included.

Main teaching points

Pupils should understand that a simple, clear and unambiguous question, with a clear choice of the possible responses, is the most appropriate and efficient way to design a data collection sheet, and that the design should include appropriate space to record the responses. This will usually be a space for tallying.

Pupils are also asked here to consider the most appropriate way to design questions and response options when designing a questionnaire. Pupils should understand the five main points that are highlighted in the text. As much discussion as possible is recommended here, so that pupils have every opportunity to consider what makes good and bad designs. Pupils should be given the opportunity to raise subjects of their own choosing for the questionnaire design, as they are more likely to have a clear understanding of the salient points. Their interest may also give them preconceived ideas about how they hope people would respond. As a result of this, they may well include leading questions and these should be clearly pointed out and opened for discussion.

Common mistakes

The most common mistake here is in the design of response options. In particular, the options to respond at either extreme are often forgotten, or not well handled. Lower achieving pupils also often find it difficult to find faults with data collection sheets or survey questions with which they are presented.

Differentiation

The questions in both these exercises are aimed at grades D and C and, as such, lower achieving pupils may well have difficulty with them. Wherever possible, it is a good idea to give pupils the opportunity to try out their own designs, so that they can experience some of the typical difficulties for themselves.

Plenary

Ask for suggested response options for the following topics (or others of your own choice): how often people use the Internet, how many days off work/school people have had in the last year, and so on. Look for a sensible range of response options, with no overlaps and the extremes catered for realistically.

Incorporating exercise:	22E
Homework:	22.4

Key words

margin of error	Retail Price Index
National Census	social statistics
Polls	time series

Learning objective(s)

⬤ understand how social statistics are used in everyday life and what information the government needs about the population

Prior knowledge

Pupils need to be able to interpret information from dual bar charts.

Starter

Ask pupils if they know how many people live in Britain. The answer is approximately 60 million.

Discuss how we know this. What is the exact figure? Can the exact figure ever be found?

Mention the National Census and discuss what sort of data this collects (number of people per house, ages, gender, religion, ethnicity, education, and so on), how often it is taken (every 10 years) and if it is compulsory (yes).

Main teaching points

Most statistics that are met on a daily basis in newspapers are 'social'. For example, percentages of unemployed, increases in the cost of living, changes in prices over time, populations and spending on the NHS.

Discuss each of these and make sure that pupils understand the idea of an index and a base number. Why is it usually 100? Review percentages if necessary, in particular the percentage multiplier.

Talk about time series. In particular, emphasise that the lines joining points represent trends and not actual values, which are generally measured at a specific time each year or month. Examples would be temperature changes, cost of houses and exchange rates.

Differentiation

This is a new topic for many and will be a difficult concept for all but the most able pupils. If necessary discuss the questions in the exercise to give pupils some idea of how to do them.

Plenary

Sketch the following graph on the board, which shows a rough distribution of ages in Britain in 1950 and 2000.

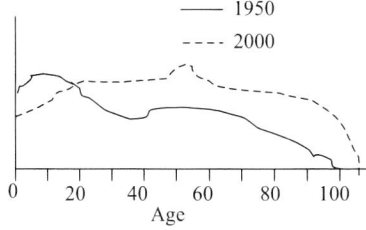

Ask pupils what use such information might be to a government? Explain that the blip is the post war baby boom.

Discuss how an aging population means pension problems and fewer young people means less school places will be needed in 5 years time.

Overview

In this chapter pupils work on some of the common sequences of numbers and learn how to recognise rules for sequences. They then learn how to express a rule for a sequence, both in words and algebraically.

Context

Finding patterns is important in mathematics. It helps to find rules for making calculations. It also helps develop the ability to work logically and in an ordered way.

Edexcel A references

Ma2 Number and algebra: Sequences, functions and graphs

23.1, 23.2, 23.3, 23.4, 23.5 2.6a "generate terms of a sequence using term-to-term and position-to-term definitions of the sequence; ..."

23.2, 23.3, 23.4, 23.5 2.6a "... generate common integer sequences (including sequences of odd or even integers, squared integers, powers of 2, powers of 10, triangular numbers); use linear expressions to describe the nth term of an arithmetic sequence, justifying its form by referring to the activity or context from which it was generated"

Route mapping

Exercise	G	F	E	D	C
A			all		
B		1	2–3	4–6	
C			1–2	3–4	5
D				all	
E				all	

Answers to diagnostic Check-in test

1 a $x - 12$ pear, $2x$ plum, $\frac{1}{2}x$ cherry

b $4.5x - 12 = 195$
c 46 apple, 34 pear, 92 plum, 23 cherry

2 a $n = 9$ **b** $n = 3.5$

3 a 10   **b** -10 **c** -6

1 A fruit farm has x apple trees, 12 fewer pear trees, twice as many plum trees as apple trees and half as many cherry trees as apple trees.

  a Write expressions to show the numbers of different fruit trees.

  b The farmer has 195 trees altogether. Write an equation that shows this.

  c Solve the equation to find how many of each variety of fruit tree the farmer has.

2 Solve the following equations.

  a $5n + 7 = 52$

  b $15 - 2n = 8$

3 Find the value of the expression $4n - 6$ for each value of n below.

  a $n = 4$

  b $n = -1$

  c $n = 0$

Incorporating exercise:	23A	Key words
Homework:	23.1	pattern
Example:	23.1	sequence

Learning objective(s)

• recognise patterns in number sequences

Starter

Write the numbers 2 and 4 on the board and ask pupils what the next number in the pattern could be. The most likely answer is 6, but give the next term as 2, 4, 6, …, or 2, 4, 8, …, or 2, 4, 7, …, and ask the pupils how these patterns are building up.
Repeat with the numbers 1 and 5. For example, 1, 5, 9, …, 1, 5, 25, …, and so on.

Main teaching points

Pupils need to look carefully at the numbers they are working with. Spotting patterns is important as it makes it much easier to carry on the sequences. It can also remove the necessity to carry out any calculations to find the next numbers in the sequence.

Plenary

Write the following pattern on the board: 1, 1, 2, 3, 5, 8, …
Ask for the next terms. Pupils find this a difficult sequence to spot. Eventually give the next term if necessary. Keep going until the rule is spotted. This is the Fibonacci sequence, formed by adding the previous two terms.
Ask pupils to give two starting numbers, for example 3, 6, and continue as a Fibonacci type sequence, i.e. 3, 6, 9, 15, 24, ….

Incorporating exercise:	23B	Key words	
Homework:	23.2	consecutive	sequence
Example:	23.2	difference	term

Learning objective(s)

● recognise how number sequences are building up

Prior knowledge

Pupils should know how to recognise number patterns.

Starter

Play 'Make me say 25'. Tell the pupils that you have a rule in your head of the form $an \pm b$, and they have to find the rule by giving you a value for n to which you give the value according to the rule. For example, if the rule is $2x-1$ and a pupil says 5, you reply 9. Eventually someone may say 13 and you reply 25. Discuss the rule. Change the rule and the 'Make me say' number.

Main teaching points

Pupils need to know that a number sequence is an ordered set of numbers with a rule that allows them to find every number in the sequence. Each number in a sequence is called a term and it has its own place in the order. The first step in finding the general rule for a sequence is to find the link between the terms. This is known as the term-to-term rule. Often the easiest way to find this link is to look at the differences between consecutive terms.

Differentiation

Exercise 23B includes questions at grades F–D.

Plenary

Play 'Make me say' again, but this time use rules of the form $n \div a + b$. Do not inform pupils of the change, but ask for only even numbers if dividing by 2 and multiples of 3 if dividing by 3, etc.

Incorporating exercise:	23C
Homework:	23.3
Example:	23.3

Key words

coefficient	linear sequence
consecutive	nth term
difference	

Learning objective(s)

- recognise how number sequences are built up

Prior knowledge

Pupils should know how to recognise number patterns and how to find differences between consecutive terms.

Starter

Give your pupils a start number and an answer, for example 3 and 16. Ask them to make up formulae of the form $an + b$ for producing the second number from the first, for example, "Multiply by 5 and add 1." ($\times 5 + 1$)

Main teaching points

To find the rule for a linear sequence you can use the difference between the terms. For example, in the sequence 7, 9, 11, 13, ... the difference is 2. The difference gives the coefficient of n. Therefore in this example the rule would include '$2n$'. Subtracting the difference from the first term gives 5. This means the rule for this sequence is $2n + 5$. With practice, pupils will become proficient at working out these sequences.

Common mistakes

When finding the 10th term, pupils often just double the value of the 5th term.

Differentiation

Exercise 23C includes questions at grades E–C. Higher achieving pupils could leave out questions 1 and 2, which are grade E, and lower achievers could omit question 5, which is grade C. All pupils should work through questions 3 and 4, which are grade D.

Plenary

Write the sequence 1, 4, 9, 16 on the board. Ask pupils to work out the next two numbers in the sequence. Ask, "What is this sequence? What will the tenth term be?"
Repeat with 1, 3, 6, 10, ... and 1, 8, 27, 64, ...

Incorporating exercise:	23D
Homework:	23.4
Example:	23.4
Resource:	23.4

Learning objective(s)

recognise some special sequences and how they are built up

Prior knowledge

Pupils should be able to recognise number patterns.

Starter

Draw the first few rows of Pascal's triangle on the board, as illustrated in Resource 23.4. Pupils may find it easier to have their own copies of the triangle. Ask if anyone can see patterns in the numbers in the triangle. Let pupils describe the patterns they see.
Continue the triangle to the 10th row.

Main teaching points

There are some sequences that pupils need to be able to recognise and for which they can state the nth term. These include the odd and even numbers, square and triangular numbers, and the powers of 2 and 10. They also need to know the first few prime numbers, although these do not have an nth term.

Plenary

Revisit Pascal's triangle. Ask pupils if they can see the counting number sequence anywhere (second diagonal: 1, 2, 3, 4, ...).
Ask pupils if they can see the triangle number sequence anywhere (third diagonal: 1, 3, 6, 10, ...).
Add up each row, for example $1 = 1$, $1 + 1 = 2$, $1 + 2 + 1 = 4$. Keep going until pupils spot the rule.
Ask for the nth term (2^{n-1}).

Incorporating exercise:	23E
Homework:	23.5
Example:	23.5
Resource:	23.5

Learning objective(s)

● find the nth term from practical problems

Prior knowledge

Pupils will need to know how to find the nth term in a linear sequence.

Starter

Show pupils the diagram from Resource 23.5. Ask, "How many matchsticks will be needed to make the pattern with four squares?" Move on to the sequence of triangles.

Main teaching points

Pupils generally like problems where they can see diagrams that show a pattern building up. They must be encouraged to be logical in their approach to solving the problems. They should start with the simplest case and move on in an ordered and logical way. They should make tables, look for patterns and then find the rules. They must check that their rules work for all cases. These skills are vital for the investigational piece of coursework pupils will be expected to do.

Plenary

Put this diagram on the board:

Ask the pupils how many squares are in the diagram (1).

Now put this diagram on the board:

Ask the pupils how many squares are in this diagram (5).
Break the five squares down into 1 of 2 × 2 and 4 of 1 × 1.

Now put this diagram on the board:

Ask the pupils how many squares are in the diagram (14).
Break the 14 squares down into 1 of 3 × 3, 4 of 2 × 2 and 9 of 1 × 1.

Introduce the homework. Tell the pupils that they should not attempt to count the squares on the 8 × 8 grid, but should instead look at 1 × 1, 2 × 2, 3 × 3 squares (as just demonstrated) and then look at 4 × 4 squares, looking for the patterns. If they do this, they should see the pattern by the time they have counted the 4 × 4 squares. (Many may already have spotted it, so discourage them from telling the rest of the class.)

Surface area and volume of 3-D shapes

Overview

24.1 Units of volume
24.2 Surface area and volume of a cuboid
24.3 Density
24.4 Surface area and volume of a prism
24.5 Volume of a cylinder

This chapter covers the surface areas, volumes and density of prisms, including the cylinder.

Context

One immediate context to which pupils may be able to reference prisms is that of confectionery. Circular prisms (cylinders) are used to hold Smarties, cuboids hold 'After Eights' and triangular prisms are the shape of Toblerones or, perhaps, the 'green ones' from Quality Street. The volume is, therefore, important to manufacturers to determine how much confectionery each container might hold. Furthermore, the surface area then becomes important as the manufacturer might like to use a shape with the smallest surface area to maintain minimal material costs.

Edexcel A references

Ma3 Shape, space and measures: Measures and construction

24.1, 24.2, 24.4, 24.5   3.4g "find volumes of cuboids, recalling the formula and understanding the connection to counting cubes and how it extends this approach; calculate volumes of right prisms and of shapes made from cubes and cuboids"

24.3   3.4c "understand and use compound measures, including … density"

Ma3 Shape, space and measures: Geometrical reasoning

24.4, 24.5   3.2k "… solve problems involving surface areas and volumes of prisms and cylinders"

Route mapping

Exercise	G	F	E	D	C
A	all				
B			1–5	6–10	
C					all
D					all
E					all

Answers to diagnostic Check-in test

1 a 24 cm   **b** 36 cm^2
2 a 20 cm   **b** 16 cm^2
3 a 26.5 cm   **b** 27 cm^2
4 a 31.4 cm   **b** 78.5 cm^2

1 What is the perimeter and area of this square?

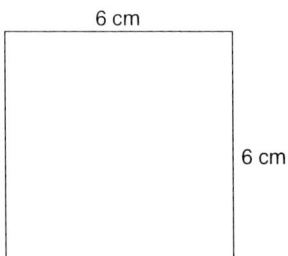

6 cm

6 cm

a Perimeter =_____cm

b Area =_____cm^2

2 What is the perimeter and area of this rectangle?

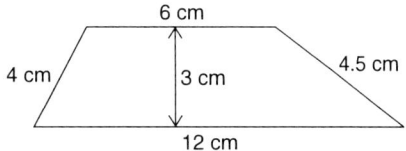

8 cm

2 cm

a Perimeter =_____cm

b Area =_____cm^2

3 What is the perimeter and area of this trapezium?

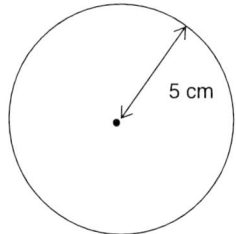

6 cm

4 cm   3 cm   4.5 cm

12 cm

a Perimeter =_____cm

b Area =_____cm^2

4 What is the perimeter and area of this circle?

5 cm

a Perimeter =_____cm

b Area =_____cm^2

Incorporating exercise:	24A	**Key words**	
Homework:	24.1	cubic centimetre	face
Example:	24.1	cubic metre	vertex
		cubic millimetre	volume
		edge	

Learning objective(s)

⚪ use the correct units with volume

Prior knowledge

Pupils need to understand the concept of 'volume'.

Starter

Draw a line on the board. Ask pupils, "In what units might this length be measured?"
Draw a rectangle. Ask pupils, "In what units might this area be measured?"
Draw a cuboid. Ask pupils, "In what units might this volume be measured?"

Main teaching points

The volume of a shape comprised entirely of 1 cm cubes may be found by counting the cubes.

Ensure the pupils' answers are given in the correct units, in this section usually cubic centimetres.

Euler's Theorem (1751) is the activity included in this section of the Pupil Book. Euler's Theorem states that, for a simple polyhedron, $F - E + V = 2$, where F is the number of faces, E is the number of edges and V is the number of vertices of the polyhedron. Although knowledge and use of this theorem is not required at GCSE, it is included here for the sake of completeness.

Common mistakes

Some pupils count only the cubes they can 'see'. At this level, it can be assumed that there will also be 'hidden cubes' included in a figure drawn on isometric paper.

Differentiation

Low achieving pupils may need help visualising the shapes through the use of multi-link cubes, if available.

Plenary

A cuboid has a volume of 24 cm³. How many different cuboids could be made (using multi-link cubes) that have this volume?

Incorporating exercise:	24B		Key words	
Homework:	24.2		capacity	surface area
Example:	24.2		height	volume
			length	width
			litre	

Learning objective(s)

- calculate the surface area and volume of a cuboid

Prior knowledge

Pupils need to understand the concept of 'volume' and be able to recall the standard conversion for lengths, that is, 1 cm = 10 mm and 1 m = 100 cm.

Starter

Draw a 2 × 3 × 4 cuboid on the board. Hand out multi-link cubes (if needed). Ask pupils to make the cuboid and calculate its volume by counting cubes. Ask them to try another cuboid themselves. Collate answers on the board into a table. Ask pupils, "Is there a quick way of calculating the volume without resorting to 'counting cubes'?"

Main teaching points

The volume of a cuboid is given by $V = lwh$, where l is the length, w is the width and h is the height. Furthermore, for a cube of length l, its volume is $V = l^3$ and $l = \sqrt[3]{V}$.

The surface area of a cuboid is given by $A = 2lw + 2hw + 2hl$.

Remind pupils of these relationships:

1 litre = 1000 cm^3

1 cm^3 = 1 ml

1 m^3 = 1 000 000 cm^3

Common mistakes

Pupils need to ensure they are working with consistent units. Difficulties also ensue whenever algebraic formulae need to be rearranged, for example when pupils are required to find the length of a cuboid, given the width and height.

Differentiation

Grade C candidates should be able to rearrange $V = lwh$, but lower achieving candidates may need to draw a diagram and 'estimate' an answer.

Plenary

Pose this problem: "There are two cuboids. One has dimensions 4 cm × 5 cm × 9 cm. The second has dimensions 3 cm × 6 cm × 10 cm. They both have an equal volume. Which cuboid has the larger surface area?"

Incorporating exercise:	24C
Homework:	24.3
Example:	24.3

Key words
density   volume
mass

Learning objective(s)

● find the density of a 3-D shape

Prior knowledge

Pupils need to be able to compute simple metric conversions, for example changing grams (g) to kilograms (kg) and vice versa, and metres (m) to centimetres (cm).

Starter

Discuss with pupils what might be meant by 'density'. What is meant when something is more or less 'dense'? Discuss the units of density.

Main teaching points

Familiarise pupils with the three arrangements of the formula:

$$\text{Density} = \frac{\text{mass}}{\text{volume}}$$

$$\text{Mass} = \text{density} \times \text{volume}$$

$$\text{Volume} = \frac{\text{mass}}{\text{density}}$$

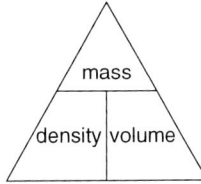

Units need to be used consistently. For example, if mass is measured in grams (g) and volume in cubic centimetres (cm^3), then the units of density will be grams per cubic centimetre (g/cm^3 or $g\ cm^{-3}$).

Plenary

For discussion, ask pupils to suggest objects that have the following properties:

a a low density and small volume (a cork)
b a low density and large volume (water)
c a high density and small volume (a gold ring)
d a high density and large volume (the planet earth)

There are many reasonable answers for each – it may prove helpful to obtain a reference list beforehand of materials and their associated densities.

Incorporating exercise:	24D	Key words	
Homework:	24.4	cross-section	surface area
Example:	24.4	prism	volume

Learning objective(s)

⚫ calculate the surface area and volume of a prism

Prior knowledge

Pupils need to be able to calculate areas of rectangles, triangles, trapezia and compound shapes.

Starter

Draw a rectangle, triangle, circle and trapezium on the board. Ask pupils to recall the formulae for areas of these shapes.
'Extend' the above diagrams into 3-D prisms by giving them depth. Label them: rectangular prism, triangular prism, circular prism, trapezoidal prism.
Ask pupils, "What are the rectangular prisms and circular prisms more commonly called? Why is it that the other two prisms do not have 'special names'?"
Have a cuboid and a triangular prism prepared from a net and held together with a small piece of Sellotape or similar. Open these out to give pupils a visual idea of the surface area.

Main teaching points

The volume of a prism is given by the product of the area of the cross-section of the prism and its length.

This might more usefully be written as $V = CSA \times$ length.

For most problems, it is therefore important to stress that pupils calculate the CSA of the prism as an essential first step.

Make sure that pupils know that the surface area is the total area of all the sides of the shape. It may help to sketch each side and put on dimensions, particularly if the shape is not a cuboid.

Common mistakes

Pupils will sometimes mistake the 'length' of the prism for a 'length' occurring in the cross-section. A good diagram and encouraging pupils to solve the problem in two distinct stages should avoid this.

Plenary

Consider the circular prism, or cylinder. Draw a diagram of a cylinder on the board, labelling the radius and height. By considering the formula $V = CSA \times$ length, ask pupils to find the formula for the volume of a cylinder. Ask pupils to find the volume of a cylinder with radius 2 cm and height 3 cm.

Incorporating exercise:	24E	Key words	
Homework:	24.5	cylinder	π
Example:	24.5	height	radius
		length	volume

Learning objective(s)

- calculate the volume of a cylinder

Prior knowledge

Pupils should know how to find the volume of a prism, as covered in Section 24.4, and be able to calculate the area of a circle, as covered in Section 16.3.

Starter

Revise or remind pupils of calculations involving areas of circles. Ask: "What is the area of a circle of radius 3 cm? What is the area of a circle of diameter 3 cm? If a circle's area is 25 cm², what is its radius?"

Main teaching points

A cylinder is a prism with a circular cross-section (CSA).

The volume of this prism is, therefore, $V = CSA \times \text{length} = \pi r^2 h$.

So, for a cylinder of radius r and height h:

$$V = \pi r^2 h$$

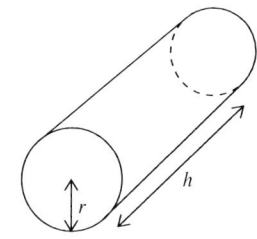

Common mistakes

Lower achieving candidates can be confused between πr^2 and $(\pi r)^2$. They may find it helpful to use a 'simpler' version of the formula in the form $V = \pi \times r \times r \times h$, until their confidence in using the formula improves.

Plenary

Ask pupils, "How can you find the surface area of a cylinder?"
First, imagine a piece of paper wrapped round a cylinder of radius r and height h. This could be 'unwrapped' to give a rectangular piece of paper, of dimensions $2\pi r$ by h.

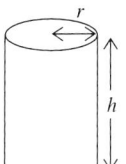 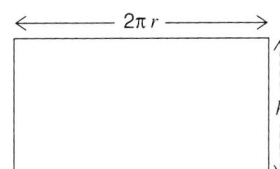

The area of this is therefore $2\pi rh$.

There are also two circles at the top and bottom of the cylinder, each having area πr^2.

The total surface area of a cylinder is therefore $2\pi r^2 + 2\pi rh = 2\pi r (r + h)$.

Quadratic graphs

Overview

25.1 Drawing quadratic graphs
25.2 Solving quadratic equations

This chapter begins by looking at drawing quadratic graphs and then moves onto solving quadratic equations from a graph.

Context

Any quadratic equation includes a term in x^2. A quadratic graph is always a parabola. Pupils will meet and use quadratic equations in science lessons when they are learning about gravity and how objects move, particularly when acceleration is involved. Other everyday applications of quadratic equations and graphs include safe braking distances.

Edexcel A references

Ma2 Number and algebra: Sequences, functions and graphs

25.1, 25.2   2.6e "generate points and plot graphs of simple quadratic functions, then more general quadratic functions; find approximate solutions of a quadratic equation from the graph of the corresponding quadratic function"

Route mapping

Exercise	G	F	E	D	C
A				1–2	3–6
B					all

Answers to diagnostic Check-in test

1 a 42   **b** 72   **c** 54
2 a 16   **b** 13   **c** 12

1 Substitute $x = 6$ into each of the following expressions.

a $x^2 + x$

b $2x^2$

c $x^2 + 3x$

2 Substitute $x = -4$ into each of the following expressions.

a x^2

b $x^2 - 3$

c $x^2 + x$

Incorporating exercise:	25A	**Key words**	
Homework:	25.1	quadratic	quadratic graph
Examples:	25.1	equation	
Resources:	25.1a, 25.1b, 25.1c		

Learning objective(s)

● draw a quadratic graph, given its equation

Prior knowledge

Pupils should know how to plot coordinate points in all four quadrants, be able to substitute numbers into a formula and know how to draw linear graphs.

Starter

Use quick-fire questions to check that pupils know the squares of numbers from 0 to 10. Then repeat for negative numbers from −10 to 0.

Main teaching points

A quadratic equation always includes a term in x^2. Before pupils can plot a quadratic curve they need to draw a table of values. Pupils need only plot two or three points for a linear graph. For a quadratic, however, it is usual to work out the value of six or seven points. In an examination, pupils are usually given the x-values and are expected to work out at least some of the y-values. The parabola drawn is symmetrical, although not all of the symmetry points may be plotted. It is important that pupils draw smooth curves; the Pupil Book gives tips for achieving this. An additional hint is, "Always look at the point you are aiming for, rather than where your pencil is." Examiners only give a tolerance of ±1 mm so it is worthwhile for pupils to practise their technique. These questions can appear on either paper, so pupils need to know that the square of a negative number is positive. In examinations, only tables of x and y values are given. The broken down tables in the exercise are just to assist calculation. Resources 25.1a, 25.1b and 25.1c may be useful when explaining the key points of quadratic graphs.

Common mistakes

Some pupils may assume that the square of a negative number is itself negative.

Pupils may fail to produce a continuous smooth curve. The most basic mistake is to neglect to use a sharp pencil.

When a graph has its vertex at a point halfway between two plotted values, the bottom of the graph is often drawn flat.

Differentiation

In Exercise 25A, questions 1 and 2 are grade D, questions 3 to 6 are grade C. Higher achieving pupils may be able to begin at question 3. Lower achieving pupils will need a lot of help to complete the tables. It may be necessary to do this as a class activity.

Plenary

Ask pupils to look at the tables they have filled in. Ask them if they can spot anything about the y-values. They should see that the y-values have symmetry about a point. Ask them to look at the graph and see if this can be related to the symmetry. They should see that the x-value about which the table is symmetrical is also the line about which the graph is symmetrical.

Incorporating exercise:	25B	**Key words**	
Homework:	25.2	quadratic	quadratic graph
Examples:	25.2	equation	solution

Learning objective(s)

- use a graph to solve a quadratic equation

Prior knowledge

Pupils should be able to complete the table of values for a quadratic graph and draw the curve.

Starter

Write on the board $x^2 - 5 = 0$ and ask pupils if they can solve the equation (± 2.2).
Now show pupils Resource 25.1a, the graph of $y = x^2 - 5$.
Ask them if they could use the graph to solve the equation $x^2 - 5 = 0$.
They should see that the graph crosses the x-axis at the points ± 2.2.

Main teaching points

Once pupils can draw quadratic graphs accurately they will be able to read from them, solving the equation for $y = 0$. In previous work, they will have already learned that $y = 0$ is the x-axis, but you may have to remind them of this. From this it follows that the equations they draw will therefore have a y-value of 0 where it crosses the x-axis. Point out that there are usually two solutions, given by the x-coordinates at the crossing points. Graphs that only touch the x-axis once have repeated roots or only one solution. Not all graphs have solutions; these do not cross the x-axis but have their turning points above or below it.

Common mistakes

Pupils may write down only one solution, where there should be two.

Plenary

Write the equation $y = x^2 + 5x - 3$ on the board.
Ask pupils to work out the value of y when $x = 0.5$ and -5.5. They should get -0.25 in each case.
Repeat with $x = 0.6$ and -5.6. They should get 0.36 in each case.
Ask them if they have met this sort of problem before. They may recall trial and improvement.
The values that make $x^2 + 5x - 3 = 0$ lie between 0.5 and 0.6 and between -5.6 and -5.5.
Discuss that from a graph, the best you could do is 1 decimal place and tell them that examiners allow pupils to read values from their own graphs.

Overview

26.1 Pythagoras' theorem
26.2 Finding a shorter side
26.3 Solving problems using Pythagoras' theorem

This chapter provides coverage for all of the work required on Pythagoras' theorem at grade C. The first section covers finding the length of the hypotenuse, the second covers finding one of the shorter sides and the final section covers using Pythagoras' theorem in context to solve problems.

Context

Pythagoras is perhaps one of the best known names in mathematics and his theorem is probably the most famous piece of maths, although many just know the name, rather than the actual theorem.

This theorem has many real-life applications. It has long been a recognised method for constructing accurate right angles, for example in building walls which need to be at right-angles to each other, a 12 foot piece of rope, marked off in 3, 4 and 5 foot sections, is used to mark the necessary directions of the two walls. Also, the lengths of restraining wires or stays can be calculated when the height of a mast or pole and the horizontal limit for the stay are known.

A useful introduction to the theorem is suggested as a discovery activity. As an alternative, the approach can be varied by asking pupils to draw squares as accurately as possible on each of the three sides of their triangles (which could be different triangles, some right-angled and others clearly not right-angled), calculating the areas and identifying which triangles lead to the sum of the two smaller areas equalling the larger one.

Edexcel A references

Ma3 Shape, space and measures: Geometrical reasoning

26.1, 26.2, 26.3 3.2h "understand, recall and use Pythagoras' theorem"

Route mapping

Exercise	G	F	E	D	C
A					all
B					all
C					all

Answers to diagnostic Check-in test

1 1, 4, 9, 16, 25, 36, 49, 64, 81, 100

2 a 97 **b** 135 **c** 324

3 a 4.8 **b** 18.0 **c** 21.0

4 a 3000 **b** 10 **c** 0.2

5 a 5.48 **b** 16.88 **c** 0.76

6 a Correct drawing: north line 3 cm, west line 4 cm **b** 10 km

1 Write down the first 10 square numbers.

2 Work out the following.

   a $4^2 + 9^2$ **b** $12^2 - 3^2$ **c** 9×6^2

3 Round these numbers to one decimal place.

   a 4.793   **b** 18.0165   **c** 20.96

4 Round these numbers to one significant figure.

   a 2684   **b** 12.678   **c** 0.1552

5 Work out the following on your calculator, giving your answers correct to two decimal places.

   a $\sqrt{30}$ **b** $\sqrt{285}$ **c** $\sqrt{0.58}$

6 a Using a scale of 1 cm to represent 2 km, draw a scale diagram of the journey of a boat which sails 6 km north and then 8 km west.

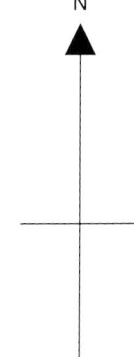

   b By measuring your scale drawing, find the distance in a direct line back from the boat's finishing point to its starting point.

Incorporating exercise:	26A	Key words
Homework:	26.1	hypotenuse
Examples:	26.1	Pythagoras' theorem

Learning objective(s)

● calculate the length of the hypotenuse in a right-angled triangle

Prior knowledge

Pupils must know how to find the square and square root of a number. It is also helpful if pupils have a familiarity with square numbers.

Pupils must also know how to round numbers correctly and should have an appreciation of what is a suitable level of accuracy given the context of the problem involved.

Starter

Display a target board of whole numbers and ask pupils to find any square numbers on it. Ask for any known square numbers which are missing from the board. Try to elicit the first 12 square numbers, with some other commonly known ones, for example 400, 625 and 1 000 000. Ask for a definition of square numbers. Ask for squares of some simple decimal numbers, such as 0.5 and 0.1.

Main teaching points

Pupils should understand that Pythagoras' theorem equates the area of a square drawn on the hypotenuse to the sum of the areas of the two squares drawn on the two shorter sides of a right-angled triangle. It should be made clear to them that the benefit of this theorem is that it allows a method to be developed for finding an unknown length. For the purposes of this section, all that is to be found is the length of the hypotenuse.

Pupils should understand that this theorem only holds for right-angled triangles and that it is incorrect to try to apply it in other situations. Therefore, unless they know positively that a triangle is right-angled, this theorem should not be applied.

It should be made clear to pupils how to identify correctly the hypotenuse of a right-angled triangle, that is, it will always be the side facing the right angle.

A formal method for finding the length of the hypotenuse should now be introduced, following the layout demonstrated in the Pupil Book, and pupils should be instructed to follow the method clearly and precisely.

It is likely that some discussion will be necessary concerning the 'suitable degree of accuracy'.

Common mistakes

Perhaps the most common mistake is forgetting to take the square root to find the final answer. This can generally be avoided if sufficient attention is paid to the layout of solutions. The other common mistake is that pupils often try to apply the theorem in unsuitable situations, such as when the triangle in question is not known to be a right-angled triangle.

Differentiation

Higher achieving pupils will finish this work quite quickly and, if time allows, they can be asked to try and find other examples of Pythagorean triples, such as those in questions 10, 11 and 12.

Plenary

Ask for a summary of key points, including how to identify the hypotenuse, an algebraic statement of the theorem and a brief summary of the method.
If some pupils have had time to look for triples, ask them to give feedback to the group.

Incorporating exercise:	26B		**Key words**
Homework:	26.2		Pythagoras'
Examples:	26.2		theorem

Learning objective(s)

◉ calculate the length of a shorter side in a right-angled triangle

Prior knowledge

As in Section 26.1, pupils must know how to find the square and square root of a number. It is also helpful if pupils have a familiarity with square numbers.

Pupils must know how to round numbers correctly and should have an appreciation of what is a suitable level of accuracy given the context of the problem involved.

For this section, pupils must first have studied Section 26.1 and be familiar with using Pythagoras' theorem to find the length of the hypotenuse of a right-angled triangle.

Starter

Give the pupils the number 100 as a target and, using a target board or a list of numbers, ask what needs to be added to each to give the target number. Repeat for other target numbers, such as 64, 81 and 25. Ask what the target numbers have in common, trying to elicit that they are all square numbers. Repeat the task using targets such as 7^2 or 12^2. Ask what type of calculation has to be done to find the required number, aiming to elicit subtraction.

Main teaching points

Pupils should understand that, from the original statement of Pythagoras' theorem, a method for calculating the length of one of the shorter sides can be obtained by rearranging the sum into a difference. It must be made very clear that, in order to avoid possible errors, the hypotenuse must be clearly identified each time. Pupils should be reminded that they must add to find the hypotenuse (longest side) and subtract to find a shorter one.

Pupils should be reminded that all uses of Pythagoras' theorem only apply to right-angled triangles and they may need to be reminded about suitable levels of accuracy.

Common mistakes

Pupils often confuse the two methods seen in Sections 26.1 and 26.2; this is usually due to a lack of care when identifying the hypotenuse. The common mistakes highlighted in Section 26.1 also apply in this section.

Differentiation

Questions 2 and 3 of Exercise 26B involve cases of both types of application encountered so far. Some require finding the hypotenuse and others require finding one of the shorter sides. Lower achieving pupils will need this pointing out and will need to be reminded of the difference between the two methods.

Plenary

Ask pupils for a summary of the two principal methods, and when to use them.
Ask pupils how to identify the hypotenuse of a right-angled triangle.

Incorporating exercise:	26C		**Key words**
Homework:	26.3		Pythagoras'
Examples:	26.3		theorem

Learning objective(s)

● solve problems using Pythagoras' theorem

Prior knowledge

Pupils must know how to use Pythagoras' theorem to find either the hypotenuse or a shorter side.

This exercise provides a wide variety of situations in which problems can be solved using Pythagoras' theorem. The extra skills required include:

● the use of compass directions
● the use of coordinates
● finding the area of a rectangle.

Starter

Ask pupils to suggest places around the classroom that have right angles.

Show pupils a coordinate grid with some points plotted. Ask pupils to show where right-angled triangles can be constructed between pairs of points. Ask how to find the lengths of the horizontal and vertical lines of the triangles.

Show pupils a variety of images which include right-angled triangles (for example, flag pole with supporting wires, sailing boat with sail or mast and stays, journey on map with a right-angled turn and gable-end of a house making an isosceles triangle that can be split by a vertical line into two right-angled triangles). Ask pupils to trace the outline of any right-angled triangles.

Main teaching points

Pupils need to be able to identify a right-angled triangle in a wide variety of situations and to understand how Pythagoras' theorem can be applied to solve problems in context.

Pupils should be encouraged to start by drawing a diagrammatic representation of the right-angled triangle involved in each situation, clearly labelling the right-angle, known lengths and the unknown side with an x.

Pupils will benefit from the demonstration of finding a right-angled triangle in as many different situations as possible. In particular, they will need a demonstration of the type of situation which involves a journey given by compass directions and of the type involving finding the distance between two coordinate points.

Pupils should be shown the converse of Pythagoras' theorem, that is, if $a^2 + b^2 = c^2$, then the triangle must have a right angle.

Common mistakes

Pupils often have difficulty identifying the appropriate information from the contextualised problem so they can apply Pythagoras' theorem. In particular, identifying the position of the right angle can cause difficulties.

Differentiation

All questions in this exercise are aimed at grade C and lower achieving pupils will have particular difficulty in seeing how to extract the relevant information from the context. These pupils will need more assistance in constructing the diagram which forms the beginning of the solution.

Plenary

Ask pupils to summarise the method for using Pythagoras' theorem. Ensure that all problems start with drawing a diagram and identifying whether the hypotenuse or a shorter side is to be found. Ask for a reminder of how the method changes depending on which side is to be found.
Use one of the activities suggested in the starter.

Homework answers

Chapter 1

Homework 1.1

Sample answers are supplied, pupils may find alternatives.

1

1	4	5
3	2	5
4	6	10

2

1	2	4	7
3	6	5	14
4	8	9	21

Homework 1.2

1 $1 \times 36 = 36$, $2 \times 18 = 36$, $3 \times 12 = 36$, $4 \times 9 = 36$, $6 \times 6 = 36$, $9 \times 4 = 36$, $12 \times 3 = 36$, $18 \times 2 = 36$, $36 \times 1 = 36$

2

$\times$	3	5	8	2
6	18	30	48	12
4	12	20	32	8
7	21	35	56	14
9	27	45	72	18

Homework 1.3

1 $12 \times 2 + 6 = 30$

2 $(6 + 7) \times 3 = 39$

3 $(9 + 7) \div 4 = 4$

4 $5 \times 9 - 1 = 44$

5 $4 \times 3 - (2 + 1) = 9$ or $4 \times 3 - 2 - 1 = 9$

6 $(12 + 3 \times 4) \div 2 = 12$ or $12 \div 3 + 4 \times 2 = 12$

7 $7 + 4 + 2 + 5 = 18$ or $7 \times 4 - 2 \times 5 = 18$

8 $5 + 3 \times (4 - 2) = 11$

Homework 1.4

1 99, 123, 250, 502, 624, 900

2 five hundred and ninety-three
two thousand and forty-six
nineteen thousand and seven
one million, two hundred and thirty thousand, nine hundred and eighty-seven

3 55, 56, 57, 65, 66, 67, 75, 76, 77

Homework 1.5

1 a *Sun*   **b** *Independent*

Name of newspaper	**c**	**d**
Express	961 000	960 700
Independent	263 000	262 600
Mail	2 407 000	2 407 100
Mirror	1 821 000	1 821 200
Sun	3 364 000	3 363 700
Telegraph	912 000	912 300
Times	648 000	648 100

2 a £5.00   **b** £12.00   **c** £10.00   **d** £6.00

3 Because a price of £19.99 sounds lower than a price of £20.

Homework 1.6

1 a 46   **b** 102   **c** 98   **d** 152

2 219   **3** 225   **4** 731   **5** 144

Homework 1.7

1 6 kilometres   **2** 182   **3** 216

4 65   **5** 120   **6** 28

Homework 2.1

Answers will vary with the pupils' diagrams.

Homework 2.2

1 Answers will vary.

2 a $\frac{4}{8}$ **b** $\frac{6}{8}$ **c** $\frac{7}{9}$ **d** $\frac{8}{11}$

3 a $\frac{6}{10}$ **b** $\frac{3}{9}$ **c** $\frac{8}{13}$ **d** $\frac{11}{16}$

4 a $\frac{4}{5}$ **b** $\frac{4}{9}$

Homework 2.3

1 Answers will vary.

2 a $\frac{1}{4}$ **b** $\frac{7}{12}$ **c** $\frac{7}{12}$

Homework 2.4

1 a $\frac{3}{4}$ **b** $\frac{2}{5}$ **c** $\frac{4}{5}$ **d** $\frac{1}{2}$ **e** $\frac{3}{4}$

2 $\frac{4}{8}, \frac{2}{3}, \frac{5}{6}, \frac{11}{12}$

Homework 2.5

1 a $\frac{9}{4} = \frac{2}{14}$, $\frac{17}{4} = 4\frac{1}{4}$, $5\frac{3}{4} = \frac{23}{4}$, $1\frac{5}{8} = \frac{13}{8}$, $\frac{10}{3} = 3\frac{1}{3}$, $2\frac{7}{8} = \frac{23}{8}$, $\frac{20}{3} = 6\frac{2}{3}$

   b $\frac{7}{4}$ is the odd one out.

2 a $\frac{36}{5}$ **b** $\frac{29}{10}$ **c** $\frac{56}{11}$ **d** $\frac{97}{10}$

3 a $2\frac{5}{6}$ **b** $2\frac{4}{5}$ **c** $5\frac{2}{7}$ **d** $9\frac{1}{2}$

Homework 2.6

1 a $\frac{3}{5}\left(\frac{9}{15}\right)$ **b** $\frac{7}{13}$ **c** $\frac{13}{18}$

2 a $\frac{9}{10}$ **b** $\frac{1}{2}\left(\frac{3}{6}\right)$ **c** $1\frac{1}{2}\left(\frac{9}{6}, 1\frac{3}{6}\right)$ **d** $\frac{3}{10}$

3 a $5\frac{7}{15}$ **b** $6\frac{1}{4}$ **c** $1\frac{1}{12}$

4 a $1\frac{3}{10}$ **b** $3\frac{5}{8}$ **c** $4\frac{1}{10}$

Homework 2.7

1 $\frac{1}{5}$ **2** $\frac{5}{12}$ **3** $\frac{1}{2}$

Homework 2.8

1 £10   **2** 180 cm   **3 a** £32   **b** £128   **c** $\frac{4}{5}$ **4** £120

Homework 2.9

1 a $\dfrac{2}{25}$ **b** $\dfrac{7}{24}$ **c** $\dfrac{2}{36} = \dfrac{1}{18}$ **d** $\dfrac{4}{42} = \dfrac{2}{21}$ **e** $\dfrac{1}{32}$

2 $\dfrac{1}{6}$

Homework 2.10

1 $\dfrac{3}{10}$ **2** $\dfrac{360}{2000} = \dfrac{9}{50}$ **3** $\dfrac{45}{180} = \dfrac{1}{4}$ **4** $1\dfrac{200}{1000} = 1\dfrac{1}{5}$

Homework 2.11

1 a 0.625 **b** 1.6 **c** $0.\dot{4}$ **d** $0.\dot{2}\dot{7}$

2 a $\dfrac{4}{5}$ **b** $\dfrac{13}{20}$ **c** $\dfrac{1}{3}$ **d** $\dfrac{2}{3}$

3 a $\dfrac{1}{7}$ **b** 50 **c** $\dfrac{5}{4}$ **d** $\dfrac{5}{8}$

Chapter 3

Homework 3.1

1 670 m   **2** Camp 2   **3** 4030 m   **4** 130 m

Homework 3.2

1

Team	Goal difference
a	+21
b	−22
c	−8
d	+22
e	0
f	−9
g	−6
h	+10
i	+18
j	−5

2 Order: d, a, i, h, e, j, g, c, f, b

Homework 3.3

1 Answers will vary.

2 a $<$ **b** $>$ **c** $<$ **d** $<$

3 $-20, -18, -16, -14, -12, -10, -8, -6, -4, -2, 0$

Homework 3.4

1 a -5 **b** -9 **c** -27 **d** -6 **e** -21 **f** -6

2 9

3 -3

4 $-12, -9, -6, -3, -2, 0, 7, 13, 15$

5 a -2 **b** 8   **c** -10

Homework 4.1

Answers will vary depending on the times tables chosen.

Homework 4.2

1 a 90   **b** 71   **c** 65

2 a 6   **b** 10   **c** 14   **d** 36

3 1, 2, 3, 4, 6, 8, 12, 16, 24, 32, 48, 96

You may want to tell lower achieving pupils that 96 has 12 factors.

Homework 4.3

1 3×5 **2** $2 \times 2 \times 2 \times 3$ **3** $2 \times 2 \times 2 \times 5$ **4** $2 \times 2 \times 7$

5 $2 \times 2 \times 3 \times 5$ **6** $2 \times 2 \times 5 \times 5$

Homework 4.4

1 9 and 16   **2** 16 and 49 *or* 1 and 64   **3** 64   **4** 40

Homework 4.5

1 13   **2** 4   **3** 12   **4** 4

5 a 13   **b** 20   **c** 25   **d** 256   **e** 361

Homework 4.6

The circle answer is 100 393, with a square root of approximately 317 ($300^2 = 90\,000$).

Homework 4.7

1 a 42   **b** 4200   **c** 4.2

2 a 986   **b** 1276   **c** 8143.6   **d** 5.93   **e** 0.1293

f 0.000 005

3 a 60 000   **b** 28 000   **c** 30 000   **d** 200   **e** 20

Homework 4.8

1 a 2×3^2 **b** $2^4 \times 3$ **c** $2^4 \times 3 \times 5^2$ **d** $2^3 \times 3$ **e** $2^2 \times 5^3$

2 216   **3** 22   **4** HCF = 6, LCM = 180

Homework 4.9

1 a 6^5 **b** 6^{13} **c** 6^{12} **d** 6^{10} **e** 6^{12}

f 6^{10} **g** 6^{15}

2 a 9^9 **b** 9^4 **c** 9^2 **d** 9^6 **e** 9^6

f 9^2 **g** 9

3 a x^8 **b** x^5 **c** x^9 **d** x^{10} **e** x^{10}

f x^2 **g** x^2 **h** x^6 **i** x **j** x^3

k x^5 **l** x^2

Homework 5.1

1 a 8 cm   **b** 14 cm   **c** 14 m   **d** 18 cm   **e** 34 cm

2 Square of length 8 cm   **3** Rectangles of dimensions 6×1, 5×2 and 4×3

Homework 5.2

Allow 1–2 cm^2 either side of the given answer. The main point is that pupils should show their working out by stating the number of complete squares in the shape being considered.

1 3 complete + 12 part, ≈ 9 cm^2 **2** 1 complete + 7 part, ≈ 5 cm^2 **3** 12 part, ≈ 7 cm^2
4 2 complete + 10 part, ≈ 7 cm^2 **5** 4 complete + 12 part, ≈ 8 cm^2

Homework 5.3

1 a 30 cm^2 **b** 40 m^2 **c** 6 cm^2 **d** 28.7 cm^2
2 a 42 cm   **b** 108 cm^2 **3** 5 cm   **4** 9 cm   **5** 5000 m^2
6 a 30 000 cm^2 **b** 150 000 cm^2 **c** 400 cm^2
7 a 500 mm^2 **b** 1000 mm^2 **c** 2 mm^2

Homework 5.4

1 a 12 cm^2 **b** 40 cm^2 **c** 26 cm^2 **d** 15 cm^2
2 a

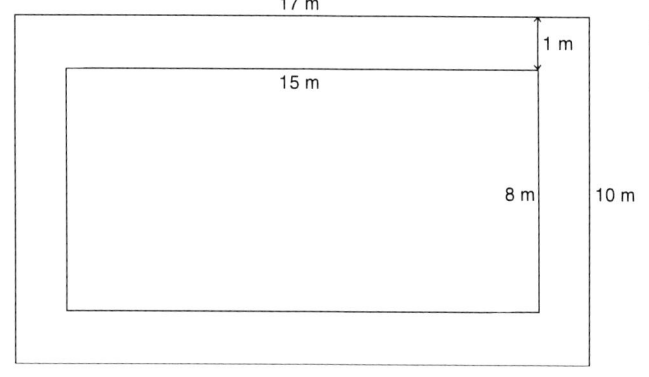

b 120 m^2

c 50 m^2

Homework 5.5

1 a 18 cm^2 **b** 45 cm^2 **c** 22.5 cm^2 **d** 2 cm^2
2 45 cm^2 **3** 104 cm^2 **4** 8 cm   **5** 10 cm

Homework 5.6

1 a 21 cm^2 **b** 17.1 cm^2 **c** 36 cm^2 **d** 15 cm^2

2 8 cm   **3** 4 cm   **4** 6 cm

5 The square, since the parallelogram has the smaller perpendicular height and $A = bh$ is used in both cases.

Homework 5.7

1 a 45 cm^2 **b** 32.5 cm^2 **c** 22.5 cm^2 **d** 354 m^2 **e** 66 cm^2

2 a 16 cm^2 **b** 27 m^2 **3** 9.3 cm

Homework 6.1

1 a Freq. column reads 4, 3, 4, 5, 8, 4, 2   **b** 7   **c** 30   **d** 180

2 a Freq. column reads 3, 4, 7, 4, 2, 4   **b** 24

3 a Sampling   **b** Accept experiment or observation   **c** Experiment

Homework 6.2

1 Numbers of chosen symbol: 6, $4\frac{1}{2}$, 3, 4, $5\frac{1}{2}$

2 a 100 satisfied customers   **b** 55 families   **c** 44 weddings

3 Answer depends on pupil choice, but a symbol representing six races would be ideal, with numbers of the symbol then being 5, 3, 4, 2.

Homework 6.3

1 a 51   **b** TV   **c** 22

2 a

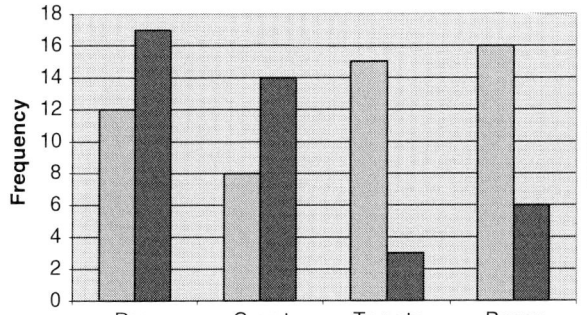

b Rose and carrot

Homework 6.4

1 a Day 7, 65 m   **b** Day 35, 26 m   **c** About 59 m

2 a

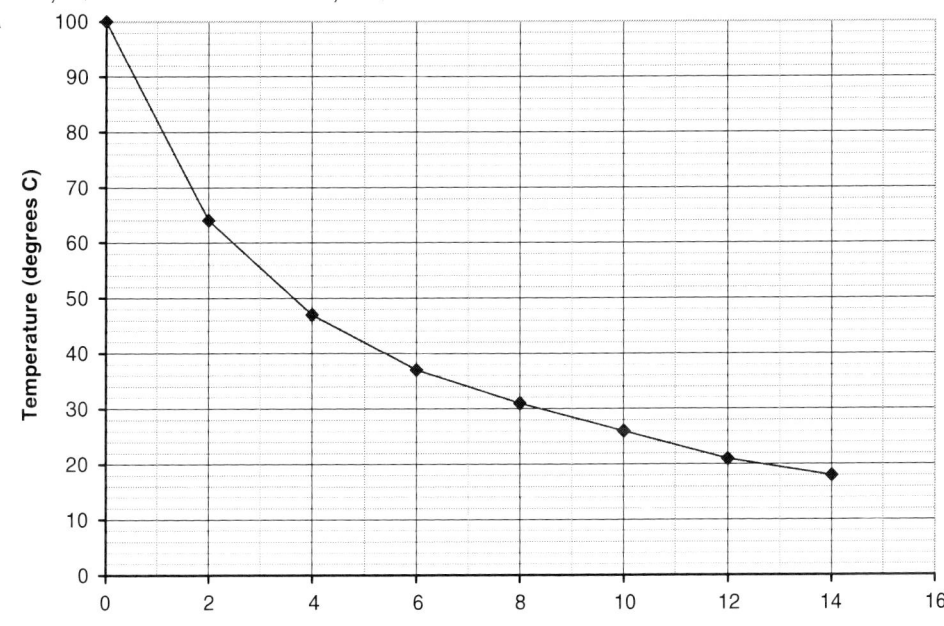

b 42 degrees C   **c** About 16 degrees C

Homework 6.5

1 a 32, 32, 37, 37, 38, 38, 38, 41, 41, 44, 44, 44, 46, 46, 47, 47, 48, 50, 53, 53

b Key   3 | 2 represents £32

3	2	2	7	7	8	8	8		
4	1	1	4	4	4	6	6	7	7	8
5	0	3	3						

c £40–£49 range, because the 4-stem has the most leaves.

2 a 18 months   **b** £48   **c** £31

Chapter 7

Homework 7.1

1 a $5y$ **b** zy
2 Bob has $s + 6$, Ali has $s - 8$, Sue has $2s$, Fran has $2s + 3$.
3 $100x$

Homework 7.2

7.2a Multiplying expressions

1 $6d$ **2** $48z$ **3** t^3
4 $6x^5$ **5** $8rs^2$ **6** $27b^2c^3$

7.2b Collecting like terms

1 $5x$ **2** $4xy + 2x$ **3** $14t^2$
4 $5ab - a$ **5** $10z + 4y^3 - 2y^2$ **6** $15ab - 7b + 6a$

Homework 7.3

7.3a Expanding brackets

1 $8a + 32$ **2** $21 - 7x$ **3** $9a + 9b$ **4** $8a - 4c$
5 $f^2 + 3f$ **6** $3d^3 - 7d^2$ **7** $4ay + y^2$ **8** $2w^2 - 8sw$

7.3b Expand and simplify

1 $11a + 44$ **2** $15 - 9x$ **3** $21a + 15b$ **4** $48a - 28c$
5 $3f^2 + 5f$ **6** $8d^2 - 10d$ **7** $-2ay - 3y^2$ **8** $-w^2 - 2sw$

Homework 7.4

1 $2(4r + t)$ **2** $6(2s + t)$ **3** $4a(1 - 3b)$ **4** $4b(4a + 3)$
5 $ac(7d - 5b)$ **6** $3t(t + 2)$ **7** $12b(ab + 2)$ **8** $9x(x^2 - 3y)$

Homework 7.5

1 $x^2 + 5x + 6$ **2** $x^2 + 11x + 30$ **3** $x^2 + 11x + 30$ **4** $14 + 9x + x^2$
5 $y^2 + 4y - 12$ **6** $s^2 - 8s + 15$ **7** $c^2 - 4c + 4$ **8** $x^2 - 4x + 4$

Homework 7.6

1 10	**2** 20	**3** 125	**4** 100
5 15	**6** 12	**7** 25	**8** 12
9 7	**10** 30	**11** 50	

Note: $2a + 2$ is the same as $2(a + 1)$.

Chapter 8

Homework 8.1

1 13 167	**2** 29 225	**3** 49 608	**4** 28 012

Homework 8.2

1 159	**2** 528	**3** 953

Homework 8.3

£5225

Homework 8.4

8.4a Decimal places

	Nearest whole number	1 dp	2 dp	3 dp
7.1568	7	7.2	7.16	7.157
12.8247	13	12.8	12.82	12.825
16.034 59	16	16.0	16.03	16.035
213.3974	213	213.4	213.40	213.397
0.9827	1	1.0	0.98	0.983
0.003 654	0	0.0	0.00	0.004

8.4b Adding and subtracting with decimals

1 27.9	**2** 67.54	**3** 83.2	**4** 94.34	**5** 21.65	**6** 28.2

8.4c Multiplying and dividing decimals by single-digit numbers

1 21.6	**2** 34.5	**3** 18.4	**4** 3.19	**5** 0.97	**6** 2.86

8.4d Long multiplication with decimals

1 230.4	**2** 878.8	**3** 532.5	**4** 12.35	**5** 315.25	**6** 446.16

8.4e Multiplying two decimal numbers together

1 4.14	**2** 15.48	**3** 87.12	**4** 2.589	**5** 41.08	**6** 282.88

Homework 8.5

8.5a Interchanging decimals and fractions

1 a $\dfrac{9}{10}$ **b** $\dfrac{9}{25}$ **c** $\dfrac{1}{8}$ **d** $1\dfrac{3}{4}$ **e** $\dfrac{41}{50}$

2 a 0.875   **b** 0.4   **c** $0.\dot{3}$ **d** 0.15

3 $0.065, \ \dfrac{1}{2}, \ \dfrac{3}{5}, \ 0.65, \ \dfrac{3}{4}$

8.5b Addition and subtraction of fractions

1 $\dfrac{3}{10}$ **2** £72   **3** 490   **4** $\dfrac{2}{3}$ of 63

8.5c Multiplication of fractions

$\times$	$\dfrac{1}{2}$	$\dfrac{5}{6}$	$1\dfrac{1}{4}$	$2\dfrac{2}{5}$
$\dfrac{1}{2}$	$\dfrac{1}{4}$	$\dfrac{5}{12}$	$\dfrac{5}{8}$	$1\dfrac{1}{5}$
$5\dfrac{1}{8}$	$2\dfrac{9}{16}$	$4\dfrac{13}{48}$	$6\dfrac{13}{32}$	$12\dfrac{3}{10}$
$3\dfrac{1}{9}$	$3\dfrac{1}{3}$	$2\dfrac{16}{27}$	$3\dfrac{8}{9}$	$7\dfrac{7}{15}$

8.5d Dividing fractions

1 $3\dfrac{1}{2}$ **2** $2\dfrac{5}{8}$ **3** $3\dfrac{1}{3}$ **4** $1\dfrac{13}{35}$ **5** $2\dfrac{31}{42}$

Homework 8.6

1 a -35 **b** -6 **c** -60 **d** 42   **e** 49   **f** -64

2 and **3** Answers will vary.

Homework 8.7

8.7a Rounding to significant figures

Number	780	5213	78	83	6.5	0.72
Number of significant figures	2	4	2	2	2	2

8.7b Approximations of calculations

The actual answers are in brackets.

1 3000 (3805.2)   **2** 313 (275.12)   **3** 200 (225.87)

4 14 (15.37)   **5** £2500 (£2681.50)

8.7c Sensible rounding

a nearest million people   **b** nearest thousand km^2 **c** nearest thousand

d nearest centimetre   **e** nearest minute   **f** nearest million miles

Chapter 9

Homework 9.1

9.1a Ratio

1 **a** 9 : 19 **b** 8 : 1
  c 7 to 8 **d** 4 to 5
  e 1 : 4 **f** 1 : 5
  g 6 to 1

2 Steve gets $\frac{5}{9}$ and Sally gets $\frac{4}{9}$.

3 Labour $\frac{7}{12}$, Conservative $\frac{1}{6}$, Liberal Democrat $\frac{1}{4}$

9.1b Dividing amounts according to ratios

1 £20, £30
2 405 g, 270 g

3 £750
4 1370 (votes)

5 12 (girls)
6 60°, 40°, 80°

7 £12 500, £37 500, £50 000, £25 000
8 159 g, 141 g

9.1c Calculating according to a ratio when only part of the information is known

1 20 (bungalows)
2 360 (girls)

3 32 litres
4 10 cm

5 18 buckets
6 2 kg

7 15 cm
8 8 (pencils)

Homework 9.2

1 55 mph
2 14 miles
3 55.6 mph
4 6 hours 40 minutes
5 11 km/h
6 **a** 165 km/h
b 50 km
c 150 km/h

Homework 9.3

1 6720 cans
2 £18.20
3 £220
4 98 (tiles)
5 £8.33
6 £135
7 £6.72
8 75 (eggs)

Homework 9.4

1 The cheapest way to buy is the two 750 g Sellots at Singhs'.
2 Khan's own-brand 500 g on offer.
3 250 g – 66p, 500 g – 81p, 750 g – 88p – 1 kg – 83p

Homework 10.1

1 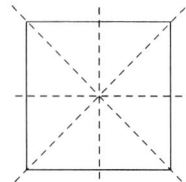   **2** 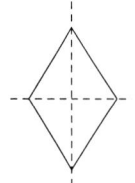   **3** no lines

4 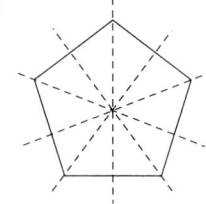   **5** 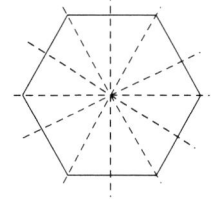   **6** 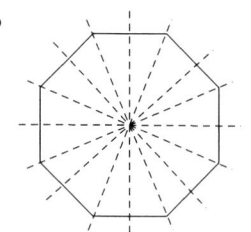   **7**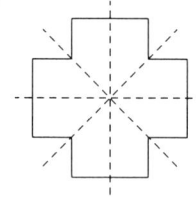

8 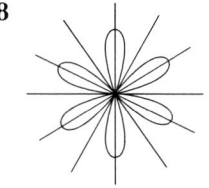   **9** 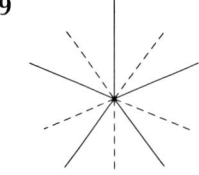   **10** 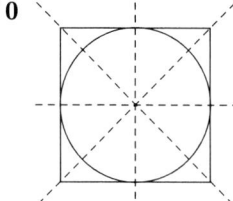   **11**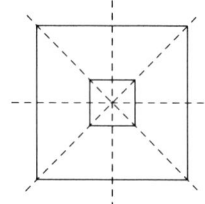

12 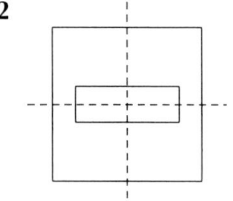   **13** 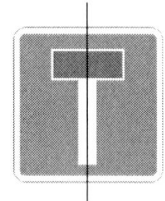   **14** no lines   **15** no lines

Homework 10.2

1 a 4   **b** 4   **c** 4   **d** 4   **e** 4   **f** 4   **g** 1   **h** 4   **i** 2   **j** 4   **k** 8   **l** 1
2 1, 1, 1, 1, 1, 2, 2, 2, 2, 1, 1, 1, 2, 2, ∞, 1, 1, 1, 1, 1, 2, 2, 1, 1

Homework 10.3

1 3   **2** 7   **3** 7   **4** 1   **5** 2   **6** 1   **7** 3
8 9   **9** 2   **10** 3   **11** ∞   **12** 2   **13** 1   **14** 0

Homework 11.1

1 a 72 **b** 4.3 and 4.9 **c** Gold **d** No mode
2 a Mode must be a data value, Daniel has used the frequencies. **b** Green
3 Any list of 6 numbers in which a 3 appears more than any other number.
4 Any list of 6 numbers in which all the numbers appear with the same frequency.
5 12 to 14

Homework 11.2

1 a 9 **b** 25 **c** 3.5
2 a 6, 7, 7, 8, 10, 12, 13, median 8 **b** 2.8, 4.0, 4.1, 4.6, 5.3, median 4.1
  c 0.28, 0.3, 0.4, 0.42, 0.5, 0.66, median 0.41
3 a 30 **b** 7
4 a 10 **b** 20 **c** 28

Homework 11.3

1 a 5 **b** 18 **c** 9
2 a 15.6 **b** 0.7 **c** 4.4
3 a 121.1 s **b** Aled, Jack, Daisy
4 a 15.6 **b** 205.6 **c** 56

Homework 11.4

1 a 10 **b** 62 **c** 8.7 **d** 8
2 a Josh: mean 234.2, range 185; Dale: mean 265.2, range 27
  b For example: Dale because his mean distance is greater and his range is lower, so he is more consistent. Josh
    hit the ball further on one occasion, but this seems to be an extreme value.
3 a Blockton: mean £79.33, range £62; Dimsdale: mean £79.50, range £10
  b For example: Dimsdale because the mean amount of money taken each week is higher and the range is low so
    the amounts are more consistent.
Note: Answers to **2b** and **3b** are opinions, which may differ depending on points of view.

Homework 11.5

1 a Data is not numbers. **b** Data has extreme values. **c** Does not use all the values.
2 a Mode 31, median 27.5, mean 23.7 **b** Mode, as it is highest. **c** Mean, as it is lowest.
  d Figures have been going up. **e** First month's figures were extreme.

Homework 11.6

1 a i 1 **ii** 1 **iii** 1
  b i 12 **ii** 12 **iii** 11.9
  c i 1.2 **ii** 1.15 **iii** 1.1
2 No; mode and mean are outside the possible range of averages; median should be 42.5.

Homework 11.7

1 a i $140 \leq w < 160$ **ii** 140.3 **b i** 21 to 30 **ii** 19.4
2 Because they use the midpoints of each group instead of the exact data.

Homework 11.8

1 a Check pupils' frequency polygons. **b** 2.7 pipes
2 a Check pupils' frequency polygons. **b** 37.3 minutes

Homework 12.1

Fraction	Decimal	Percentage
$\frac{2}{5}$	0.4	40%
$\frac{3}{10}$	0.3	30%
$\frac{3}{100}$	0.03	3%
$\frac{4}{5}$	0.8	80%
$\frac{3}{8}$	0.375	37.5%
$\frac{3}{50}$	0.06	6%
$\frac{7}{10}$	0.7	70%
$\frac{3}{5}$	0.6	60%
$\frac{1}{20}$	0.05	5%
$\frac{21}{100}$	0.21	21%
$\frac{7}{100}$	0.07	7%
$\frac{21}{100}$	0.01	1%
$\frac{2}{3}$	$0.\dot{6}$	$66.\dot{6}$%
$\frac{9}{10}$	0.9	90%
$\frac{1}{5}$	0.2	20%
$\frac{7}{8}$	0.875	87.5%
1	1	100%
$\frac{5}{8}$	0.625	62.5%

Homework 12.2

1 12	**2** 6	**3** 14	**4** 90	**5** 20
6 48	**7** 8.5	**8** 2	**9** 6	**10** 6
11 72	**12** 66	**13** 280	**14** 87.6	**15** 18

Homework 12.3

1 a £5	**b** £9.36	**c** £24	**d** £4.60
2 £3080	**3** 330 ml	**4** £17.25	**5** £30 000
6 £30	**7** £2	**8** £7.80	

Homework 12.4

1 a 30%	**b** 75%	**c** 10%	**d** 25%
2 53.3%	**3** 45.2%	**4** 93.$\dot{3}$%	**5** 66.7%

Chapter 13

Homework 13.1

13.1a Inverse operations and inverse flow diagrams

1 $y = 4$	**2** $z = 5$	**3** $c = 7$	**4** $s = 30$
5 $x = 2$	**6** $d = 5$	**7** $y = 2$	**8** $c = 36$

13.1b Doing the same to both sides and dealing with negative numbers

1 $u = 7$	**2** $d = 10$	**3** $e = 9$	**4** $p = 30$
5 $h = 9$	**6** $u = 2.5$	**7** $y = 6$	**8** $x = -4$

13.1c Rearrangement

1 $u = 9$	**2** $d = 7$	**3** $e = 9$	**4** $p = 56$
5 $h = 11.5$	**6** $u = 12$	**7** $y = 64$	**8** $s = 45$

Homework 13.2

1 $x = 9$	**2** $x = 12$	**3** $x = 15$	**4** $x = 2.2$
5 $x = -1$	**6** $t = -3$	**7** $x = -1.5$	**8** $y = -3.5$

Homework 13.3

1 $x = 4$	**2** $x = 2$	**3** $x = 5$	**4** $x = 7$
5 $x = 3$	**6** $x = 10$	**7** $x = 6$	**8** $x = 4$

Homework 13.4

Letters may be different from those given in the answer.

1 $P = rh + b$; £130   **2** $P = rh + b$; £137.50   **3** $C = 3d$; 180 cm
4 $C = pn$; £4.25
5 $22h + 50 = 204$; 7 hours
6 $4m + 14 = 82$; Fred has £17, Bill has £34, Jack has £31.

Homework 13.5

1 $x = 5.1$	**2** $x = 2.5$	**3** $x = 3.4$	**4** $l = 4.6$ m

Homework 13.6

1 $x = \dfrac{y-c}{m}$ **2** $x = \dfrac{c-r}{a}$ **3** $x = \dfrac{2g+h}{3}$ **4** $x = \dfrac{k-u}{6}$

5 $x = \sqrt{\dfrac{y}{2}}$ **6** $x = \dfrac{f-d}{3}$

Homework 13.7

1 $x > 3$ **2** $x \le 4$ **3** $x < 6$
4 $x \ge -2$ **5** $x \ge -3$ **6** $-3 \le x < 2$

Chapter 14

Homework 14.1

1 a i £50 **ii** £70 **iii** £60 **b** 6 hours **c** Check pupils' explanations.
2 a 18 litres **b** 25 litres **c** 6 gallons **d** 4.4 gallons **e** 90 litres **f** Check pupils' explanations.

Homework 14.2

1 a 1.5 hours **b** 20 mph **c** 100 miles **d** 5 hours **e** 20 mph
2 a 1 hour **b** 12 kph **c** 20 km **d** 4 hours **e** 5 kph

Homework 14.3

1 A straight line passing through (0, 1), with a gradient of 4.
2 A straight line passing through (0, –6), with a gradient of 1.
3 A straight line passing through (0, 3), with a gradient of 0.5.

Homework 14.4

1 A straight line graph that passes through the point (0, –3) and has a gradient of 2.
2 A straight line graph that passes through the point (0, 1) and has a gradient of 0.5.
3 A straight line graph that passes through the point (0, –1) and has a gradient of 2 and a straight line graph that passes through the point (0, 1) and has a gradient of 1.

Chapter 15

Homework 15.1

Allow 1 degree either side of the correct answer.

1 46° **2** 134° **3** 227° **4** 20°
5, 6 Check pupils' answers.

Homework 15.2

All answers are in degrees.

1 a 142 **b** 105 **c** 85 **d** 40
  e 58 **2** 180 **3** 120 **4** 10

Homework 15.3

All answers are in degrees.

1 69 **2** 79 **3** 125 **4** 60
5 30 **6** 46 **7** 60 **8** 132

Homework 15.4

All answers in degrees unless otherwise stated.

1 a 85   **b** 120   **c** 100   **d** 36
   e 105   **f** 305   **2 a** 720   **b** 135   **3** 15 sides

Homework 15.5

Answers are in degrees unless otherwise stated.

1 a 18   **b** 162
2 177
3 24 sides
4 36 sides
5 No; each exterior angle is 70°, so the number of sides would be $\frac{360}{70} = 5.14$, which is not a whole number.

Homework 15.6

Answers are given in degrees.

1 a $x = 110$; allied angles   **b** $x = 35$; alternate angles
   c $a = 40°$, $b = 140°$; angle opposite to angle a corresponds to 40, so a is 40 (vertically opposite); b and a lie on a straight line, so b is 140 (angles on a straight line add to 180).

2 a $a = 30$, $b = 70$, $c = 80$ **b** $x = 70$ **c** $a = 40$, $b = 60$, $c = 40$
3
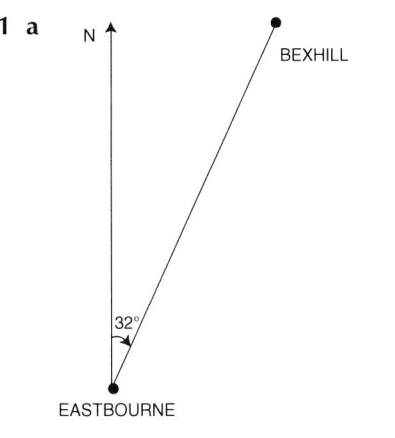

Homework 15.7

All answers are given in degrees.

1 $a = 65$, $b = 115$, $c = 65$ **2** $a = 100$, $b = 80$, $c = 100$ **3** $a = 55$, $b = 125$, $c = 55$
4 $a = 100$, $b = 30$ **5** $a = 40$, $b = 40$, $c = 20$ **6** $a = 68$, $b = 60$

Homework 15.8

1 a   **b**

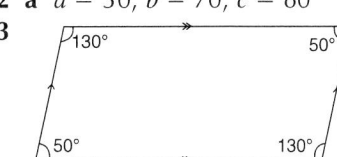

2 a 047°   **b** 090°   **c** 338°
3 195°
4 040°

Homework 16.1

1 Check accuracy of pupils' drawings.

2 Check accuracy of pupils' drawings.

3 Segment, radius, circumference, chord, semicircle, sector, arc, tangent

4 a 4   **b** 3   **c** 2   **d** 1

Homework 16.2

1 a 62.83 m   **b** 8.17 mm   **c** 125.66 m
2 31.4 cm
3 a 1885 mm   **b** 1885 m   **c** 531 revolutions
4 32 cm
5 a 17.9 cm   **b** 25.7 cm

Homework 16.3

1 a 314.16 m^2 **b** 39.27 cm^2 **c** 58.90 cm^2
2 78.5 cm^2
3 a 1134 mm^2 **b** 48
4 0.080 m^2 or 795.775 cm^2

Homework 16.4

1 $C = 20\pi$ m   **2** $A = 16\pi$ mm^2 **3** $C = 40\pi$ m   **4** $A = 9\pi$ cm^2

5 $d = \dfrac{50}{\pi}$ cm   **6** $r = \sqrt{\left(\dfrac{25}{\pi}\right)} = \dfrac{5}{\sqrt{\pi}}$ cm   **7** $A = 400 + 50\pi$ m^2

Homework 17.1

1 a 2 kg   **b** 6 kg
2 a 2 l   **b** 54 l
3 a 5 g   **b** 15 g
4 a 5 g   **b** 65 g
5 a 2.5 g   **b** 12.5 g
6 a $\dfrac{1}{4}$ kg   **b** $\dfrac{1}{4}$ kg
7 a 2 mph   **b** 66 mph
8 a 0.2 °C   **b** 36.9 °C
9 a 5 °C   **b** −6 or −7 °C

Homework 17.2

1 Car 3.4 m, bus 6.8 m   **2** 14.4, so allow 14 m, 14.4 m or $14\frac{1}{2}$ m   **3** 50 g

4 Bus 6 m, bike $1\frac{1}{2}$ m   **5** 0.6 kg   **6** Car 4 m, bike 2 m   **7** 1 kg (Read the question!)

Homework 17.3

1 100 cm (1 m), 5 cm   **2** 150 m   **3** 6 km   **4** 200 cm (2 m)

5 2000 cm (20 m)   **6** 50 000 cm (500 m or 0.5 km)   **7** 200 km

8 240 cm (2.4 m)   **9** 120 km   **10** 46 cm

11 3 000 000 cm = 30 000 m = 30 km   **12** 14 cm (0.5 × 28 cm)

Always encourage the pupils to use a sensible unit – 50 km is a more sensible answer than 5 000 000 cm. They must remember to put an '=' as they change units, as in question 11 (GCSE rules).

Homework 17.4

1 One of the nets of a cube shown in the Starter, all sides 2 cm.

2 Triangular-based pyramid or tetrahedron

3 Triangular prism or right-angled triangular prism

4

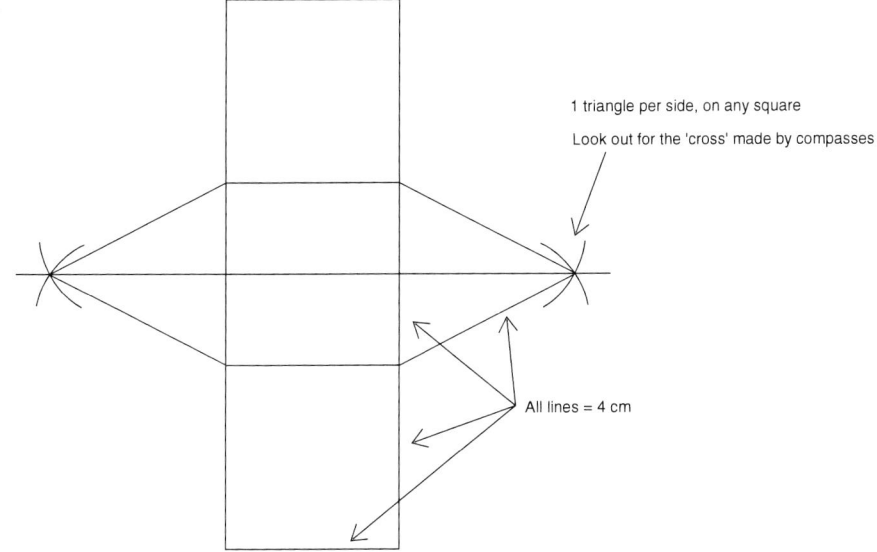

1 triangle per side, on any square

Look out for the 'cross' made by compasses

All lines = 4 cm

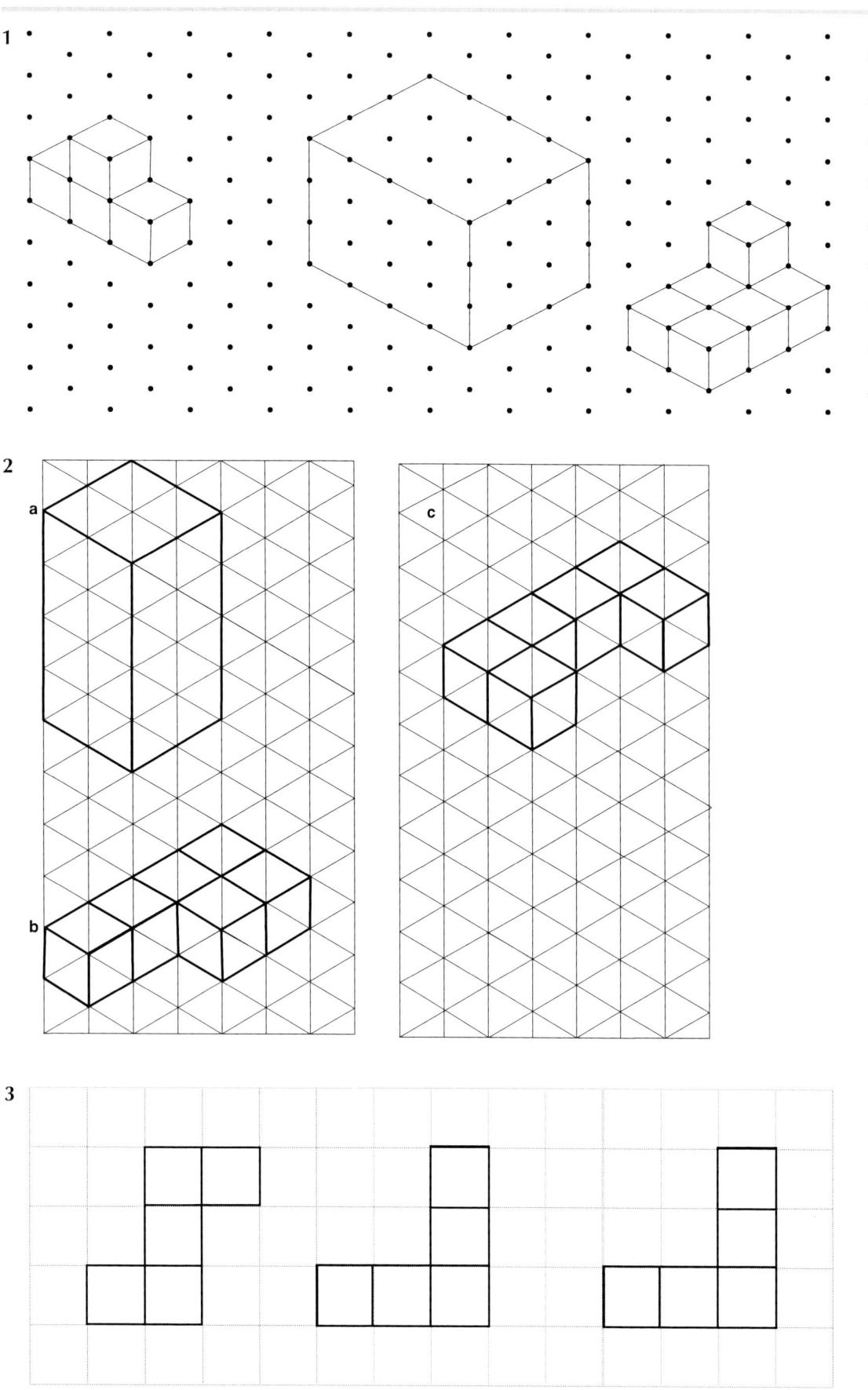

Plan   Front   Side

Chapter 18

Homework 18.1

1 Answers may differ, but suggestions are: **a** even chance **b** likely **c** unlikely **d** unlikely **e** likely
2 Pupils' own answers.
3 Order (from left to right): B D C A E

Homework 18.2

1 a $\dfrac{7}{15}$ **b** $\dfrac{1}{3}$ **c** $\dfrac{1}{5}$

2 a $\dfrac{1}{52}$ **b** $\dfrac{1}{2}$ **c** $\dfrac{3}{13}$ **d** $\dfrac{3}{52}$

3 a $\dfrac{2}{5}$ **b** $\dfrac{4}{5}$ **c** $\dfrac{7}{10}$

4 a ET, EA, EM, TA, TM, AM   **b** $\dfrac{2}{3}$

Homework 18.3

1 Events are not exhaustive.

2 Events are not mutually exclusive.

3 a $\dfrac{1}{26}$ **b** $\dfrac{25}{26}$ **c** $\dfrac{1}{13}$ **d** $\dfrac{12}{13}$

4 a $\dfrac{2}{7}$ **b** $\dfrac{5}{7}$ **c** $\dfrac{4}{7}$ **d** $\dfrac{3}{7}$

    e $\dfrac{4}{7}$ **f** $\dfrac{3}{7}$ **g** $\dfrac{4}{7}$

Homework 18.4

1 a $\dfrac{1}{3}$ **b** $\dfrac{4}{15}$ **c** $\dfrac{3}{5}$

2 a $\dfrac{3}{10}$ **b** $\dfrac{3}{10}$ **c** $\dfrac{2}{5}$

3 a $\dfrac{1}{12}$ **b** $\dfrac{1}{8}$ **c** $\dfrac{19}{24}$

4 Events are not mutually exclusive and therefore probabilities cannot be added.

5 a 35%   **b** 40%   **c** 53%

Homework 18.5

1 a White $\dfrac{7}{20}$, red $\dfrac{17}{120}$, yellow $\dfrac{3}{10}$, blue $\dfrac{5}{24}$ **b** White 7, red 3, yellow 6, blue 4
2 a 0.10, 0.09, 0.11, 0.10, 0.09, 0.11, 0.11, 0.10, 0.09, 0.09 (all to 2 d.p.)
   b Results are fairly close, but you might expect a little closer after 1500 trials; may require more evidence.
3 a $\dfrac{13}{20}$, $\dfrac{19}{25}$, $\dfrac{31}{50}$, $\dfrac{33}{50}$, $\dfrac{297}{500}$ or 0.594   **b** 11 or 12 times

Homework 18.6

1 a

6	6	6	6	6	6	12
5	5	5	5	5	10	6
4	4	4	4	8	5	6
3	3	3	6	4	5	6
2	2	4	3	4	5	6
1	2	2	3	4	5	6
	1	2	3	4	5	6

Red dice (left), White dice (bottom)

b $\dfrac{14}{36}$ or $\dfrac{7}{18}$ **c** $\dfrac{3}{36}$ or $\dfrac{1}{12}$ **d** $\dfrac{14}{36}$ or $\dfrac{7}{18}$

2 a

Fruit, F	L, F	C, F	S, F	P, F
Sponge, S	L, S	C, S	S, S	P, S
Trifle, T	L, T	C, T	S, T	P, T
	Lasagne, L	**Chicken pie, C**	**Sandwich, S**	**Roast pork, P**

Dessert (left), Main meal (bottom)

b $\dfrac{3}{12}$ or $\dfrac{1}{4}$ **c** $\dfrac{4}{12}$ or $\dfrac{1}{3}$ **d** $\dfrac{5}{12}$

Homework 18.7

1 a $\dfrac{2}{5}$ **b** 120   **c** 240

2 a i $\dfrac{3}{5}$ **ii** $\dfrac{1}{100}$ **iii** $\dfrac{2}{5}$ **b** 1/4   **c** 100   **d** £50

Homework 18.8

1 a 75   **b** 44%   **c** 140

2 a 28%   **b** 14%   **c** $\dfrac{27}{100}$ **d** $\dfrac{69}{100}$ **e** 2400

Homework 19.1

1

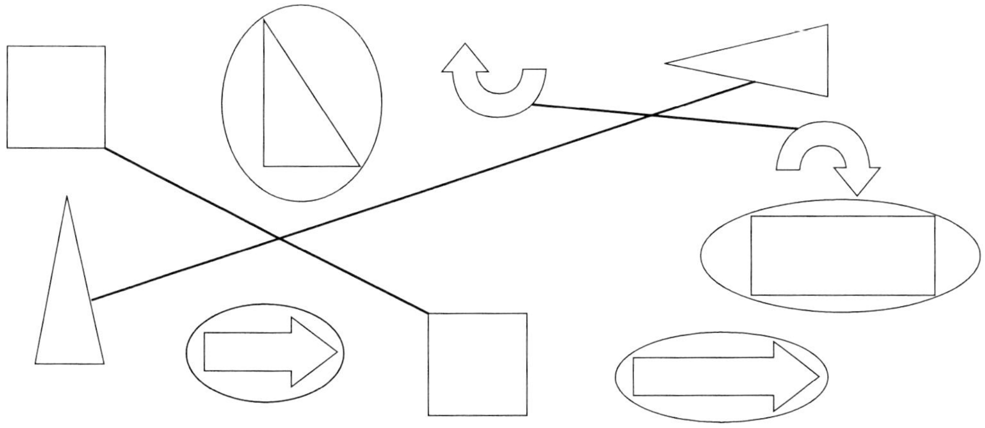

2 a  **b** 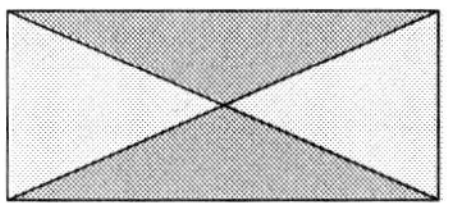 **c**

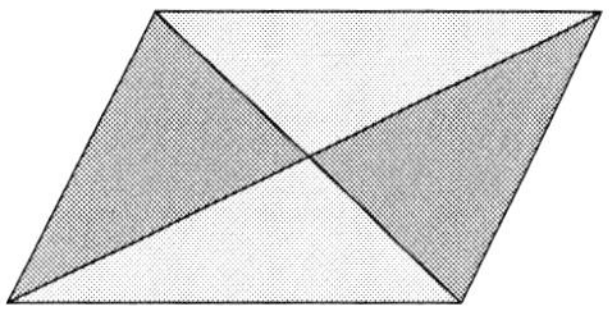

d 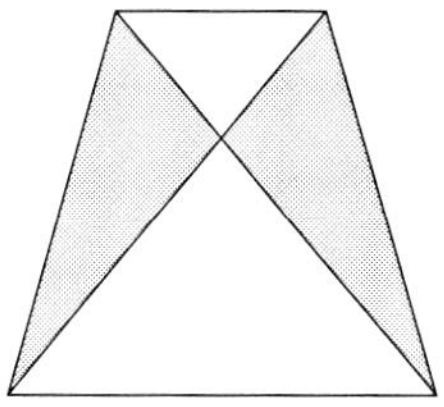 **e** 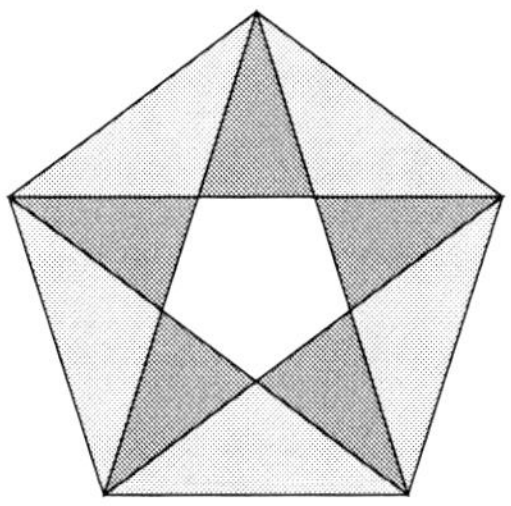 **f**

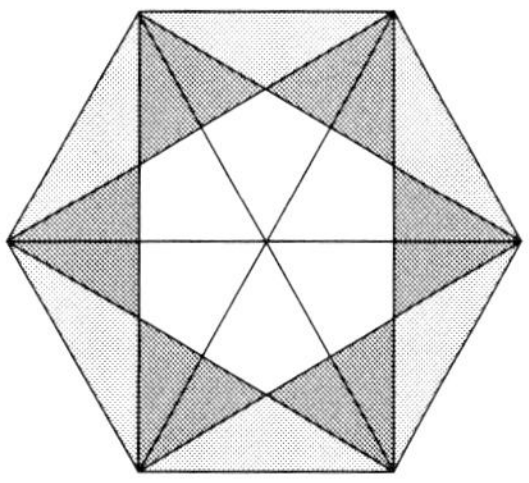

g 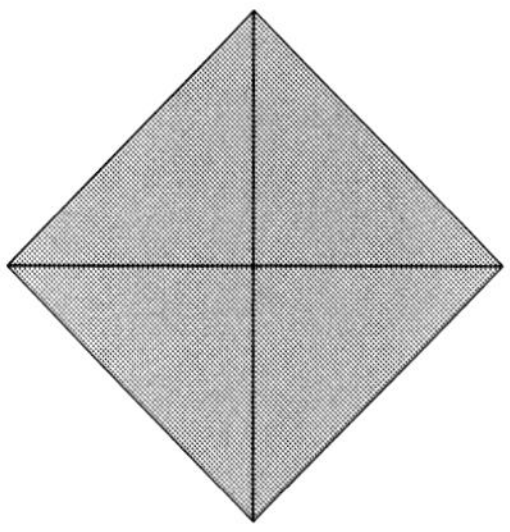 **h** 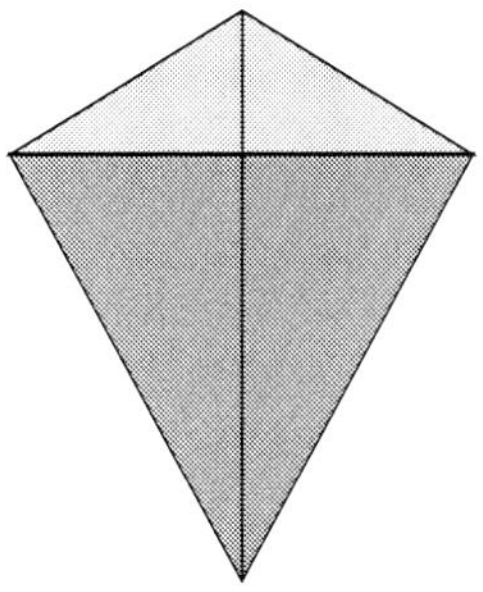 **i**

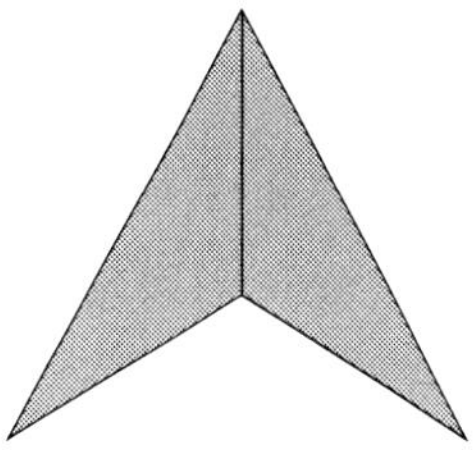

Homework 19.2

Check pupils' work on the tessellations of the given shapes.

Homework 19.3

1

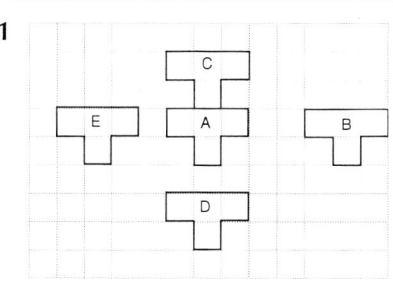

2 a $\begin{pmatrix} 3 \\ 0 \end{pmatrix}$ **b** $\begin{pmatrix} 5 \\ 1 \end{pmatrix}$ **c** $\begin{pmatrix} 1 \\ 7 \end{pmatrix}$ **d** $\begin{pmatrix} -1 \\ 4 \end{pmatrix}$ **e** $\begin{pmatrix} 1 \\ -4 \end{pmatrix}$ **f** $\begin{pmatrix} 6 \\ 0 \end{pmatrix}$ **g** $\begin{pmatrix} 2 \\ 3 \end{pmatrix}$ **h** $\begin{pmatrix} -2 \\ -3 \end{pmatrix}$ **i** $\begin{pmatrix} 4 \\ -3 \end{pmatrix}$ **j** $\begin{pmatrix} 3 \\ 0 \end{pmatrix}$ **k** $\begin{pmatrix} -3 \\ 0 \end{pmatrix}$ **l** $\begin{pmatrix} 0 \\ 3 \end{pmatrix}$

Homework 19.4

1 a 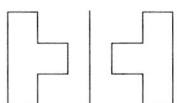   **b** 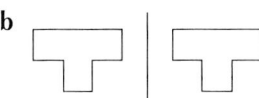   **c** 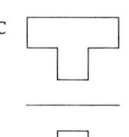   **d**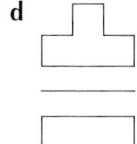

2 a 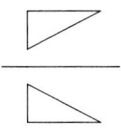   **b** 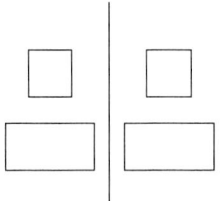   **c** 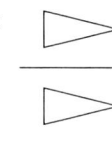   **d**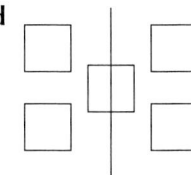

3 a 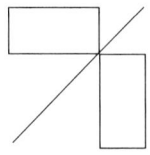   **b** 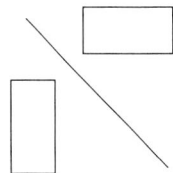   **c** 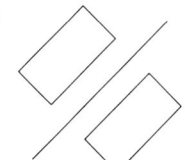   **d**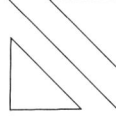

4

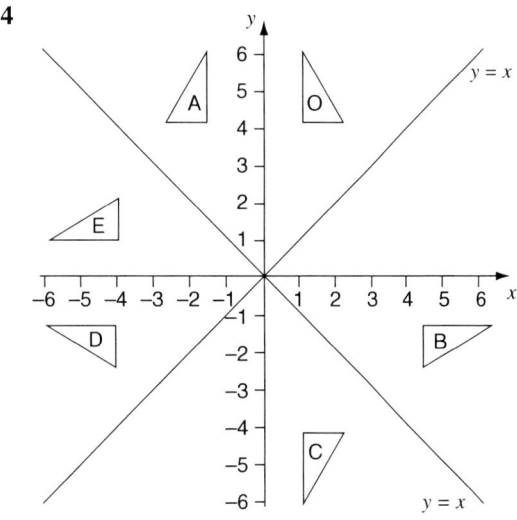

Homework 19.5

1 a   **b**   **c**   **d**

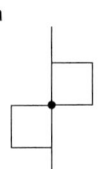 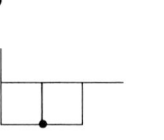 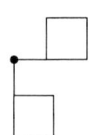 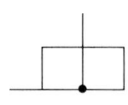

2 a   **b**   **c**   **d**

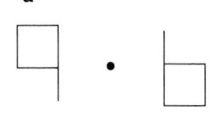 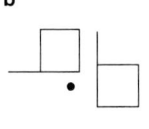 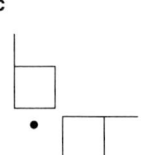 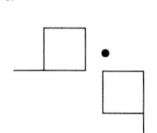

3 a B$(2, -3)(5, -7)(2, -6)$ **b** C$(-1, 0)(-4, 0)(-5, -3)$ **c** D$(-2, 1)(-5, 5)(-2, 4)$

Homework 19.6

1

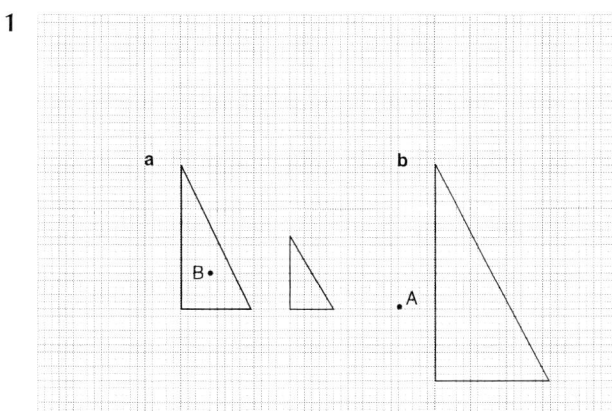

2

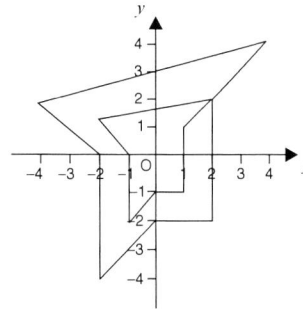

3

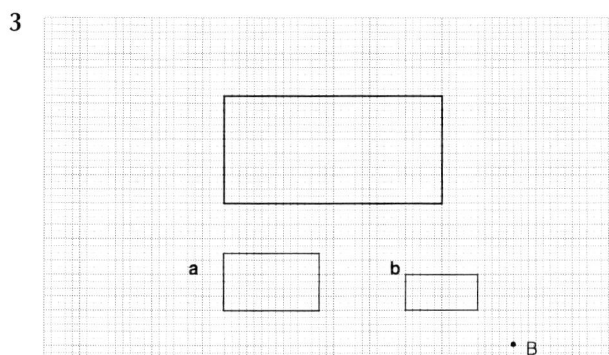

Chapter 20

Homework 20.1

The best way to mark the pupils' work is to draw the triangles on tracing paper and use it as an overlay (as is done in GCSE and SATs exams).

Homework 20.2

1 Each half of the line = 3 cm.
2 a Large angle 60°   **b** Both smaller angles 30°
3 To check their bisections are accurate, get pupils to draw the circumcircle using the intersection of their three lines as centre. All three vertices should touch the circle.
4 Get pupils to draw the inscribed circle and check that all three sides of the triangle are tangents to the circle.

1

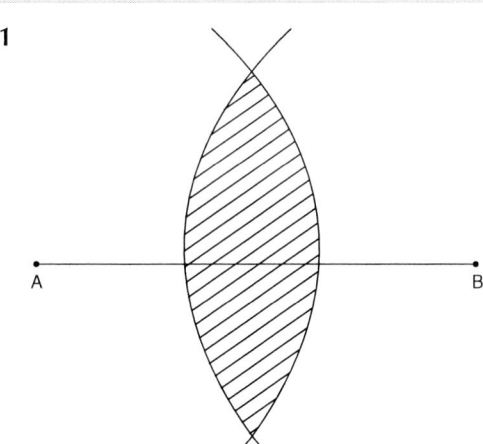

2

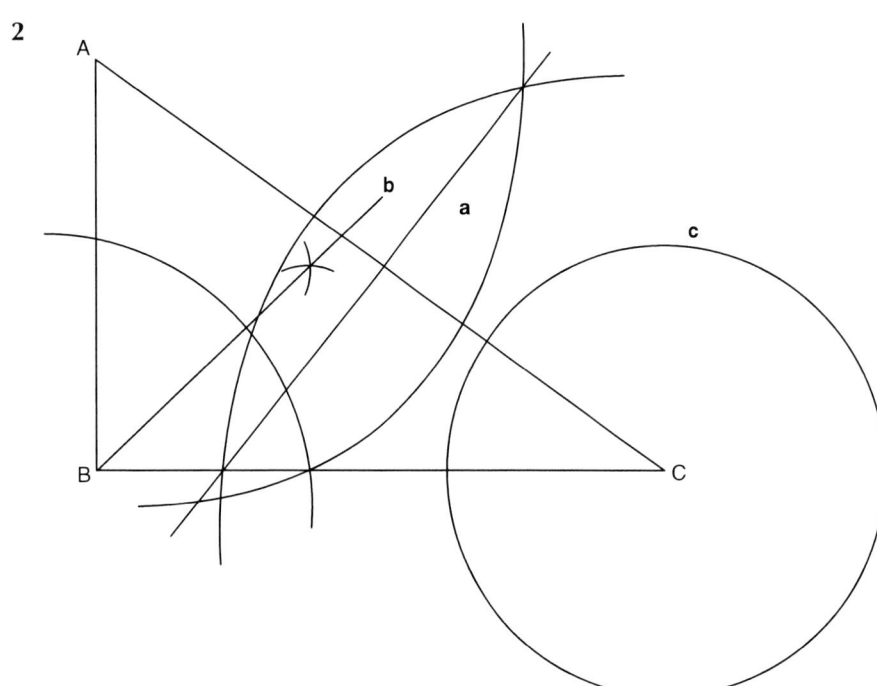

3

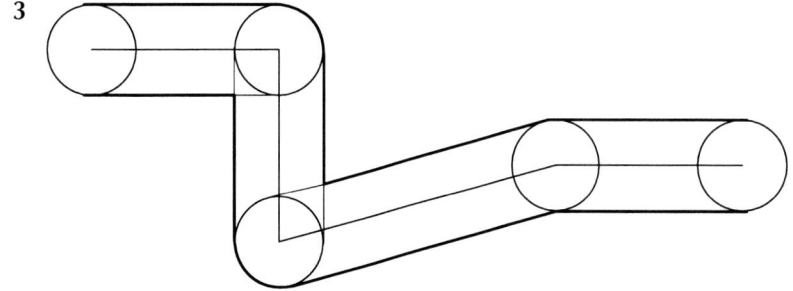

Homework 21.1

1 m (or km)	**2** mm	**3** m
4 mm (or cm)	**5** g	**6** tonnes
7 ml	**8** l	**9** km
10 kg	**11–15** Class discussion	

Homework 21.2

1 1.75	**2** 800	**3** 8.1
4 7	**5** 0.755	**6** 2050
7 700	**8** 45	**9** 0.075
10 1300	**11** 11.75	**12** 500
13 43	**14** 50	**15** 0.43
16 5500	**17** 4.3	**18** 43 000
19 5	**20** 1750	**21** 27.5

22 1000 ($1000 \, cm^3 = 1000 \, ml = 1$ litre)

Homework 21.3

1 12	**2** 36	**3** 2
4 8	**5** 1760	**6** 17 600
7 $\frac{1}{2}$	**8** 36	**9** 16
10 80	**11** 3	**12** 14
13 2	**14** 1120	**15** 8

16 $2\frac{1}{2}$

Homework 21.4

1 9	**2** 47.3	**3** 10
4 4.9	**5** 4.4	**6** 158.4
7 10	**8** 454.5	**9** 16
10 42	**11** 150	**12** 625
13 15	**14** 31.3	**15** 2.4
16 5		
17 a 155	**b** 75	**c** 2 h 4 min

Homework 22.1

1 a

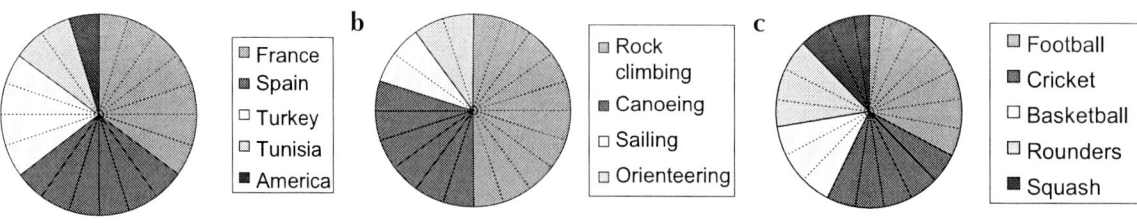

Legend a: France, Spain, Turkey, Tunisia, America

Legend b: Rock climbing, Canoeing, Sailing, Orienteering

Legend c: Football, Cricket, Basketball, Rounders, Squash

2 a

Age range	Frequency	Fraction	Fraction of 360°
11 to 20	12	$\dfrac{2}{15}$	$\dfrac{2}{15}$ of 360°=48°
21 to 30	40	$\dfrac{4}{9}$	$\dfrac{4}{9}$ of 360°=160°
31 to 40	24	$\dfrac{4}{15}$	$\dfrac{4}{15}$ of 360°=96°
41 to 50	8	$\dfrac{4}{45}$	$\dfrac{4}{45}$ of 360°=32°
51 to 60	6	$\dfrac{1}{15}$	$\dfrac{1}{5}$ of 360°=24°

b

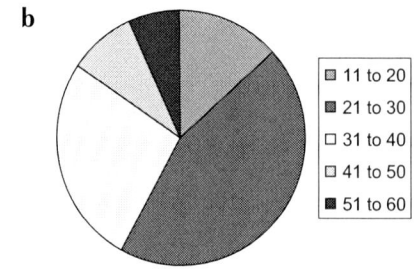

11 to 20, 21 to 30, 31 to 40, 41 to 50, 51 to 60

3

Category	Size of angle	Fraction	Amount spent
Music	60°	$\dfrac{60}{360}=\dfrac{1}{6}$	$\dfrac{1}{6}$ of £240 = £40
Clothes	120°	$\dfrac{120}{360}=\dfrac{1}{3}$	$\dfrac{1}{3}$ of £240 = £80
Going out	90°	$\dfrac{90}{360}=\dfrac{1}{4}$	$\dfrac{1}{4}$ of £240 = £60
Mobile phone	45°	$\dfrac{45}{360}=\dfrac{1}{8}$	$\dfrac{1}{8}$ of £240 = £30
Computer games	30°	$\dfrac{30}{360}=\dfrac{1}{12}$	$\dfrac{1}{12}$ of £240 = £20
Travel	15°	$\dfrac{15}{360}=\dfrac{1}{24}$	$\dfrac{1}{24}$ of £240 = £10
Totals	360°		£240

Homework 22.2

1 a Positive
  b Suitable line of best fit added to graph.
  c About 42 m (depending on line of best fit).
  d 1.69 m to 1.70 m (depending on line of best fit).
2 a Points plotted correctly.
  b Negative.
  c Suitable line of best fit added to graph.
  d £1800 to £1900 (depending on line of best fit).
  e About 40 000 miles (depending on line of best fit).

Homework 22.3

1 Variety of answers possible. Ensure a single, simple and appropriate question, with all possible responses catered for, and space for tallying answers.
2 Variety of answers possible. Questionnaires should have two questions relevant to the matter in question, following the guidelines in the textbook, with response options which are unambiguous and cater for all eventualities.

Homework 22.4

1 Yes, because the lowest level of support is 51%.
2 a

Year	1980	1985	1990	1995	2000	2005
Index	100	108	115	119	122	130
Price	26p	28p	30p	31p	32p	34p

  b 1980–1985
3 a 1990–2000 **b** 1950–60 **c** 130 million

Chapter 23

Homework 23.1

1 $2\frac{1}{4}$ **2** $6\frac{1}{4}$ **3** $12\frac{1}{4}, 20\frac{1}{4}$

4 The pattern is: "Multiply the whole number (n) by $n + 1$ and just add a quarter."

5 $30\frac{1}{4}, 42\frac{1}{4}$

Higher achieving pupils might like to use algebra to express this.

$(n + \frac{1}{2})^2 = n^2 + n + \frac{1}{4}$

Homework 23.2

1 18, 22, 26; rule is "Add 4."

2 8, 5, 2; rule is "Subtract 3."

3 3, 3.5, 4; rule is "Add 0.5."

4 2, 1, 0.5; rule is "Halve."

5 11, 16, 22; rule is "Each time, add 1 more than you added last time."

6 16, 32, 64; rule is "Multiply by 2."

7 $\frac{4}{5}, \frac{5}{6}, \frac{6}{7}$; rule is "Add 1 to both numerator and denominator."

8 15, 21, 28; rule is "Each time, add 1 more than you added last time."

Homework 23.3

1 a $2n + 1$ **b** $6n$ **c** $11 - 2n$ **d** n^2
   e $3n + 2$ **f** $21 - 4n$ **g** $5n - 2$ **h** $n^2 - 2$
2 a $5n - 2$ **b** 498
3 a $3n + 4$ **b** 304

Homework 23.4

1 a 1, 8, 27, 64, 125   **b** n^3
2 a $3n + 6$, 306   **b** $10 - 2n$, -190 **c** $4n + 19$, 419   **d** $3n - 7$, 293
3 a 31, 63   **b** $2^n - 1$

Homework 23.5

$204 \ (1^2 + 2^2 + 3^2 + 4^2 + 5^2 + 6^2 + 7^2 + 8^2)$

Chapter 24

Homework 24.1

1 $12 \, \text{cm}^3$ **2** $28 \, \text{cm}^3$ **3** $18 \, \text{cm}^3$ **4** $14 \, \text{cm}^3$

Homework 24.2

1 a $72 \, \text{cm}^3$ **b** $108 \, \text{cm}^2$
2 $8 \, \text{cm}$
3 a $8 \, \text{cm}$ **b** $384 \, \text{cm}^2$
4 $1.89 \, \text{m}^3$ or $1 \, 890 \, 000 \, \text{cm}^3$
5 27 litres
6 a $72 \, \text{m}^2$ **b** 144 000 litres

Homework 24.3

1 $11.3 \, \text{g/cm}^3$
2 $750 \, \text{g}$
3 $435 \, \text{cm}^3$
4 a i Platinum   **ii** Silver   **b i** Silver   **ii** Platinum
5 $2.3 \, \text{g/cm}^3$

Homework 24.4

1 a i $168 \, \text{cm}^2$ **ii** $120 \, \text{cm}^3$ **b i** $492 \, \text{cm}^2$ **ii** $504 \, \text{cm}^3$
2 a $270 \, \text{m}^3$ **b** $1500 \, \text{cm}^3$
3 $28 \, \text{cm}$
4 $15.5 \, \text{cm}^2$
5 $57.6 \, \text{kg}$

Homework 24.5

1 a $141 \, \text{cm}^3$ **b** $137 \, \text{cm}^3$ **c** $14 \, 700 \, \text{cm}^3$
2 $50 \, \text{cm}$
3 $100 \, \text{m}^2$

Chapter 25

Homework 25.1

The graphs are supplied as Resources 25.1a–c.

1 $y = x^2 - 5$

x	−3	−2	−1	0	1	2	3
x^2	9	4	1	0	1	4	9
y	4	−1	−4	−5	−4	−1	4

2 $y = 2x^2 + x$

x	−3	−2	−1	0	1	2	3
$2x^2$	18	8	2	0	2	8	18
$+x$	− 3	− 2	−1	0	+1	+2	+3
y	15	6	1	0	3	10	21

3 $y = x^2 + x - 2$

x	−3	−2	−1	−0.5	0	1	2
x^2	9	4	1	0.25	0	1	4
$+x$	−3	−2	−1	−0.5	0	+1	+2
-2	−2	−2	−2	−2	−2	−2	−2
y	4	0	−2	−2.25	−2	0	4

Homework 25.2

1 a 0   **b** −2 and 1

2 a

x	−4	−3	−2	−1	0	1	2	3	4
y	−9	−2	3	6	7	6	3	−2	−9

Check points plotted correctly.

   b $x = -2.7$ and $x = 2.7$

Chapter 26

Homework 26.1

1 h marked on side facing right angle.
2 a 18.4 cm   **b** 4.7 m   **c** 111 cm

Homework 26.2

1 a h **b** s **c** h **d** s **e** s
2 a 28.7 cm   **b** 5.7 m   **c** 16.4 cm

Homework 26.3

1 1.73 m (2 d.p.)
2 4.5 km (1 d.p.)
3 Points plotted correctly   **a** 5.1 cm (1 d.p.)   **b** 11.2 cm (1 d.p.)   **c** 6.7 cm (1 d.p.)

Chapter 1

1 a i 1459   **ii** 9541   **b i** 9 + 5 = 14   **ii** 0

2 a 17 252   **b** 5400   **c** 4000

3 a Twenty nine thousand, seven hundred and sixty-five   **b i** 700   **ii** 9000   **c** 29 800

4 a i 54 073   **ii** 54 100   **b i** Twenty one thousand, eight hundred and nine   **ii** 22 000

5 a i 28 000 000   **ii** 2800   **b i** 100   **ii** 10

6 Murray did the addition first, Harry did the multiplication first.

7 a One million, two hundred and eighty-seven thousand, two hundred and twelve   **b** 795 400

8 a 54 000   **b** 50 000

9 a £6.55   **b** £7.38   **c** 96   **d** 32   **e** £3.31   **f i** 8   **ii** 2   **g i** 1080   **ii** 15

10 a 7750   **b** 7849

11 a i 105   **ii** 23   **b i** 72   **ii** 31

12 a He used BODMAS and did the power first, then the multiplication before the addition.

   b i $(2 \times 3)^2 + 6 = 42$ **ii** $2 \times (3^2 + 6) = 30$

13 a Adam has calculated 5×2 instead of 5^2, Bekki has added 3 to 5 first, instead of doing the power first.

   b 26

Chapter 2

1 a $\frac{1}{2}$ **b**
                                             2 $\frac{1}{3}, \frac{2}{5}, \frac{1}{2}, \frac{3}{4}$

3 $\frac{3}{10}$ **4** 111

5 a £72.96   **b** 87   **6 a** $\frac{1}{2}$ **b** $\frac{2}{5}$

7 $\frac{3}{10}$ **8** 77

9 a i 105   **ii** $\frac{1}{2}$ **b** $\frac{1}{4}$ **c** $\frac{3}{5}$ **10** £4.80

11 172 g   **12** 27 kg

13 $\frac{2}{3}$ is larger.   **14 a** 20   **b** $\frac{7}{10}$

15 a 0.2   **b** $0.\dot{3}$ **16** 660 grams

17 a $0.\dot{1}4285\dot{7}$ **b i** 0.5555 … or $0.\dot{5}$ **ii** 0.6666 … or $0.\dot{6}$

Chapter 3

1 a Tuesday   **b** Friday

2 a Moscow   **b** 16°   **c** −10°C

3 a 8   **b** −9   **c** −7

4 a 90   **b** 540   **c** Jupiter   **d** −230 °C

5 i 9, 37, 56, 59, 75   **ii** −10, −6, −4, 2, 5   **iii** $\frac{2}{5}, \frac{1}{2}, \frac{2}{3}, \frac{3}{4}$

6 a −2, −1, 0, 1   **b** 3 degrees

7 a i 8   **ii** 9   **iii** −7   **b i** −7   **ii** 8   **iii** 8

8 i Any number between −196 and −210, e.g. −200

   ii Any number over −196, e.g. −10 or any positive number

   iii Any number below −210, e.g. −250

9 a i Hydrogen   **ii** 70 degrees   **b i** 21 degrees   **ii** 91 degrees

Chapter 4

1 a 99   **b** 102

2 4, 16, 25, 36, 49, 64, 81

3 a 90   **b** 105

4 i 6, 12   **ii** 4, 16   **iii** 3, 4, 6, 12   **iv** 8, 27

5 a 4, 6, $4 \times 4 \times 4 \times 4 \times 4$, 1024, 4   **b** 4

6 a 6, 12, 18, 24, 30   **b** 1, 2, 3, 4, 6, 12   **c** 25   **d** 23, 29

7 a 4, 8   **b** 5, 10   **c** 5, 11   **d** 4, 9   **e** 8   **f**

10	5	6
3	7	11
8	9	4

8 a 13.69   **b** 53, 59

9 i 8   **ii** 8

10 40

11 5

12 a 80 000   **b** 200   **c** 2

13 i 5^6 **ii** 5^3

14 a $2 \times 2 \times 11$ **b** 132

15 36

Chapter 5

1 a 29 cm^2 **b** 24 cm   **2 a** 212 m   **b** 2448 m^2

3 24 cm^2 **4** 32.3 cm^2

5 10 m^2 **6** 70 cm^2

7 a volume   **b** length   **8 a** volume   **b** length   **c** area

Chapter 6

1 a 20   **b**

Thursday	☺ ☺ ☺ ☺
Friday	☺ ☹

2 a 12   **b**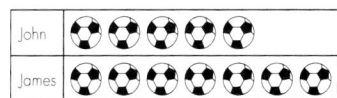

3 a 12   **b** 33   **c** 15   **4 a** 13   **b** Salt 'n' vinegar   **c** 6   **d** 75

5 a Deep Space 9 6, Voyager 2, Enterprise 3, Next Generation 4

6 a i 1.2, 1.9, 1.2   **ii** The average height for the boys is always greater than for the girls.

   b Because the graph only shows the very most top of the bars and so exaggerates the differences.

7 a $\frac{3}{4}$ **b** £15   **c** Iron and cook set

8

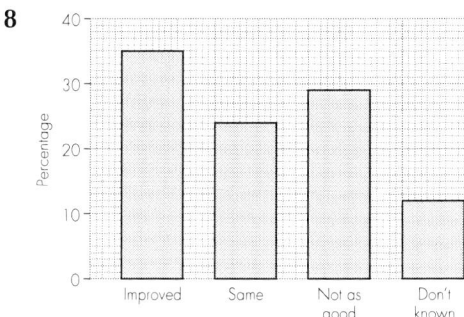

9 a Sheffield, Bristol   **b i** 8   **ii** 9

   c Manchester: home 22, hospital 30. Chosen because hospital is clearly seen to be only a few more than home.

10 a 2   **b** 37   **c** 27

11 a 160   **b** 2004–2005

12 b 115 cm

Chapter 7

1 a $18 \rightarrow 90$, $34 \rightarrow 170$, $27 \rightarrow 135$ **b** Multiply by 5 **c** $5n$

2 a $3t$ **b** $12pq$ **c** $-4x$ **3** $2(y + y)$ and $2y + 2y$

4 $-6\,°C$ **5 a** $55x$ **b i** $2x$ **ii** $160x$

6 a $4a + 7b$ **b** $5p + 10q - 15r$ **7** 26.8

8 a $x + 8y$ **b** 1 **c** 25   **9 a i** £2.40 **ii** £7.60 **b i** $20c$ **ii** $15d + 20c$

10 a $5 + y$ **b** $\dfrac{5 + y}{2}$ **11 a** 125 **b** 9 **c** $4p + 6q$

12 a 229.1 **b** 299.5

13 19.1

14 a $7x + 16$ **b** $2x + 3y$

15 a i $a + 3b$ **ii** $2x^2 + x$ **b i** $8x - 12$ **ii** $pq - p^3$ **c** $5p + 16$

16 a $4x + y$ **b** $3(2c + 3)$ **c** $z(z + 6)$

17 a i $5x - 5$ or $5(x - 1)$ **ii** $n^2 - 2n + 1$ **b i** $a(6a + 1)$ **ii** $2xy^2(3xy - 2)$

18 a $p(p + 6)$ **b** $x^2 + 3x - 28$

19 a $9x - 13$ **b** $x^2 - 5x + 6$

Chapter 8

1 a £3.40, £4.35, £2.30, £10.05 **b** 50p **c** £7.30

2 a 9 **b** 36   **3 a** 250 000 **b** 7 (million)   **4 a** 0.625 **b** $\frac{3}{5}$

5 855.4 kg   **6 a** 450 **b** 2800   **7 a** 34 **b** 150

8 When $n = 2$, $n^3 + 3 = 7$, odd

9 Chuck $(30 + 14) \div (1.3 - 0.5) = 44 \div 0.8 = 55$

10 $1\frac{11}{15}$ **11** 800   **12 a** $-19, 37$ **b** -60

Chapter 9

1 Small is 0.42p per g, large is 0.44p per g, hence the smaller is better value

2 a 93.6 mph **b** 5 hours 12 minutes   **3 a** 3.75 miles per hour **b** 3.33 mph

4 a $\frac{3}{10}$ **b** 56   **5** 62.5 cm

6 £4800   **7 a** B and C **b** Jack, 24; Kenny, 28

8 a $3 : 7$ **b** 2   **9** 35

Chapter 10

1    **2 a** 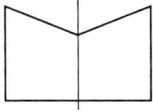 **b** 2   **3 a** 18 **b** 11 or 88 **c** 69

4 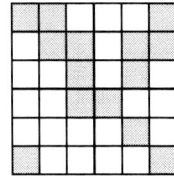   **5** 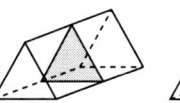   **6** 4

Either of these or rotations of these

Chapter 11

1 a 24   **b** 2   **c** 2   **d** 2.3   **2 a** 6   **b** 9

3 a 3   **b** 4   **c** 8   **d** 4.9   **4** 62

5 6.834 375

6 a i 74   **ii** 25   **b** They are quick growing   **ii** They are of even height

7 a 37   **b** 52   **c** 48

8 a i 84 kg   **ii** 53 kg   **iii** 77.2 kg   **b** Median, since only 1 weight is lower than the mean

9 a £210   **b** £360   **c** £459   **d** The mechanics get lower than the average pay.

10 1.9

11 3.55 km

12 a 150–200   **c** Tom's were generally smaller, but more consistent.

13 a 246 kg   **b** 57 kg

14 6.08 hours

Chapter 12

1 25%   **b** 23%   **c** $\frac{21}{50}$ **2 a i** 30%   **ii** 70%   **b** $\frac{7}{10}$ **c** 0.6

3 a i 0.4375   **ii** 0.27   **b** 0.095, $\frac{6}{10}$, 65%, 0.7   **4 a** £30   **b** £220

5 a $\frac{2}{5}$ **b** 0.98   **c** 7 500 000   **d** 25%   **e** 60%

6 $\frac{3}{5}$ of £25 = £15 so is larger than 40% of £30 which is £12

7 £332.80   **8 a** 13.9   **b i** Amy   **ii** Charlotte

9 £141

10 HTV cost £17.60, CVS cost £20.16, so HTV is the better deal.

11 50%   **12** 20%

13 £14734.50   **14** 32%

15 a £56   **b i** £44.80   **ii** 56%

16 20% off £300 = £240, 10% off 240 = £216, 30% off 300 = £210

Chapter 13

1 a $x = 6$ **b** $y = 9$ **c** $t = 2$ **d** $m = 9$ **2 a** $x = 2$ **b** $x = 6$ **c** $x = 5$

3 a $x = 7$ **b** $x = 7$ **c** $x = 22$ **4 a** 23   **b** 5

5 a $z + 4$ **b** $4z + 4$ **c** $4z + 4 = 60$, $z = 14$p

6 a i $x = 4.5$ **ii** $x = 7$ **iii** $x = 3$ **b i** $13q$ **ii** $7n + 3p$

7 area $= 2w \times w = 2w^2 = 128 \rightarrow w^2 = 64 \rightarrow w = 8$, hence $2w = 16$ cm

8 $a = 5$, $b = 7$, $c = 3$, $d = 2$ **9 a** $30x + 160$ **b** 5

10 a $x = 3$ **b** $m = 2$ **c** $k = 3$ **11 a** $x = 1$ **b** $p = 3$ **c** $t = -17$

12 a $x = 2.5$ **b** $x = 0.5$ **13 a** $3x + 1$ cm   **b** $3x + 1 = 22$, $x = 7$

14 a $4x + 8$ **b** 15.5 cm   **15** $x = \frac{1}{3}$ (note, no mark for 0.3 or 0.33)

16 a $3x + 120$ **b** 20°   **17 a** 3.5   **b** $x = 7$

18 a 0   **b** −4   **c** $x = \frac{1}{3}(y - 12)$ **19** $x = \dfrac{6y - 7}{5}$

20 $m = 4p - 1$ **21** $x = 3.3$

22 $x = 4$ cm   **23 a** $p = \dfrac{T}{5}$ **b** $t = \sqrt{\left(\dfrac{V}{5}\right)}$

24 $x = -0.8$ **25 a** $\frac{3}{5}$ **b** −3, −2, −1, 1, 2

1 a 4.8 km   **b** 6.9 miles

2 a

x	−1	0	1	2	3
y	−5	−3	−1	1	3

3 a

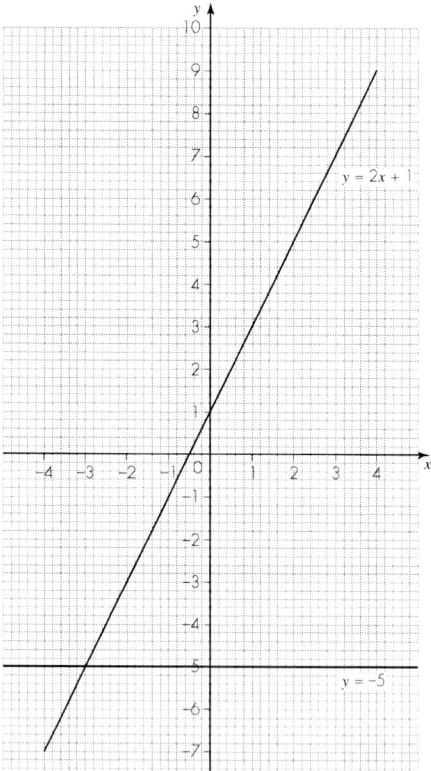

b (−3, −5)

b

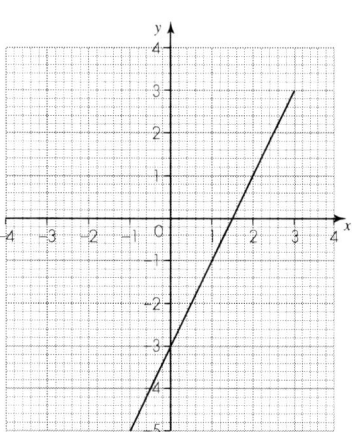

c $x = 0.5$

4 a 15 minutes   **b** 15 km   **c**

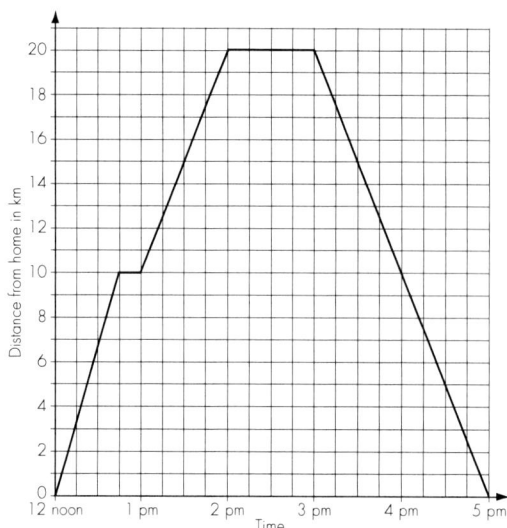

5 a 40 km/h   **b**

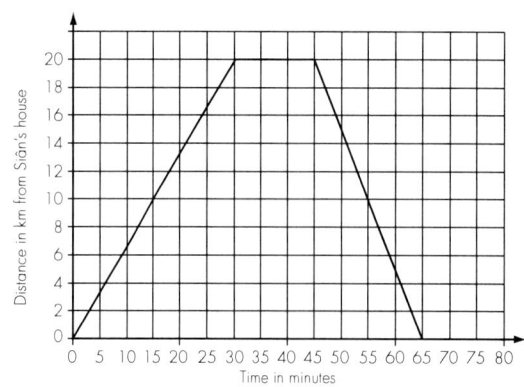

Chapter 15

1 **a** 60°   **b** 110°

2 **a** Isosceles   **b** $a = 65°$, $b = 50°$

3 110°

4 100°

5 108°

6 **a i** 72°   **ii** Alternate angle to angle ADB
b i 58°   **ii** Angle BEC = 50° (angles on a line), so $y = 58°$ (angles in a triangle)

7 Angle CDE = 35° (alternate angles), angle CED = 105° (angles in triangle), so angle ACE = 75° (angles on straight line). There are other methods.

8 Exterior angle is 60°, interior angle is 120°, $6 \times 120° = 720°$. There are other methods.

9 **a** 135°   **b** 12

Chapter 16

1 **b** 10 cm

2 7.7 cm

3 40.2 cm

4 16π m^2

5 **a** 113.0 cm^2 or 113.1 cm^2 **b** $(5\pi + 10)$ cm

Chapter 17

1 a 6.3   **b**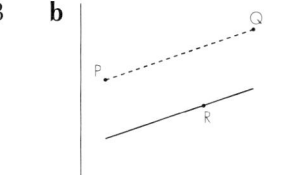

2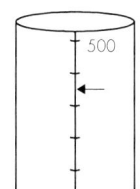

3 a 38 °C   **b**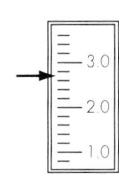

4 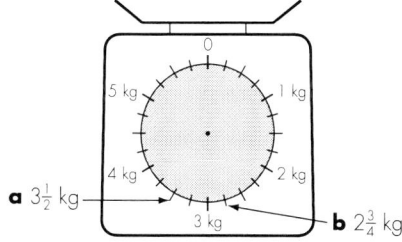   **a** $3\frac{1}{2}$ kg   **b** $2\frac{3}{4}$ kg

5 D and C

6 a i 12   **ii** 8   **b**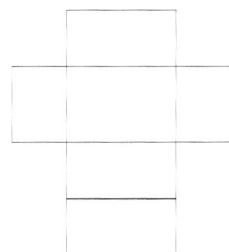

7 a 8 litres   **b** £29.10

8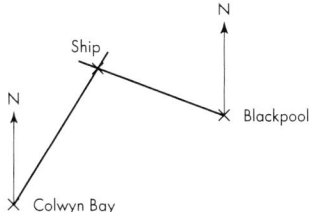

9 a   **b**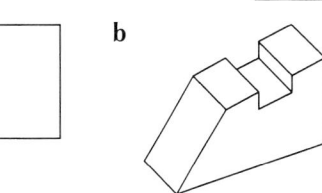

10 a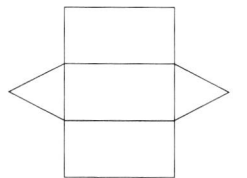

b 4.5 cm   **c** 216 cm^2

11 30 cm^2

12 a 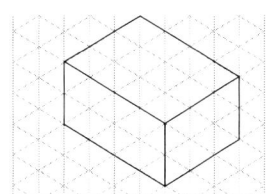   **b** 24 cm^3

Chapter 18

1 a April and May   **b** Daffodil   **c** February   **d** Crocus   **e i** $\frac{1}{5}$ **ii** ├──────×──┼──┤
0   0.6   1

2 a ||||| ||||| ||||| ||||| ||||| || **b** 3   **c** 3

3 a $\frac{29}{30}$ **b** 3

4 Carol (20), Bill (14), Ann (12)

5 a Palmers, a smaller range   **b** Sturroks, smaller mean weight   **c** 79g

6 a Usually takes less time to do the journey than route Y.
   b You know how long the journey will take. It's always about 20 minutes.

7 a 1   **b** There are five possible outcomes and only two of them are 2. The probability is $\frac{2}{5}$.

8 a 16   **b** 21

9 $\frac{5}{12}$

10 a

2	4	5	8
5	7	8	11
6	8	9	12
9	11	12	15

   b 8   **c** $\frac{1}{8}$ **d** $\frac{5}{16}$ **e** $\frac{1}{2}$

11 a $\frac{14}{25}$ **b** $\frac{21}{50}$

12 a 1H, 2H, 3H, 4H, 5H, 6H, 1T, 2T, 3T, 4T, 5T, 6T   **b** $\frac{1}{4}$ **c** $\frac{3}{4}$

13 a 0   **b** $\frac{3}{8}$ **c** 12

14 a 0.4   **b** 275

15 a 0.25   **b** 60

Chapter 19

1 B, E and F   **2** 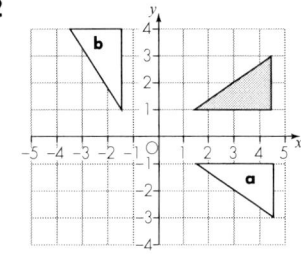   **3**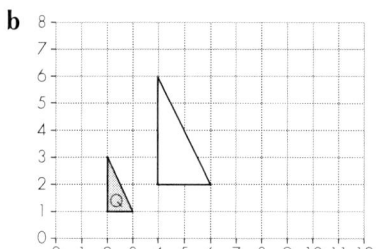

4 A rotation of 180° about O

5 a   **b**   The enlarged triangle can be anywhere on the grid.

6 A reflection in $y = x$

7 a and b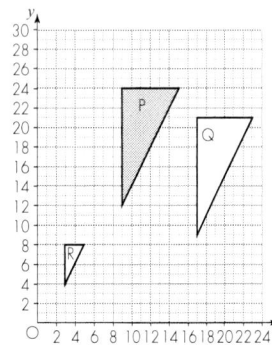

1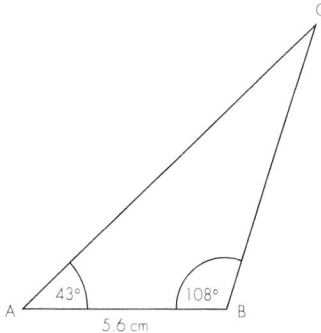

2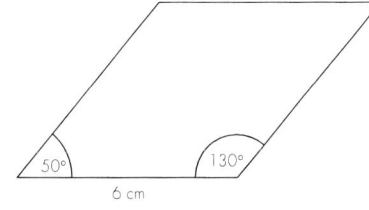

3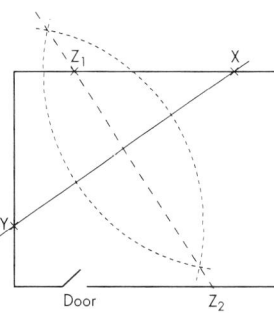

4 a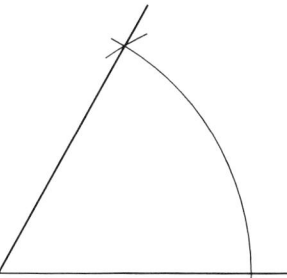

b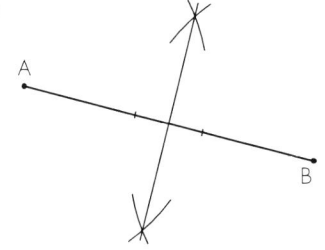

5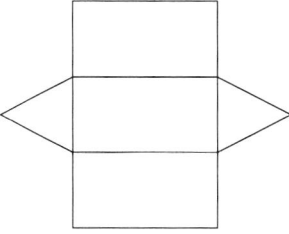

6 a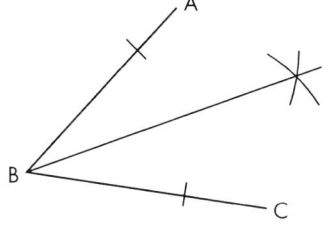

b-c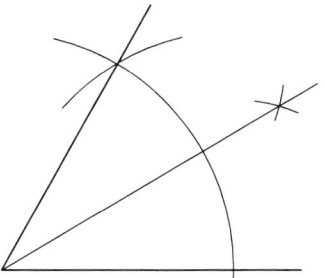

7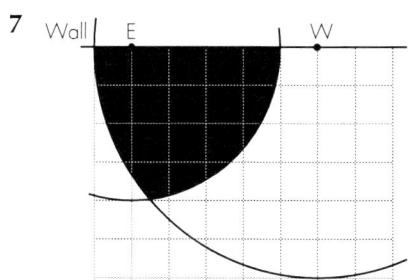

Chapter 21

1 Metres, kilograms, inches

2 **a i** Kilometres   **ii** Grams   **b i** 24 cm   **ii** 3800 ml

3 **a** 1.2 kg   **b** 1750 g

4 **a** 40 000 m   **b** 25 miles

5 **a** $\approx 9\,l$ **b** $\approx 16\,l$

6 Yes. 30 pints $\approx 30 \times 1.75 = 52.5$ litres

7 75 mph

8 **a** 1 m   **b** 2.82 m

1 a

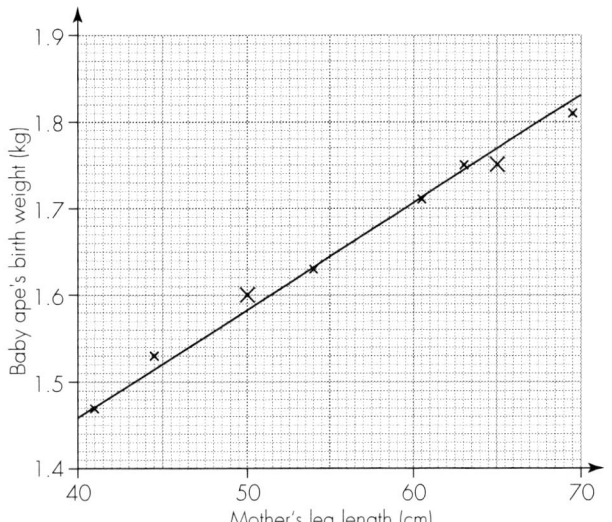

b 66

c i 60   **ii** $\frac{7}{18}$

2 a

F, French
S, Spanish
I, Italian
G, Greek
A, American

b 20%

3 Burger: 80°, Hot dog: 10, 40°, Kebab: 15, 60°, Total: 360°

4 The angles for the pie chart are: 60° (gold), 80° (silver), 220° (bronze).

5 a

Do not understand at all
Understand a little
Total understand
Understand some
Understand
Women

b Women had a better understanding. Around 85% of the women had some understanding or better, while of the men, the figure was only 75%.

6 a i Diagram C   **ii** Diagram A   **iii** Diagram B   **b** Diagram A

7 The categories overlap.

8 a

	Eat vegetarian food	Do not eat vegetarian food	Total
Boys			
Girls			
Total			

b Yes, as 53% of the girls said they ate vegetarian, whereas only 45% of the boys said they did.

9 a It is very subjective and there is not a big enough range of possible responses.   **b** This is a biased sample.

10 a

11 a 128 kg   **b** a positive correlation

c

d 194 kg

b positive   **c** 1.65 kg

12 Answer depends on pupil's plotting

13 a It's a leading question. There is no option to disagree.

b There are only the two possible responses of yes or no. The numbers of shows is a complete set, so that no matter how many shows someone goes to, they can complete the questionnaire.

1 a  **b** 10, 15 **c** The difference increases by 1 each time.

2 a i 9, 5 **ii** Subtract 4. **b i** 122 **ii** 20 **iii** –7

3 $m = 6n$

4 a Always even **b** Could be either odd or even.

5 a 3, 7 **b** 5th
c If 78 was a term, then the term number would be given by the solution of $4n - 1 = 78$. This solution is $n = 19.75$, not a whole number, hence there is no term that totals 78.

6 a If $E = 4$, then $\frac{1}{2}E + 3 = 2 + 3 = 5$, which is not even.
b No, because all the prime numbers are odd apart from the number 2, so you could choose 2 and any other prime number, giving you an odd number.

7 a $A + B$ is odd. As odd + even is always odd, then odd + 1 is always even.
b Because if $A = 2$ and $B = 1$, then $A + B - 1 = 2$, which is prime.

8 a $4n - 5$ **b** All the terms in the first sequence are odd, while all in the second are even.

9 a i 3, 7, 11 **ii** No, 133 is not a multiple of 4. **b** $4n + 1$

10 a $\dfrac{4 \times 5}{2}$ **b** $\dfrac{8 \times 9}{2}$

11 a ⁝ **b** 15, 21 **c i** 25 **ii** square numbers **iii** 100

12 The square of any positive fraction less than 1, for example.

13 a For any value of n, $2n$ is even, so $2n + 1$ is odd.
b The square of an odd number will be odd, the square of an even number will be even.

1 48 m³

2 200

3 a 264 cm² **b** 216 cm³

4 300π cm³

5 170.1 g

1 a y-values: 4, –1, –4, –5, –4, –1, 4

2 a y-values: 9, 3, –1, –3, –3, –1, 3
c –3.2 or –3.3

3 a y-values: 0, 36, 56, 60, 48, 20, –24
c 2.8

4 a 3
b The graph moves 2 squares down.

1 150 m **2** 4.1 m **3** 13.4 cm

4 13.7 cm **5** 5.1 m **6** 5.74 cm

7 39.1 km **8 a** 1.8 km **b** 3.8 km